SEEKING SHELTER

A Working Mother,
Her Children, and a Story
of Homelessness in America

◆

JEFF HOBBS

SCRIBNER

New York Amsterdam/Antwerp London Toronto Sydney New Delhi

Scribner
An Imprint of Simon & Schuster, LLC
1230 Avenue of the Americas
New York, NY 10020

This is a work of nonfiction. Some names and
identifying characteristics have been changed.

First Scribner hardcover edition February 2025

SCRIBNER and design are trademarks of Simon & Schuster, LLC

For information about special discounts for bulk purchases,
please contact Simon & Schuster Special Sales at 1-866-506-1949
or business@simonandschuster.com.

The Simon & Schuster Speakers Bureau can bring authors to
your live event. For more information or to book an event, contact
the Simon & Schuster Speakers Bureau at 1-866-248-3049
or visit our website at www.simonspeakers.com.

Interior design by Jason Snyder

Manufactured in the United States of America

1   3   5   7   9   10   8   6   4   2

Library of Congress Cataloging-in-Publication Data has been applied for.

ISBN 978-1-6680-3482-8
ISBN 978-1-6680-3484-2 (ebook)

To Sugar Ruth Goldstein,
for a life devoted to homes and families

Author's Note

THIS BOOK IS PRIMARILY A work of reconstructive journalism. Most of the events were described to me after they occurred and were verified to the deepest extent possible. I undertook this process with the consent, trust, and courage of those who chose to share their stories.

During the period right after pandemic social restrictions had begun to ease in California—late summer 2021—I began spending much of my time in different transitional housing organizations around Los Angeles that were geared toward serving families. The public school districts were just reopening in full at the onset of the 2021–22 school year, and I was also spending time in a number of high schools that provided resources for students with unstable housing situations. In these contexts, I was meeting some of the vast numbers of unsheltered families with school-aged children in one of the epicenters of America's ongoing housing crisis.

The disaster of homelessness in Los Angeles and many other cities is often reduced in news reports as well as in common conversation to a binary: housed or unhoused. Some descriptive gradations exist—*episodic, chronic, hidden*—but even those modest systemic efforts toward nuance tend to fold into the dominant presumption that most people who end up without shelter do so as a result of drug addiction, mental-health challenges, and general shortcomings of competence. The country's influential privileged class, policymakers, and news outlets together propagate this terribly facile framing of what homelessness is and whom it afflicts.

In contrast, this project began with parents who worked and children who went to school: people of sound mind and without substance issues who carried the typical kinds of aspirations that parents and children have, yet who could not always manage to remain housed in the neighborhoods where they lived. These voices and journeys are rarely put forward in the media—in part because of the media's bias toward the grimmest narratives, in part due to valid fears of the systems in place to help—and I sought to learn how adults and youth in these situations define themselves, meet the demands of day-to-day American life, sustain dreams, and bear the unique psychic load that each carries across a stark socioeconomic line drawn by others. That is how I encountered the individuals who trusted me to tell their stories in these pages.

The majority of our conversations took place in a small nonprofit organization's office over a period of more than two years. Sometimes we walked and talked outside or sat in local parks. Frequently, we drove to a certain setting where a segment of the story occurred or to meet with other people, such as educators and social workers, who had insights to share. I recorded most of these conversations with permission.

Nearly all the physical spaces described, including specific street corners and motel rooms, were visited in person.

Memory is subjective and malleable, especially when terror and trauma are involved. Many events in these pages could be cross-checked to a degree with others who were present. Some could not.

The same holds true for dialogue.

The same holds true for descriptions of interior feelings that may have changed over time and reflection.

Primary participants were given access to these pages before publication as a method to further authenticate the writing, to affirm their comfort with the story's structure and style, and to aid an author who does not share their heritage, race, class, or very many experiential threads at all.

Some surnames have been omitted, and some names and identifying characteristics have been changed to protect privacy.

PART I

Monterey Park

Evelyn and Her Family
August–September 2018

THEY LIVE NEAR THE BOUNDARY where the city gives way to the high desert. The landscape unfolding into the northeasterly distance is brown and dry and unending, while the compact front yards along the curve of their street remain an impossible green, courtesy of the state's vast system of water conveyance.

Evelyn holds one end of the bed frame and walks in choppy steps forward along the short driveway. Manny holds the other end and walks backward.

"Hold up, wait, I need to put it down for a sec," she says.

Manny continues backpedaling, yanking her along. "It's like ten more steps," he says.

Evelyn abruptly stops and drops her end of the frame. The wood scrapes on the concrete. She begins shaking out her cramping fingers. Manny sets his end down and makes a performance of crouching to inspect underneath for scratches. "Who cares?" she asks preemptively. "We're giving it away anyway."

"That's not a reason to bust it up," he replies.

After a few deep breaths and finger flexes, they transport the frame the remaining distance to the curb, leaning it lengthwise against the couch, table, and bunk bed that already comprise a heap there. These big furniture items are surrounded by a few large boxes overflowing with kids' toys—themselves mostly thrift store purchases—as well as a miniature slide and swing set, a tangle of kitchen chairs, and all their belongings that won't be making the journey from Lancaster to Los Angeles: from their old life to their new life.

The reason Manny is in a sour mood with her has to do with his ongoing claim that they don't have to toss possessions so ruthlessly—that with some puzzling he would be able to stow and rope down everything they own in towers on his small pickup truck and the roof of her Toyota SUV. Evelyn remains insistent that they leave behind all their cheap stuff, all the castoffs of parents and aunts and cousins. She desires to freshly furnish their new space, once they actually secure a new space.

She is sweating heavily, her hands and forearms are cramped, her back and shoulders hurt badly, her husband is pissed at her and her landlord has been leaving borderline threatening messages about her breaking the lease agreement and her kids are acting like little crazies, but Evelyn feels fantastic today—and never more so than when she tapes to the front of the junk pile the sheet of paper that her five-year-old daughter, Sofia, crafted that reads: FREE STUFF!!! COSAS GRATIS!!! surrounded by multicolored firework explosions.

◆　◆　◆

In this late summer of 2018, Evelyn is twenty-nine years old and is the mother of five children aged twelve, ten, seven, five, and three. She has been married for five years to Manny, the father of the youngest three of these children. She has lived in Lancaster, California—a city of almost two hundred thousand people at the southern end of the Sierra Nevada mountain range—for her entire life. After severing from the gang culture that circumscribed many of her teenage years, she has worked as a waitress and bartender for her entire adulthood. She is a member of the second generation of an El Salvadoran–American family. Her father died of liver cirrhosis years earlier. Her mother is a serious Catholic. Her four older siblings all still live around town and, like their parents and most members of their extended family, tend to be either alcoholic or religious or both. The city of Lancaster seems sometimes to be half-populated by her cousins and nieces and nephews ranging in age from babies to forty-somethings. She can feel as if not a moment of her life has ever passed without being observed and commented upon by a relative.

Evelyn is really tired of the desert and its people. She is tired of serving food and drink to the broke, angry, lustful, and wasted of the Antelope Valley—many of whom she has known since childhood. She is tired of mournful songs on the radio seeming to embody her life. She is tired of the complaining from different people about different subjects—work, school, wind, dirt, other people—that permeates each day. Above all, she is tired of observing her various children in their various day-to-day lives and seeing clearly the direction those lives are taking—a direction parallel to that which hers has taken thus far, a direction that has left her this tired.

She and Manny have almost $4,000 saved. They did not sequester this amount arbitrarily or casually. Each dollar in their joint account is the result of double shifts worked, discount stores scoured, small extravagances deferred, arguments had, a cumulative and unpleasant effort undertaken over years of wanting to leave this place.

Coupled with this money, the email she received from the city of Los Angeles at the end of July 2018 granting them qualification for a Section 8 voucher means, in her yearning imagination, that things can change.

❖ ❖ ❖

5

The kernel of the dream, for Evelyn, grew directly from an online resource that educators nationwide beseech parents to ignore: school rankings on the internet. She did not need a website to inform her that her kids' school district in Lancaster was impoverished in both instruction and resources. Even with her different jobs and complicated relationship history, Evelyn has always been devoted to dropping off and picking up all her children from school. So twice a day for almost a decade as her family grew, she stood outside the fencing and watched children emerge from school structures that looked like repurposed shipping containers and cross the blacktop recess area. The younger kids in her daughters' elementary classes were generally cheerful; small children only need the company of one another to be happy. But as her oldest son progressed through elementary and into middle school—he is going into seventh grade now, his little brother into fifth—she watched as he and his peers became progressively downcast and unruly. They would pass through the gate and she would catch and hold her own kids while many of the others rushed past her this way and that unsupervised into the neighborhood, pulling on vape pens and throwing rocks at cars. Such young people without purpose saddened her.

Two years ago Evelyn began spending far too much of her time on a popular school rankings website. A few clicks would fill her screen with a map of Lancaster, dense with yellow dots all containing a C or a C–, plus a spackle of red dots containing Ds, in reference to the quality of various district schools. The site unveiled more granular rankings, too: academics, teachers, programs, sports. Her kids' school graded C– in every category except diversity, in which the school received a B. The overall math proficiency at the time was 27 percent. The reading proficiency was 23 percent.

One day in the spring of 2016, she typed into this site a school district near Los Angeles called Monterey Park. One of her aunts lived there and had worked in the school system. Evelyn marveled at the green circles that proliferated across the website's map of the few square miles comprising this easterly wedge of Los Angeles: uniform A grades for all the public K–12 schools in Monterey Park, both overall and in most subcategories. The school nearest her aunt's address was ranked forty-first out of all public elementary schools in California.

After that epiphany, Evelyn spent a few weeks toggling between these two maps, cross-referencing the densities of Lancaster's yellow Cs and red Ds with Monterey Park's green As. The contrast gripped her, clawed down, anchored in for good. She showed them to Manny and demanded that he see what she saw, which was that even though their own lives were set in terms of education—both quite thin—the children's lives were not. The online maps represented two trajectories for the five humans in their care. Evelyn's grand idea of relocation was born out of the stark comparison, oversimplified as it was via the internet. Beginning then, she saved what she could to actualize the change.

That Americans sweepingly, loudly spoke of education as an equalizer while states like California tied public school funding to local property and income taxes—both overarching indicators of disparity—was a national fallacy as well as an inescapable reality. For a family like Evelyn's, decent schools meant high housing costs. The average monthly rent within the Monterey Park district had reached over $2,000 for a one-bedroom—and since averages took into account rent-controlled units, the prices of apartments available to them were in an even higher tier. No amount of frugality that Evelyn and Manny were capable of with their earnings could render this area affordable, so the notion of a high-quality education for their kids became contingent on some form of housing assistance. Evelyn placed them on any waiting list that her searches turned up, including many that they didn't even qualify for due to age or family size. She found that the more specific she was in describing her family, the narrower her family's options appeared.

Section 8 was the first of these applications that returned positive news.

In the popular national program for low-income renters, voucher recipients can secure legitimate lease agreements from participating landlords. Then the renters pay no more than one-third of their income toward housing costs. The government covers whatever monthly rent remains. As such, the program is popular with tenants, who are unbound from the limitations of designated low-income housing. It is less popular with landlords who have to weigh the unpredictable means of residents on the economic margins of modern American society against the guarantee of government payments. The demand and supply within this effective but finite social safety net are increasingly imbalanced, the waiting lists in cities like Los Angeles tens of thousands of names long.

In her eagerness and because her application was completed over the internet using mostly her cell phone and the guidance of an automated system, Evelyn has not researched thoroughly enough to understand that qualifying for Section 8 and actually receiving a voucher are two separate processes.

◆　◆　◆

"How far is it?" Iris, her third child, seven years old, asks. She is scrunched in the middle row between Sofia and Marisol in their car seats, with multiple bags of clothes and shoes and bedding bulging over their heads from the trunk space.

"*Enough!*" Evelyn snaps back. She immediately softens because she doesn't want her kids to remember this important drive by her short temper: "Maybe less than an hour now."

The trip from Lancaster to Los Angeles is less than two hours without traffic. But they are traveling on a Sunday afternoon and so partaking in a clogged lattice of freeways that converge from the west, north, and east. The whole entanglement swings around the San Gabriel Mountains into the San Fernando Valley, where the satellite desert communities begin to cluster closer together to form exurbs and then suburbs: Sylmar, Pacoima, Burbank, a continuum of denser populations. The maps application on her phone is all dark red veins. She does her best to stay close behind Manny's truck, not for any practical reason but as a symbolic gesture to making this passage together. But people are driving angry today, and Manny is, too, and she eventually loses track of him amid the constant jockeying for faster-moving lanes.

Their 2008 Toyota Highlander is a large vehicle, over fifteen feet long, that is difficult to maneuver but easy to bully others around with in traffic. Evelyn felt uncomfortable driving it when Manny first brought it home two years before in 2016, proud of the deal he'd gotten and the fact that it had logged less than a hundred thousand miles in eight years. The passenger side wears multiple small dents that are the result of unfortunate right turns. But over the past year she has come to feel almost overconfident behind its wheel. Evelyn is five feet three inches tall and rarely experiences any inkling of height or physical power over others the way she does in the driver's seat of this vehicle. She also likes knowing that in the event of a minor accident, her kids will be well armored—though she loathes the size of the gas tank, which she has to stop to refill just north of Los Angeles proper at a cost of seventy-five dollars, plus chips and juice for the kids.

❖   ❖   ❖

Orlando and Gabriel ride with Manny in the pickup ahead of the girls, the three of them tightly shoulder to shoulder across the bench in front. Their stepfather hates this drive and doesn't seem thrilled about the reasoning behind it. Orlando, at twelve, is growing old enough to consider—if not to fully understand—the currents that run between his mother and stepfather. At the root of their dynamic is the fact that his mom is a fast thinker, talker, and planner. She can push a passing thought into an actionable directive in just moments. A lot of his friends' homes in Lancaster feel static in comparison: one adult drinking beer and watching TV, kids drinking soda and playing games on a different TV, another adult staring at the phone. His mom is always prodding Manny to *do* things such as dig a hot tub or paint the fence Miami colors. Manny is a pliant man at home and basically has always done what she wants until he reaches a point in the project that proves her idea to be untenable or unaffordable—like the hot tub—and then he stops and grumbles about time and effort wasted. That is how the two of them coexist. But they've never reached this level of dramatic action before: relocating their lives based on an exciting notion that they know where "better" is and its direction is south toward Los Angeles. He has a sense that all of Manny's cursing in Spanish at the drivers of cars around them has more to do with the family's upheaval than anybody's road manners.

They cut a stairway pattern south and east through Glendale, South Pasadena, and Alhambra. These are all outlying northeastern townships to downtown LA. The homes are a mix of Spanish bungalows, larger Craftsman houses, and cheaply built apartment buildings. The terrain is hilly and they can't even see any markers that signify being in America's second-most-populous city until a short run on I-10 reveals the striking downtown skyline receding in the truck's side-view mirrors. Then Manny exits into the township of Monterey Park.

"Everyone's Chinese," Gabriel, who is ten, observes with some degree of quiet wonder at the dozens of people of Asian extraction moving on foot up and down both sides of the commercial street.

"Don't say stuff like that," Orlando tells him in what must be an irritatingly high-and-mighty tone for a twelve-year-old. "It's not everyone."

"It's a lot."

"Some can be like Korean, or Japanese."

"Wherever they're from, they can't drive for shit," Manny mutters. Along the main thoroughfare, Garfield Avenue, he alternately pumps the brake and gas hard, lurching the boys forward and back. Their entry into Monterey Park is violent in this way.

◆　◆　◆

Evelyn's aunt Talia, her deceased father's sister, has offered to take them in for a couple days while they firm up a housing situation. The girls are cramped and tired when Evelyn double-parks the Highlander in front of the apartment complex a mile south of the interstate. Manny's truck is in a spot in the complex's lot. He and her two boys lean against the hatch with matching expectant expressions.

"She isn't home!" Manny yells back, as if her aunt not being there is squarely Evelyn's fault—and it might be, actually, since Evelyn has neglected to specify a time of arrival. She texted her aunt while knowing her aunt does not really communicate via text or check her cell phone hardly at all.

"Let's get something to eat, then," Evelyn poses.

"I can't just leave all this." Manny gestures toward the tall hump of their possessions strapped in the truck bed.

Iris chooses this moment to declare her need to pee, which in turn sparks

11

the same need in Sofia. Evelyn is sorting this situation out when the driver of another large SUV that can't fit past hers leans on his horn. The abrupt noise causes Manny to bound into the street and confront that driver. Evelyn gets out to yell at Manny; rarely does he wind himself up this tightly, but when he does he is capable of real trouble. He's been beaten up badly twice while out with friends at Lancaster bars, and she's had to pick him up at police stations twice more for nonviolent belligerence.

She apologizes to the driver with her hands closed in front of her face as if in prayer, commands Manny to stay here and wait for Aunt Talia, asks the boys to go look for a taco truck or something else cheap for dinner, and then drives the Highlander around the block to look for a parking space. These streets are very narrow and heavily trafficked. But by luck she crosses Garfield Avenue and runs into a sprawling green space called Barnes Park. Children swarm over the playground structure and ride scooters along the walkways. Elderly people circle the perimeter for exercise. A few homeless people look filthy and grim but comfortable enough in this atmosphere. The park has decent public bathrooms the girls use, and an ice cream vendor. Dusk is falling now and Evelyn buys a Popsicle for herself and Disney-themed frozen concoctions for the girls. They sit on a bench in the coral light and look across the swell of cared-for land. Here, with her little girls, Evelyn feels all right again.

◆   ◆   ◆

Aunt Talia's one-bedroom is about five hundred square feet, and all the discord that immediately besets them seems to further shrink the space. Manny expresses continuous stress about the stuff tied in his truck. Evelyn does a poor job of calming him down and her efforts are agitated in and of themselves. Talia likes this set of grandnieces and grandnephews more than most of her relatives in Lancaster—together Evelyn's kids are loud but they are also polite and interesting—yet having them here filling the majority of the physical space in her apartment after a long car trip, with all their natural energy having no outlet, is quickly regrettable.

Talia actually forgot which day they were supposed to come. Possibly, her niece misstated or never specified the date. She was planning to reheat lasagna and watch *Survivor* before coming upon Evelyn's clan and all their possessions on her building steps. Her life here as a widowed, retired schoolteacher is thoroughly quiet. But what she has gleaned from her exchanges with Evelyn over the last few months stirred her enough to offer to help this family.

A mother wants her kids to go to a decent school. This particular neighborhood might be their only access point to one. Talia understands these interlacing core truths to underlie this specific unfolding situation: as plain as a mother's hope, as knotted and psychotic as America's racist, classist education system.

Talia is averse to surprises and change but she cannot *not* try to help these kids and this modest, well-intentioned quest.

But as Evelyn settles in that evening and explains in her typically overexcited staccato speech rhythm what her plan is for the next few days, Talia feels a stabbing unease as to how very thin that plan seems to her.

◆ ◆ ◆

Evelyn assigns to Manny the job of bringing armloads of bags upstairs and packing them into corners. He is a task-oriented person and she knows the exercise will calm him. In the meantime she sits with Aunt Talia in the kitchenette and reassures her that they will be here a maximum of three nights.

13

"I'm concerned about the landlord here," Aunt Talia confides. She is a frail woman with a voice worn thin by age, but she still conveys authority when she speaks. "And the noise."

"Everyone *shhh!*" Evelyn calls generally to the room to little effect.

With his possessions secure, Manny sits with them. He bought beers at a corner deli while Evelyn was at the park and now opens his second or third. He is calmer now and generous with compliments on Aunt Talia's appearance and her home. Evelyn assures her that in the morning she will be first in line at the closest city housing-authority office to sort out whatever paperwork her Section 8 application requires. Her understanding is that the most onerous stage of the process—securing a housing voucher— is already complete and they basically will spend the day touring available Section 8 homes, signing forms, and making deposits. She tells Aunt Talia that they will never forget this incredible gift and that Talia in turn will now have a whole new family nearby to help her.

Later, the TV is off and Evelyn and Manny lie on a makeshift mattress made of layered clothes. The limbs of children are splayed and tangled all around them. Manny is drunk and half asleep. Evelyn snuggles against him. She feels wired and hopeful already just being here in the city.

"Just a few hard days and we'll be settled in our home," she whispers.

"Then all we gotta do is find jobs," he replies sarcastically.

Evelyn does not worry about that. Throughout her whole life, she has always found jobs, even if they are typically lousy ones. She has always earned enough. She believes that gathering the courage to leave the old place was the hardest moment of the journey they have undertaken. She's had so many girlfriends and boyfriends and coworkers and cousins over the years who swore they were leaving Lancaster for San Diego, Orange County, Los Angeles, San Francisco, or even farther-flung places like Seattle or Vegas. They outlined timetables to save money and people they could rely on. They obsessed over highly specific, reachable American dreams. Then what invariably happened was time passed and money failed to accumulate and those dreams grew increasingly vague and distant. Then a random day unfolded in which the dream was not mentioned at all. Then a week, then a month. And then the dream was no longer. Very few actually left.

Yet here they are: Evelyn and Manny and the kids, together on the floor in a new city.

◆　◆　◆

Evelyn's version of this dream has not wavered much in the two years since first taking shape as an abstract vision of her kids thriving in school. The way she still sees it, her and Manny's savings would cover the security deposit and about three months' rent on a subsidized apartment near Aunt Talia's and within Monterey Park's school district. Even with housing assistance, they would no doubt have to pay a lot for a small place with boys and girls sharing rooms. She would work around thirty hours per week at minimum wage, plus $100 or so in tips, and earn roughly $450 per week—significantly more if she could find a spot behind a restaurant bar. Manny might need some time to establish himself as a construction laborer, but he eventually would be working full-time at slightly above minimum wage. And so together they would be making nearly $4,000 per month as their living baseline—which according to Los Angeles guidelines would place them just barely above the Extremely Low Income level of $46,950 for a family of seven. Per Section 8 standards, no more than $1,333 of their monthly earnings would be spent on rent and utilities. Around the same amount would pay for food and other basic household supplies. Evelyn calculates about $400 per month on gas and car maintenance, depending on how close their jobs are, and roughly the same amount on the unfortunate necessities of modern existence such as cell phone service and home Wi-Fi, $200 per month on insurance, and $200 more for fun additions like beer, ice cream, and forays to the beach and the movies. According to her math and without accounting for exigent circumstances, Evelyn envisions the family living well and still saving in the vicinity of $500 a month for future educational expenses. She cheerfully imagines that number to be on the rise as Manny becomes a certified craftsman, she ascends toward managerial work, and the girls' childcare costs decrease with age. Within five years, in her estimation, they wouldn't even need to rely on the government's housing vouchers anymore; with luck, they might even be able to contemplate buying their own home.

She isn't the kind of person who writes a lot of things down, but for over a year now she has been keeping this financial table in her mind, where its allotments feel motivating and elegant.

◆　◆　◆

The Housing Authority of the City of Los Angeles has offices throughout the city. All of them are busy, but the main office, in the city's Koreatown neighborhood, is a nexus point of civic need. Evelyn and the girls arrive nearly an hour before the time of opening and the line already reaches down the block along Wilshire Boulevard. The building is large and imposing with its opaque glass paneling. Across the street, like a mirror image, a separate line of people wait for the county social services office to open. On one side is a massive Catholic cathedral, on the other a Korean day spa.

Evelyn is dressed up nicely but she hasn't been able to shower in the crowded apartment. As is often the case, she spent time brushing and braiding the girls' hair to the detriment of her own. Generally, she feels a little gross and stiff. But everyone in line looks gross and stiff, even those who have made an effort to appear businesslike as she has. A great number of children join their parents here. They form small groups and then larger groups to play tag games along the building's hedge. Iris and Sofia yearn to join, but Evelyn is wary of the hectic street. She mostly holds her toddler, Marisol, to keep her from running off. But her back hurts and by the time the office opens and the line begins moving, Evelyn is worn and snappy.

Inside the door, people follow signs that categorize their problems. Evelyn assumed coming here that since she had completed so many forms online, she would be fast-tracked to an actual human being for a formality of a meeting. But the line for current voucher holders in search of housing seems to be the longest of them all. Nylon straps turn a large space off the building's main foyer into fifteen rows of anxious people clutching thin reams of documents to their chests as if someone might steal their old pay stubs, birth certificates, and utility bills. Employees occasionally shout for people who have made an appointment to go to a different room; Evelyn did try to make one herself but the available slots are months away. The primary job of the people shepherding the line seems to be yelling at children to stay next to their parents.

For the next three hours, Evelyn and her daughters shuffle along. Some people in the line mutter bitterly or carry on harried cell phone conversations, but most move in an orderly, muted state and seem resigned by past experience. Even now, on this dry, hot morning in August 2018, awaiting her turn in this brutal line with her miserably bored daughters, Evelyn carries an optimistic view about finding a home today. She equates the housing authority with the DMV: inefficient and understaffed but capable of providing people with what they need within the span of a crummy morning.

Then she finally reaches a clerk, and he states bluntly that Evelyn is mistaken in presuming her qualifying confirmation to be an actual Section 8 voucher. All she actually has right now is a provisional placement on the waiting list, which itself is dependent on providing a legitimate address within Los Angeles; Evelyn has brought documentation involving her aunt's apartment, but—unbeknownst to her until this moment—Monterey Park is part of Los Angeles County but not the city of Los Angeles proper, and this form of housing assistance does not carry over those boundaries. Monterey Park has its own much smaller Section 8 program with a separate wait list that is currently closed until next June, ten months from now.

Evelyn listens, nods, and strives to present calmness. Her mind and spirit loosen and tumble around within. The clerk is trying to coax her along so that he can help keep the line moving. He isn't mean exactly, just curt and unapologetic. She has about a hundred questions but is unsure how many of them are useful. Most involve schools and district boundaries, because her whole plan revolves around the education system of Monterey Park, which is far superior to that of the adjacent Los Angeles Unified School District, but she has a sense that whatever this man might have to say about that subject will fully crush her.

Instead she asks how long the whole housing-assistance process might take once she has all her information resituated. He tells her that people are waiting six years on average for a voucher in Los Angeles. He adds that the city and most of its surrounding independent townships are on the verge of closing their wait lists entirely and indefinitely because of this backlog. Evelyn thinks that this man must feel either very sad or very stupid having to apply normal words such as *process* and *backlog* to describe numbers and time frames so dire as to sound barbaric. She wonders why this office upon receiving her original application did not reply immediately with a message in bold, bright text instructing her not to bring her family here because there were no homes available to poor people.

Evelyn leads the girls out of the building. She has forgotten to validate her parking garage ticket and has to pay the maximum fee of twenty-two dollars. She nearly weeps—not about the parking cost or the clerk's blunt dismantling of her vision or the terrible morning as a whole, but rather about the experience of being faced directly by her own naivete and foolishness in believing anything might be easy.

❖　❖　◆

The immediate numbers that inform Evelyn's life decisions are always close at hand: the five children she is raising, the few thousand dollars she has saved, her hourly wages in the service sector, the assortment of costs she must cover each month.

Beyond these basic family economic figures, she hasn't thought or researched much about the greater landscape she has entered in the nation's most populous county because on the surface, aside from crushing traffic and the occasional *Los Angeles Times* piece about housing scarcity, the area appears to be thriving. Large homes peer down from hillsides across busy residential neighborhoods. Dense islands of tall buildings dot the county. The traffic itself indicates the vast circuitry of commerce. Construction is happening everywhere: residential lots, apartment complexes, office parks, retail centers, warehouses, university campuses, hospitals, skyscrapers. Part of her confidence and optimism stems from the fact that the sheer volume of building projects in every direction virtually ensures Manny's continued employment.

In all her school, job, and apartment research, she hasn't yet come across the region's scary numbers—particularly the way that in Southern California in the early 2010s, as home prices stabilized and then rose very fast following the Great Recession, the number of people without homes began a parallel, prolonged upward rise: 39,461 officially counted on a given night in Los Angeles County in 2013 rising to 44,359 in 2015 and to 55,048 in 2017. Of this latter number, 8,279 were recorded in the "family" demographic and 5,070 were under the age of eighteen.

And she definitely knows nothing of the truly horrific numbers—the murkier, unofficial, unsettling ones that frame reality for the less fortunate, less visible segment of this metro region's twelve million inhabitants. These numbers lie in neighborhoods hidden by freeway barrier walls and tents lining the streets beneath the towers. They lie in the zoning laws that for generations favored single-family dwellings in desirable locations. They lie in East LA, South LA, Pico, and other neighborhoods that are high-density and multigenerational but still deemed unsafe for investment. They lie with the impoverished people who are bound to the city through service to the affluent; in the consistently abysmal ratings of its public school system, which wealthy families don't patronize; in the hours working-class people spend in their daily commutes; in stagnant wages within the service industry; in the rising rates of anxiety, depression, addiction, domestic abuse, and other forms of violence; in the current strain on welfare and other social safety nets; in the hundreds of thousands of applications the county's various Section 8 and other housing-assistance programs receive each year, the wait times that are lottery based but can stretch past a decade for qualified families, the prerogative to build more low-income housing clashing with all the influential, monied interests profiting from the monumental peak value of property.

These trends are not limited to this one city and are not driven by capitalism alone; they are a reflection of a national exigency anchored by the inequities of ownership, engineered across centuries of policy, and magnified by a sprawling disparity fixed to this place and moment in urban America—a place and moment Evelyn has entered with a few Google searches, a ninth-grade education, a strong work ethic, and an overbearing hope for the education and future of her five children.

◆ ◆ ◆

The boys spend the day driving around to the filming locations of different movies and TV shows: *The Fast and the Furious, Independence Day, San Andreas, Transformers*. Orlando is excited at first before realizing that these are mostly just regular houses and buildings that some actors have been paid loads of money to run in and out of. They circle Paramount Studios, and aside from the grand columned entrance, the famed film lot is surrounded on the three less visible sides by a tall, plain yellow perimeter wall stretching for blocks and blocks, against which dozens of homeless people's tents are propped. Orlando envisions TV shows starring household names that cost millions of dollars being shot directly on the other side, a cinder block's width from anonymous dirty people who can't afford to eat. Reality here bums them all out. Then the afternoon becomes a lot of driving and getting lost. Gabriel is not interested in these things even a little bit; Gabriel likes art and drawing, sitting quietly in out-of-the-way spots. Orlando would have much preferred skateboarding in a parking lot, but a day in the city has shown him that open space is much less available here than in the desert.

Both boys have learned over the years that when they are assigned to their stepfather's care, time passes more smoothly if they just go along with his plans. Anytime they object or suggest alternatives, Manny has a way of sulking and then growing prickly and then finding beer. And the boys are often assigned to Manny while their mother takes the girls. Such is their family dynamic: either everyone together or the girls and boys apart.

◆　◆　◆

"Did we really give up our lease?" This is Manny's most pertinent question once Evelyn has the kids set up with screens so that she can relate the day to him. He asks it multiple times in different forms and tones, and he treats her consistent reply of *yes* as a possible misunderstanding.

Evelyn loves Manny very much. She has been with him for eight years, has borne three children with him, has seen him at his most angry, lazy, exhausted, bitter, and dumbfounded. But she still sometimes falls into the grip of those childlike feelings of love that place him as the lens through which all the world must filter before reaching her perception. Her boys are not biologically his—in fact they are the sons of a gang guy Manny despised and feared growing up—but he pays them more attention and is more interested in teaching them things than virtually any father she has observed in her world. He is a little pudgy, a little unkempt, a little full of himself, a little bit of a drunk—but he is very loyal. Maybe he listens to her too devotedly sometimes, with a habit of saying *yes* without really thinking through whatever he might be agreeing with. In these instances, he becomes especially disappointed, even contemptuous, when her plans do not turn out as proposed. But prior instances have never approached the stakes they contend with now.

His suggestion is to call the landlord and beg for their lease back, then return to Lancaster tomorrow. "Maybe our shit is still on the street where we left it," he says.

Evelyn already received a message earlier today relaying that the land-lord has had their stuff cleared away. But that doesn't matter. She is not going back to the desert. She strives to explain in practical terms that they have already given up their home and many of their belongings as well as her job. But in her mind's unspoken argument, she isn't going back home because people who leave and then go back do not tend to leave again. She neither wants to grow old there nor wants her children to grow up there.

"We have savings," she insists to Manny. "So let's find jobs, and find an apartment, and make it so we don't even need the city's help to live."

◆ ◆ ◆

To look for employment in a totally new landscape with five kids on sum-mer break, three of them younger than eight, proves from the outset to be laborious and logistically complicated. The boys can watch the girls up to a certain point—maybe as long as two hours. Past that she cannot bring her-self to quite trust her sons in the event of some pressing need. The thought of her baby girl, Marisol, wanting something important and Evelyn not being there is still terrifying.

Various bosses, girlfriends, and family members have told her that five kids is too many, that she should have stopped at two or three; this judg-ment has been incessant in her life even from people with more children than she. With the first two kids—her boys—she was young and uned-ucated, associated with a Lancaster gang, wrapped up in delirious ideas of a romantic life with her sweetheart in that gang, who turned out to be philandering and abusive. But having two babies as a teenager somewhat organically removed her from that life, and the boys' father ultimately ran out on them. That he did so before she could gather the courage to leave him would always make Evelyn feel like a coward, but at any rate he landed in prison not long after and she has never had contact with him since. From that segment of her young adulthood grew a determination never to remain for too long in a situation she knew to be repressive or dangerous; from that determination grew her ambitious plan to leave Lancaster.

When she became involved with Manny she'd already known him most of her life. Very quickly he fastened himself to the idea of taking care of her, and with him she had the two girls and they seemed to have a perfectly balanced, well-sized family. Marisol, Evelyn's fifth baby, was unplanned but arrived in a way that felt destined somehow because they were managing pretty well all around at that time. Her beautiful children and the attention she loved giving them felt redemptive every day, and in that context—and in a wide extended family of Catholics—she was accustomed to treating the judgments of others with defiance. But these judgments further propelled the idea of fleeing Lancaster.

Now she has fled and the onus to validate the decision economically not only is an imperative for her kids' sake but also will permit her to tell dozens of people who once made a pastime out of questioning her life choices that they had been wrong all along.

Monterey Park lies at the westernmost end of a band of densely populated suburbs that stretches about sixty miles between Los Angeles and San Bernardino. Within these contiguous neighborhoods are hundreds of restaurants: Chili's, TGI Fridays, Applebee's, Buffalo Wild Wings, Outback Steakhouse, and other localized versions of mid-tier chains. In short excursions over the course of three days, she submits applications throughout the area and then, despite being nonreligious in her adulthood, prays.

Manny's job situation was always going to be both harder and potentially more lucrative. He is experienced in most areas of light construction, but he remains unlicensed and lacks artisan skills. In Lancaster, where his father's and his own relationships spread wide, he could find a real job when he wanted with one or two phone calls. Evelyn has assumed that building anything close to such a network in a new area will take months at least. Manny believes that he has enough loose contacts to begin that process by taking undesirable gigs like digging trenches. From there he will gradually prove himself and form dependable relationships. The plan then will be to earn a license in drywall, start his own business, and branch out into other specialties such as plumbing and electricity. This arc made him act confident and heroic when they were talking about it hypothetically late at night with drinks in their outdoor area in the desert. But after a few mornings of waking up on the floor of Aunt Talia's one-bedroom entangled with five kids, and with the new pressure of recent developments, he has fallen far out of its enchantment.

Manny drives off in his truck in the mid-morning and she doesn't hear from him for the rest of the day. At night, they don't have the time or space to talk about anything that transpired in between.

◆　◆　◆

They are just children. This is Aunt Talia's assessment both hosting and observing the family's first frenetic week in the city. In her mind she is not referring to Marisol, Sofia, Iris, Gabriel, or Orlando. She thinks of Evelyn and Manny this way: so maniacally busy with their bodies and their voices and momentary *to-dos* without ever pausing to think more than a few moments ahead of the service jobs they seek. Talia believes in the worth— the nobility even—of her niece's foundational desire for her kids to attend schools of opportunity rather than sparsity. And she definitely knows the need to leave Lancaster and the layers of family history there, much of it toxic. She once made the same exit and at roughly the age Evelyn is now. Her late husband was more enterprising than Manny, and Talia herself had a clear, obtainable ambition to earn a teacher's certificate and work in schools, which she did mostly as a special education assistant. Rents were cheaper then in the late 1980s; life was simpler and its decisions less consequential. Two working-class people could reside in the city then with small comforts. That basic bearing is no longer accessible without some serious preexisting advantages, of which Evelyn and Manny have none. She isn't sure now that she sees a way through here for this family at this time—a way to pull the fraying edges together and establish a sustainable existence. Talia knows in her heart that in the current iteration of what America is, people of their background, with their skin color, with their means do not have a route of entry to spaces in which their children can have a solid education. Evelyn is trying to force that truth to be untrue and Talia foresees trouble. There is no reinvention here—not anymore.

Talia wants to help shepherd them, but already, after just a few days, she is receiving calls from her landlord's office regarding too many people in her apartment, lease violations, fire code infractions. Only for another night or two can she claim a brief family visit. The neighbors who saw all the luggage being carried in do not help her argument. She's been living here for over twenty years and her rent is probably more than $2,000 below market. That deviation makes her a target in her own home.

◆　◆　◆

Evelyn understands that the time frame of her modest goals no longer aligns with the time frame their situation demands. Her aunt needs calmness.

Her kids need exercise and stimulation. And Evelyn needs to use her aunt's address in order to place her kids in school here. She does not desire to press a tense situation toward rupture.

At any rate, on Thursday afternoon—five days after arriving in the city—Evelyn returns home to a serious chaos of bickering children. She wades through them and gently knocks on her aunt's bedroom door and leans her head inside. The bedroom is very small, maybe six feet by eight. Her aunt sits in a chair crammed between the bed and the window, struggling to shut out the racket. Evelyn understands that they all need to be out of the apartment this afternoon.

She sets her kids to packing what clothes and things they have brought upstairs while Evelyn does her best to tidy the place, to soften the footprint of their stay. The kids are all helpful; they have a way of banding together with Orlando as leader in times when she needs some order.

In the late afternoon, with bags on their laps and in the footwells, Evelyn pulls the Highlander away from her aunt's building. Some neighbors observe the departure with satisfaction from railings and doorways. Talia waves as Evelyn enters the city's terrible traffic patterns in search of somewhere to stay that night.

In this moment, she has over $4,000 in a standard Citibank checking account. She is not addicted to any substances or diagnosed with any mental disorders. She's had a job since she was sixteen years old. She's paid some form of rent for the majority of that time. She is capable of hard work. She owns a car and has a wide extended family on which to rely in an emergency. She is in a supportive marriage. The very notion of homelessness—as it is for the majority of housed people across the urban landscape of the city of Los Angeles, the state of California, and the nation of America—remains a sad abstraction for her. Her children have always known rooms with their own beds in them, meals prepared in the mornings and evenings, a sanctuary to which they could always return together no matter what kind of day they'd had.

They will not have a stable home again for nearly five years.

◆   ◆   ◆

The American Inn Motel is a low-slung horseshoe of rooms. The doors open directly onto the parking lot. Located two blocks south of Interstate 10, the main east-west artery serving this sector of Los Angeles County, the American shares a well-trafficked corner with a taqueria and a Mobil gas station. Their room has two double beds, a breakfast table with two chairs, a bathroom, and a mini refrigerator and microwave that together serve as the "kitchen" advertised on the road sign. The room costs seventy-three dollars per night, a low-end figure for the area. The lot seems to attract working people like them and not people needing rooms for drugs or sex or both. This is important to Evelyn. The family is in a predicament, and the kids understand that the situation is far from ideal. But they open the door in the morning and encounter people who are clearly going to work—almost as in a legitimate apartment complex—and so life does not appear entirely out of hand.

The parking lot is not gated and they move all their things inside from the SUV and truck. Bags fully layer the floor and pile up in the four corners. Evelyn has not yet succeeded in potty training Marisol and this is a problem for everyone. Evelyn has always kept an extremely clean home. Her friends label her OCD; she considers herself prideful. The American Inn Motel room gives her nothing to feel proud of.

She hasn't slept all that well for most of her adult life since giving birth to her first child, Orlando, because there was always some worry or fear to stir her mind even at rest—perhaps especially at rest. Initially these were gang- and relationship-related. After those dual ties were severed, the orbit of her angst shifted to the insecurities of single motherhood, which for some reason lingered even after she moved in with Manny. For a few years working night shifts in bars during her early twenties, she'd relied on drinks during and after work to sleep. But after having her third child, Iris, who was her first with Manny and symbolic of a new beginning in Evelyn's personal life, she didn't really have the bandwidth to drink anymore. She'd grown accustomed to fitful sleep and actually took comfort in knowing that she could be awake more or less instantaneously if one of the kids needed her.

But in the motel room, even semi-sleeping is scary. The corner outside is loud with middle-of-the night pedestrian traffic and loiterers. Only a pane of glass and hanging vinyl shades separate her children from whatever muttering madman or shrieking woman happens by on a given night. More unsettling still in her active imagination are the people she can't hear, the people who might case the lot and figure that a family of small children crammed into a cheap motel with no security features signifies easy prey. At times throughout the nights here she disentangles herself from the little ones in bed with her and sits at the table by the window, peering through the slanted shades into the shadowed lot. She thinks of herself as keeping watch. But in truth she spends those hours wondering how they have reached this state of affairs so quickly.

Nights like these—which is to say every night they remain at the American Inn Motel—find her exhausted come morning, when her job search resumes.

◆ ◆ ◆

Orlando will not ultimately remember many details regarding the American Inn Motel, only that the name is redundant, he is not really allowed to leave it, they eat too much fast food, and his mother rustles around in and out of bed throughout the night. Once he wakes and sees her unsuccessfully trying to wedge all their extra bags in the closet, out of sight; the piles she makes keep collapsing outward through the door, and each time that happens she emits a defeated little gasp into the darkness. On another night he sees her sitting atop the air-conditioning unit by the window with her knees clutched tightly to her chest, staring outside.

Orlando tries to make games for his younger siblings to play on the narrow strip of sidewalk that separates the parked cars from the motel room doors: relay races and obstacle courses and such. But one of the motel managers tells them that it isn't a playground.

◆ ◆ ◆

In the afternoons, using her phone for guidance, she drives wider and wider circles around the region, filling out applications. Some forms are fully online, but most restaurant managers still work with hard copies and Evelyn likes showing her face to them even in passing. Her glossy hair and big hoop earrings, huge and authentic smile, and fluent English make an overall terrific impression on people, she thinks. She usually leaves her sons to look after themselves at the motel or at the park near her aunt's house for these time blocks. Her daughters, being dragged along, despise these hours even with the steady stops for candy affording moments of respite from their boredom.

"Did you get the job, Mama?" Iris and Sofia ask in unison when she emerges from a restaurant—not in tones of supportive curiosity but rather in pent-up longing for the search to conclude.

"Get jobba, Mama?" the little one takes to imitating.

"I don't know yet," Evelyn replies at first. After a few days, she begins telling them gently to stop asking. At the end of a week with no callbacks at all, her response is silence. She simply puts the car in gear and drives.

◆　◆　◆

She refers to them often as *my boys* or *the boys.* She reduces her first two children to a single entity this way because together they are the reason she escaped gang life in Lancaster, the reason she escaped their father, possibly the reason she is not now in prison like that man is. The boys are intimately connected through this shared experience and identity, and Evelyn is connected to them through those early years of having one tucked within each of her arms. For some reason she liked to have Orlando in her right arm, and Gabriel in her left. She holds so many memories of late, late at night in the apartment on the outskirts of Lancaster, holding them with the TV on, waiting for their father to come home and hoping he'd had a good enough day to want to sit with them and hold them, too—and not a day so bad that he might be impelled to curse her and strike her. Those nights—the uncertainty of those nights—comprised their first years of childhood. And maybe as a means to endure that passage in her life, she envisioned that her sons would always remain a bundle in each arm. She treats them that way sometimes still.

Yet the two of them are so distinct in personality that to blanket them together is almost comical. Orlando is small in stature but he has a forceful attitude that draws stronger kids to him. Beginning in day care, he tended to be the self-proclaimed leader of all his groups. He was not a well-behaved kid and he always had a scheme, but he rarely was in trouble because he found minions to absorb consequences. "The crime boss," Evelyn called him. But Orlando did not become a bully. He was never especially physical or inclined to antagonize others. Teachers thought he was funny and Orlando liked school. For these reasons, Evelyn—who was always highly watchful of school dynamics due to her own mostly terrible experiences and eventual dropping out—did not worry about his tendencies as a ringleader. As he moved into early elementary school, even as his home life and family unit began to rend apart, his self-confidence and magnetism seemed to strengthen.

In contrast to Orlando, Gabriel remained her baby. She felt that connection with him even as he grew almost as tall as her, even as she raised three more babies after him. He was simply the one who seemed the most thoroughly and consistently happy to be close to his mother. The others and particularly the girls found elements to complain about within any given moment, even within the family's very best days. But Gabriel seemed geared toward contentment. When he was very young, Evelyn worried that he might have some sort of mental disorder characterized by tranquility. Autism was her primary concern, and late-night internet searches amplified it. She could reduce any aspect of his demeanor to a word or two in a symptom search box—*doesn't cry* or *high pain tolerance* or *gentle*—and within two clicks she'd arrive at a list with autism near the top. But once he entered school situations, Gabriel proved himself to be simply a kid who gave easily to the tides of childhood and school days, one who played well and got along with something of a stoic demeanor. Released from concerns over autism, Evelyn worried next that her son was doomed to be a pushover, the pawn of more dominant types—kids like his older brother but meaner. This fear went unsubstantiated, too. From an early age, Gabriel neither sought the approval of others nor seemed moved by any active disapproval. From Evelyn's perspective, he was more or less immune to most aspects of childhood that had made childhood torturous for her. He was glad to see her each afternoon. He was understanding when she had to leave for work in the evenings. Gabriel was and remains all-around wonderful in her estimation.

She has now a sense that she over-relied on her boys for emotional support when they were young and that each himself became a bit too needy in his own way. Yet another motivator for leaving the desert was the blanket observation she'd made that children there—especially boys—were growing up faster than they should because of the people and the lifestyles around them. A hardening occurred, a desensitization. It happened to her brothers and cousins. It definitely happened to the boys' father and, to a lesser extent, Manny. She doesn't want it to afflict Orlando and Gabriel; she wants them always to remain themselves.

◆　◆　◆

Her children need to have nice shoes when they begin a new school year at a new school. Neither Evelyn nor Manny has a job yet, and two and a half weeks in the American Inn Motel has reduced their savings by over one-third, into a territory of alarm if not total disaster. But in the meantime Aunt Talia has agreed to lend her address so that the kids can enroll at her local kindergarten-to-eighth-grade school—which happens to rate highly online in the categories that Evelyn values. This aspect of her larger plan—the central and most important aspect—remains intact. In spite of the current hardship and close quarters, Evelyn manages to experience gratitude.

Evelyn grew up mostly clothed by Goodwill. The soles of her sneakers were often starting to become unglued before she even wore them. For a few years she carried the nickname "Floppy" because of that slapping noise the rubber made against the ground when she walked. In the meantime, she knew kids from totally broke families who showed up in brand-new, brightly colored on-brand basketball shoes. Those kids did not have disparaging nicknames.

On the Saturday before school starts, she takes them all to a suburban mall called the Plaza West Covina, which is old-fashioned in the sense that the structure is massive, windowless, and filled with food and jewelry pagodas in between the anchor stores. Manny considers this outing to be foolish and does not join them. Evelyn agrees that she is being foolish, but she thinks that she can still afford to be that way for a good cause once in a rare while.

There is a special feeling when a family as large and wide-ranging in age as hers comes through the door of a public setting—a sensation of bursting forth, of assuming ownership, of somehow altering in a major way the reality of the physical space by virtue of their entering it. This perceived takeover of the mall issues within her a feeling of immense pride and also something like power, as if she were a general with a small army. She deeply loves doing this, even when the metaphorical land they are metaphorically invading is a somewhat grim shopping mall where they can't afford what they have come here to buy.

They browse Foot Locker and the Nike store. Evelyn's mental ceiling of thirty-five dollars per kid isn't really applicable to the stock at either. But when they check out Target and Macy's, the kids make off-putting faces at everything she shows them. Now they are all tired. The food court is a pleasant diversion where Marisol can roam a bit. Then they try the big sporting goods store and find an end-of-summer discount wall with enough options such that Evelyn is just slightly over her budget and the kids are pleased.

She is not actually prepared for how painful the expenditure feels, and the shock of it does not fully land on her until they are almost back to the American but still locked in traffic on the interstate. Marisol is asleep and the other kids are weary and quiet. Evelyn's hands clench the wheel tightly. Her fingers are stiff. She cannot rid herself of that fleeting but impactful dose of actual fear that passed through her as the cashier rang up the boxes. Life has always tended to balance out before, and she is behaving as if it will balance out still. But buying shoes is unnerving.

◆　◆　◆

The day before school begins, all seven of them go to a public pool together. The pool is part of the park Evelyn and the girls visited that first evening in the city. The line to enter is long due to the hot day and the facility's capacity rules. But once inside at a cost of $1.50 each they all have a beautiful time. They spread a few towels from the American on the concrete. Evelyn lies in the sun with Marisol while Manny and the boys take turns jumping off the side. Iris is able to pass the lifeguard's test to swim in the deep end but decides not to so that Sofia does not feel left out. The kids begin playing with other kids and Manny comes to lie out with Evelyn. Their shoulders press together in the sun. They hold hands. Evelyn dozes for a time while Marisol naps against her. When they both wake to that ultra-tiredness that comes with having slept in the hot, bright sun, Evelyn takes Marisol in the pool. She swirls the toddler around the shallow section. The other kids surround them and splash. Manny dangles his legs off the side and just watches them all with a warm, fond smile that feels more typical of the person he is than the irritable flashes that have been distinguishing him since the motel stay began. For these hours, Evelyn is the matriarch of a vibrant family.

❖ ❖ ❖

Orlando takes to sleeping within the room's closet with the mirrored accordion door closed, and now all the younger kids emulate him and try to stake out their own "rooms": behind the table leg for Iris, in the bathtub for Gabriel even when it is residually wet from people showering, behind the corner of the AC unit for Sofia, with a rampart of bags forming a crib-like space. They fight over which spot is more private and thus more desirable.

❖ ❖ ❖

"You all look amazing," Evelyn tells them as they emerge from the room in their new sneakers on the first day of school. Against the usual grumpy protest she lines them up youngest to oldest in front of the Highlander and takes a photo.

She notices immediately while approaching their new school that most kids' shoes look ratty—not with a sense of fashionable intention but in a way that suggests nobody actually cares about shoes here. What stands out in the line of students waiting for the gates to open are the backpacks slung over their shoulders: mostly brand-new with sequins and reflective silvery swatches. Evelyn realizes quickly that she invested in the wrong accessory. These first moments in their new school become stressful for her even though her children don't seem to notice or care. She feels as if she has failed them and—just as regretfully—wasted a lot of money in doing so.

More than a decent job or even a decent apartment, she yearns now to be a mother who puts her children in a position to be successful in school: the one who knows how best to study each subject and craft standout art projects and wear acceptable clothes. She observes other such parents in the line as the gate opens and kids begin filing inside, leaving the adults outside. As she holds Marisol and they wave frantically at the other four receding across the yard—Sofia to kindergarten, Iris to second, Gabriel to fifth, Orlando to seventh—she consoles herself with the fact that at least she has delivered them to school washed, dressed, and on time. The fundamentals on this day represent triumph. Her heart also swells with the way Sofia seems to unconsciously reach for the hands of Iris and Gabriel on either side of her, and they all walk behind Orlando: the older kids usher the younger one into school until teachers break them away toward different sectors.

Evelyn and Marisol linger outside for a few minutes after the other parents disperse. Together they point and marvel at the stunning murals painted on the school's outer walls, brightly colored depictions of childhood happening beneath rainbows and alongside unicorns.

◆   ◆   ◆

The Applebee's in east Alhambra is one of the many, many restaurants that initially did not call her back. When she followed up exactly a week after leaving her application, someone there informed her that they'd hired another. But at the end of August, Evelyn's phone lights with a number she doesn't recognize and she learns that since a couple new hires "didn't work out," she can begin waitressing that night if she is available. This conversation occurs in the midafternoon just as school pickups are happening. The weather is hot and dry and the Toyota Highlander's old cooling system feels weak as she idles in a long line of cars around the corner from school. She blurts that, yes, she can absolutely be there to work by 4 p.m., a little over an hour from now. Then she leaves a slew of messages for Manny—first in celebratory tones and then more sternly pleading with him to be back at the motel by 3:30 to watch the kids.

She fusses over her hair and makeup in the bathroom, excited not only to work and earn money and make their life feel sensible again— but also to have somewhere to be outside this room, people to be with, a purpose beyond the immediacies of childcare. In fact, she is giddy. But as the minutes elapse toward her shift, that feeling passes over into concern and then dread as Manny continues not to come back and not to answer his phone.

It is 3:30, then 3:35, then 3:45. The Applebee's is probably twenty minutes away in modest traffic. She looks casually great but already she will be late. Orlando, at twelve, is not the most reliable kid but he is competent enough to handle a few hours of real caretaking. And it is Orlando, not Manny, who saves her on that first evening of employment. The moment is simple: she asks him if he would mind watching the younger kids, and without question he replies, "Sure." Maybe its simplicity is what quietly moves her and makes the exchange one she will remember and hold close through all the years of trials that follow: the good-natured smirk he gives her, the genuine happiness and pride he exudes toward her when he learns she has landed a job, the way he sweeps Marisol up in one arm while urging his mother out the door, Marisol's belly laughter as she paws at his face.

That first night at Applebee's, though fretful about the childcare situation, she definitely impresses with her ability to fold somewhat seamlessly into the shift. Every restaurant she's ever worked at—which number many and range from summers at sweltering taco counters to a six-week stint at a moderately priced sit-down restaurant that catered to Los Angelenos passing through Lancaster en route to Mammoth and Tahoe and other upstate ski destinations—operates not just to its own rhythm but with what she considers its own personality. Some places carry tones of anger and desperation. Others are sort of harmlessly frantic, and others are dull. This Applebee's immediately feels like a place with a low pulse, a spot where people come in some manner of retreat from the too bright, too hot, too loud, too demanding world outside.

The manager is a man in his twenties, a little younger than her but portly, balding, with bad skin and maybe a sweating problem. He seems the type to be overly sharp toward people who work under him but not with enough authority to be hurtful, most likely because he is insecure. His hands and arms are always up to something: pointing at spaces or futzing around with tableware or gesticulating with words. He leads Evelyn urgently around the half-full restaurant—slow-eating elderly singles at the bar and couples at the tables—and she nods and smiles throughout her tour.

What Evelyn knows about herself—what has rarely failed her throughout her life—is the way she has of disarming people. She is short, which makes others feel strong around her, men and women both. And she is full-figured and over-perfumed with thick black hair and snugly fitting clothes and a smoky voice. These accoutrements can make men feel virile even in completely nonsexual situations. She asks questions in a way that puts others in the role of being an expert. Everyone loves that. And in this precise moment in her life, Evelyn feels like her gratefulness must be radiating off her. She is immediately popular. Historically this first impression does not tend to last long once she grows louder with her thoughts, but it is always a nice way to begin a job.

Discreetly, she checks her phone whenever she is not active on the floor. Orlando is responsive and taking good care of her family.

❖ ❖ ❖

The first days of seventh grade make for a jarring, nearly bizarre experience for Orlando. Each aspect of the school day here feels novel to him. At his old school, the hundreds of students milled around the yard in confrontational friend-group clusters until the first-period buzzer sounded. Here, he is assigned to a homeroom with seventeen other classmates in his grade. They sit at desks all facing forward and their homeroom teacher checks in with each of them one by one, permitting them to share thoughts and feelings out loud if they care to. At his old school, one harried teacher taught every subject. Here, they move from class to class learning from instructors who specialize in what they are teaching. His classmates used to be uniformly Latin American. Now roughly half of them are Chinese and the rest are, at a glance, an even mix of Latino, Black, and white kids. PE class changes from being recess with some lackadaisical calisthenics to organized sports. Seventh-graders have art three times a week. Textbooks are up-to-date within a year or two. Club sign-ups are offered for band, chorus, and theater.

He is overwhelmed to be given this amount of individual attention and this many choices within his education each day. He experiences these days in a slightly nervous state perhaps attributable to decision-fatigue and to anxiety over how far behind he is academically, particularly in math.

He does not raise his hand during any of the homeroom sharing opportunities, but he enjoys passively listening to his new classmates talk about their summers, robotics camps they attended, and trips made to their parents' home countries. The ease with which new classmates are vulnerable with one another is astonishing to him.

◆ ◆ ◆

A few cans of beer are lined up on the ground right outside the motel room door when she arrives there close to midnight at the beginning of her second week of work. She throws the cans away and then enters the room to find Marisol and Gabriel awake and watching something on a cell phone. Manny, Iris, and Sofia are all asleep together on the bed. Manny snores. Orlando is propped up against the side wall of his closet thumbing on his phone, the screen of which has about a hundred cracks webbing it.

"Thank you again," she whispers to Orlando, who has been babysitting all week. They don't even wait for Manny to text excuses anymore; her oldest kid caring for her youngest kids is now routine. He nods and shrugs. His pleasant, helpful mood must have been worn away by the hours of childcare. She is also quite tired between the effort of being extra cheerful to everyone all night and the physicality of serving; people tend to over-order at Applebee's and the trays she shuttles around are huge. She presses no more conversation on him.

She is confident that their time at the American Inn Motel, sleeping in closets and bathtubs, has almost reached its end. She is just as confident that the tensions that have grown here within her family will dissolve upon leaving.

During these nights after work shifts, her internet usage revolves almost entirely around housing. Craigslist, Zillow, Redfin, and myriad other rental sites have her scrolling down for long stretches of time, until her eyes throb from fixating on the glowing screen in the darkness and her spirit aches from the margin between what is listed and what they can afford. Apartments the size of Aunt Talia's, even smaller and dumpier than hers, even directly abutting the freeways, are renting for $2,000 or more per month in Monterey Park.

The city provides housing aid besides the Section 8 voucher program. She searches these .gov and .org sites multiple times a day, too: programs as simple as affordable-housing units spread throughout the city and as off-putting as emergency family services. So much text and so many numbers surround the descriptions of these programs. All the semi-permanent options carry warnings of long waiting lists. She is not sure which they might qualify for or if the act of reaching out and asking would threaten to expose the family's address misrepresentation to the school district, expelling her kids and causing Aunt Talia trouble. The whole genre of affordable-housing research is scary. Each night spent wrapped up in its figures and potential consequences causes Evelyn to decide anew that the status quo is by far the least perilous option in terms of her kids staying in school.

◆   ◆   ◆

In 2017, the Los Angeles Homeless Services Authority—LAHSA—counted the number of school-aged children who were homeless as fewer than five thousand in the county of nearly ten million. That same year, a separate civic entity called the LA County Office of Education—LACOE—estimated the same category to exceed fifteen thousand. And the Child Welfare League of America cited roughly sixty-three thousand school-aged children in greater Los Angeles facing housing instability at some point over the course of the school year. The disparity has to do with methodology. The federal definition of *homelessness* used by LAHSA is a person living on the street, in a car, in a shelter, or in a motel. LACOE's designation casts a wider net that includes all youth lacking a stable home residence: those who move between friends and relatives and significant others, maybe, or otherwise carry on a fluid existence. The Child Welfare League uses still a broader categorization of youth homelessness. All these numbers have been rising at double-digit rates year by year since 2010. The counts are used as data points to set budgets and allot resources. Such dramatic differentials between numbers lead not only to funding gaps but to a dissonance in public awareness, a salient confusion as to who really qualifies for resources, who merits sympathy, and how significant the problem actually is.

Orlando, Gabriel, Iris, and Sofia fit all definitions but are counted by none, because they present well and are told sternly by their mother not to allude to their circumstances to anyone, ever, at school—not their nicest teachers, not their best friends. An increasingly paranoid Evelyn fears that doing so will prompt the district to initiate an intervention, learn about their overcrowded motel room and lack of childcare, and force them to change schools or far worse. Evelyn has learned that the Los Angeles Department of Children and Family Services is the largest child protective services agency in the United States and processes more than one hundred and fifty thousand cases per year. She wants the city's social workers nowhere near her kids.

From the very beginning of their new life in the city, these children carry on a dual, stealthy, evasive existence. Even Sofia, five years old and absolutely loving her new school, understands that this is for her benefit, that the consequences of honesty or of asking for help can be grave. In order to maintain the precarious foothold they have managed to gain in a better America, they must lie convincingly and they must lie often.

◆　◆　◆

The neighborhood's terrain is a little hilly for Orlando's skateboard in contrast to the unfailing asphalt flatness of the desert. But he meets some kids his age at school who frequent the two area skate parks. Since he's been building up so much goodwill with his mother by babysitting during her evening work shifts, she permits him to leave school with these friends for a couple hours in the afternoon before making his way to the American by 4:45 p.m. so she can leave for Applebee's.

Orlando is skilled at adjusting to new environments and making friends as he goes. He changed schools in Lancaster a few times growing up. By his own reckoning at age twelve, Orlando has never been very attached to any one person or group. He is socially liquid. While establishing himself in a new school always makes for a puzzle to be solved, this school and neighborhood present a specific canvas in which by virtue of being Latino and from the desert and a little rough in his manners, his new peers regard him as intimidating. Back in Lancaster, Orlando was always considered a mama's boy and a nerd.

The situation at the long-stay motel remains brutal, as does Manny's drinking and simmering anger, as does his mother's blithe faith that when Manny is gone all day but not bringing home any money, he is truly establishing a network of certified crews and not hanging out in bars with other unemployed men or probably just sitting in his truck on side streets working through six-packs. Orlando feels angry about the dynamic when he is dealing with Marisol's bedtime and Sofia's overtired grievances and Iris's hyper demands on a given night. But he primarily feels sadness for his mom and sisters.

The skateboarding community of any neighborhood is slow to accept new regulars. A person has to appear daily and not only display the mastery of certain tricks but also show the reckless daring required to attempt newer, harder tricks. He has to exhibit success and failure and persistence in a certain performative balance in order for skate park kids to cede space. Orlando is nothing more than an average skater at the beginning of the school year, but he devotes most of his free time to improving upon both his skill and reputation. This focus also helps him to minimize the exponentially growing burden of having a place to sleep but not a home.

◆   ◆   ◆

The only non-necessity that Evelyn really spends money on—a very small but meaningful perk, she believes—is a flower arrangement kept in one of her mother's passed-down vases on the loud AC unit that serves as the windowsill in their motel room. Near her Applebee's is a flower vendor: a couple of old Asian ladies working out of a shedlike rotunda surrounded by the huge asphalt coverage and big-box stores of suburbia. The first time that Evelyn stopped there on a whim, she simply spent a few minutes standing in the fragrances of lavender, lilies, sunflowers, bluebells. Then once she felt confident in the longevity of her job at Applebee's, she permitted herself to purchase a few stems for $7.99. She supplemented these with some of the baby's breath turned out every couple of days by the Applebee's check-in stand. And the vase in their motel room, modest as it is, makes her feel now like they are home. Of all the two dozen windows at the American, all the families and individuals in the various unique straits that have landed them here, theirs is the only one to feature such a flourish. She notices this each time she pulls in and the sight of the blossoms means that they are not yet truly desperate.

◆   ◆   ◆

The weekday serving shift from 10 a.m. until 5 p.m. works best with her kids' schedules—including Marisol's all-day Head Start preschool program—but is less busy. The shift from 5 p.m. until midnight earns significantly more money in tips that she can immediately take home, but those hours lay pressure on Orlando and her kids and Manny. They also wreck her for drop-offs the following morning. Because she is new, she does not necessarily have much influence on when she works. Flexibility is absolutely vital when starting out at a restaurant. A degree of autonomy comes only after months of subjecting herself to the dictates of others.

She earns $12.66 per hour in wages, and California taxes bump that figure down to just below $10—missing money that she will retrieve in tax refunds but not until after the new year. Tips vary, but at the moment she averages the figure to $40 per shift and four to six shifts a week. All those numbers will rise with time and seniority. But for the fall of 2018 she projects her earnings to be a little less than $550 per week, or $2,200 per month. This number is more than she anticipated earning here and on its own would *almost* cover the average rent and utility costs of a basic low-end one-bedroom apartment in Monterey Park—omitting car maintenance, gas, cell phone plans, insurance, and other foundational costs of living that must be counted even before feeding and clothing seven people.

Evelyn always disliked math in school. She hates talking about math with her husband now.

"If you keep on with it, then whatever I make is just going to cover whatever you spend," she says to Manny in a tone that—she feels—is matter-of-fact and non-accusatory.

Manny blows air sharply through his lips. "So I can't spend money here? I'm *not allowed*?"

He sits on an overturned plastic trash can outside the door to their motel room. He uses this spot to smoke sometimes. This is the place where they usually argue now. He isn't drunk tonight, and she is energized by a busy work shift, so she thinks it would be as decent a time as any to attempt an adult conversation. She misses their little patio in Lancaster where they would form big dreams late at night.

"You can spend money, just not *all* the money." Their nest egg has eroded now well below the point of affording the first month/last month cost of securing any legitimate place to live. The motel room is a relentless driver of the dwindling. Just as damaging are the chunks Manny has been withdrawing from their checking account: forty or sixty dollars every few days. He claims gas and food and the prerogative not to seem like a broke person around people who can potentially hire him. "I want to get out of this place," she states. "Do you?"

"Of course I do."

"So just, like, watch it. The money, the beer, the way you talk around the kids sometimes—"

"Wait, what do I say around the kids?"

"The way you talk to *me* around the kids," she clarifies. "You're not very respectful sometimes."

"I respect you!" he hollers.

"I know that. It hurts when you talk down to me. It's embarrassing when the boys are there. I can see it makes them upset or even mad."

"I'm not trying to make anyone mad at me," Manny says. He pulls hard drags off his cigarette and shakes his head toward the concrete. He seems glum and sincere. "I'm just struggling, you know."

"We're not going to struggle for much longer," she says quietly to both him and herself. "It's just hard right now."

◆   ◆   ◆

Iris has a forceful personality and Evelyn does not worry about her: if Iris is not receiving attention at school, she demands it one way or another.

Teachers do not always appreciate this trait, but it means that Iris never feels overlooked.

Sofia is Evelyn's greater concern. She did not like any aspect of school in Lancaster; she cried most mornings; she attracted tormentors; she starfished around her mother's thigh at drop-off and sagged into her mother's arms at pickup. She wilted there throughout preschool, and Evelyn's heart shattered anew each morning when, no matter what day it was, Sofia asked upon waking if it was a school day and then, learning that indeed it was, bunched her face into an expression of pure hopelessness.

Her first two weeks of kindergarten have her beaming now. Her teacher's name is Ms. Agatha, and Sofia speaks her name constantly, with reverence, like that of a secret connection to a world of power and influence. Her new best friends are named Hsun and Feng. She renames stuffed animals after these people and can't wait to see them each day. Sofia heaves herself into the Highlander before the others each morning, kicking her feet excitedly against the back of Evelyn's seat.

August has turned to September and the kids are all firmly embedded in the school year. They each have friends whom they talk about, kids they avoid, teachers whose quirks provide hilarity and consternation, some homework. They each have a daily slew of both high and low emotions that call for a mother's attention. That attention, when asked for, is Evelyn's great happiness throughout these days. She treasures the act of giving it—of learning all the different players' names and personality traits, of making exaggerated expressions of delight or dismay to mirror those of her children, of devising tactics by which to earn a teacher's good graces or undermine the power wielded by a bully. She takes interest in the ways that problems grow more sophisticated as children grow older—but also don't. She is a true and thorough sucker for a child who needs a hug, including

Gabriel, who needs many but is embarrassed about needing them in front of his younger siblings and Manny. In these instances, Evelyn asks Gabriel to come help her fetch bags from the car; she opens both the passenger and rear doors of the Highlander to form an alcove in which she can still hold him and call him her baby. Each small incarnation of these moments—each tender need—possesses its own overwhelming gravity that assures her that, contrary to the popular refrain in Lancaster, she has not borne too many children.

She truly believes her kids to be a major force of good in the world and thus valuable to all the spaces they inhabit. When she is with them, despite the driving and errands and bickering—the vast amount of physical and emotional energy demanded by five little people—she feels as if her existence follows an order and purpose greater than those determined simply by the grisly economics of lower-class American life. She is inspired.

The rest of the time she frets over those economics and how she is not earning as much as their lives cost.

Manny finally secures some work here and there. Two or three times per week she now returns to the motel room and finds him deep asleep in bed, reeking and covered in paint or Sheetrock particles. But she doesn't really see what he is earning because he is paid in cash and spends that cash on his own. Asking him for specifics upsets him.

Near the end of September, the number in her and Manny's checking account—the full monetary value of her family of seven aside from the truck and SUV, which has taken years of consistent effort to build—falls from four figures to three figures.

◆ ◆ ◆

Orlando's new friends submit themselves to multiple high-velocity colli-sions against concrete surfaces while trying to invent new rail tricks at the skate park. Their joints are ever bruised and abraded. As a group they can be a little loud and obnoxious while alternately whooping for and deriding one another's efforts. They strut around the eight or nine blocks between the park and their apartments with the posture of vivacious teenagers. But they are not tough kids; they are really a quartet of skinny, gangly chil-dren in baggy clothes who don't want to upset their moms. Orlando doesn't have the technology or know-how, but the others in the group spend vast amounts of time editing video clips of their skateboarding exploits into YouTube and Snapchat content. This activity comprises most of what the group talks about even though the resulting videos are nearly unwatchable.

None of them know where Orlando lives at the moment. He is embar-rassed—of course he is, since he sleeps each night in a motel room closet—and he also clings to some faith in his mother's wild positivity, her constant assurances that the motel is a temporary stopover.

Their current video-in-progress features Orlando standing atop a steep ramp flexing his small muscles, then descending and weaving, a little wob-bly, across a level section of the park before attempting to leap onto a rail while performing a 180-degree turn. Over and over, he either misses the rail entirely or hits it at an odd angle. Over and over, he topples forward. The nature of the trick makes landing on his feet difficult because he first has to clear the rail without the wheel fixtures catching on it. So his succes-sion of failures ends time and again with awkward plummets and rolls on the ground followed by the acid jeers of other skaters and Orlando goofily X-ing his arms to signal a bad take. The whole effort is fairly pointless, and he is pretty sure that his pals are all aware of that. But he feels wonderful to be a part of something creative.

At the American Inn Motel, when his mother is working and he is watching his siblings in the small space, he brings these cringe-inducing falls onto his phone screen and watches them over and over with the girls, sharing their laughter at his own expense. Hypothetically, the video will end with a successful landing of the trick—if he ever manages to land it. In the meantime, in his daydreams, he can only imagine the video going viral and bringing him fame.

On a midweek evening, their mother is excited to switch a day shift for a night shift with another server. So Orlando comes straight to the motel from school and takes over for her. In her absence, the kids all settle into the typical night. Gabriel and Iris sit at the table. Gabriel begins his homework, which he is always annoyingly diligent about, and also helps his sister memorize a poem that she will recite in front of her class tomorrow.

Orlando reclines on the bed and allows Marisol and Sofia to huddle around his phone watching the day's outtakes. He is involved in a few different text message threads and in between videos he spends a few minutes responding to those. Marisol keeps whining during these interludes, Sofia goading her on. He has trouble concentrating. Iris and Gabriel are bothered by the noisy bickering and soon all of them grow short with one another.

These situations usually end with laughter once they vent some severely pent-up energy. But Manny bursts into the room before they reach that point. He is stumbling, slurring, and squinty-eyed, causing Orlando to be embarrassed for him.

Manny tells them that he can hear their bullshit from the parking lot and they need to shut up. For whatever reason, he singles out Gabriel with his tirade. Orlando finds a protective instinct activated within him. He often feels jealous of Gabriel because their mom treats him with the most affection even though Orlando assumes the most responsibility, but he also knows that Gabriel needs him more than most little brothers need older brothers. So when he watches the grown man jab his finger at the ten-year-old and his books, and he registers how genuine and deep Gabriel's fear is, Orlando steps in between them.

Orlando pushes Manny's finger away.

Stop with your bullshit, you fucking drunk piece of shit, he says, or something like that. The siblings will remember the rest of the night in very different ways as far as what is said and in what order. But they will each remember Gabriel murmuring for Orlando to stop and step away. Orlando instead steps forward, toward Manny. Though the adult is soft around the middle, his arms and chest are strong from most of a lifetime of manual labor. He pushes Orlando with some intention and Orlando tumbles over the bed past Sofia and Marisol and onto the floor. Working his way back to his feet amid the piled clothes along the wall, maybe Orlando curses Manny out again, or maybe that only happens in his mind. Manny then hits him with a closed fist in the face.

Orlando falls and this time remains huddled on the floor, his arms covering the impacted bone swelling beneath his eye, his spirit shocked still. Manny goes about manhandling Orlando out the door of the room, and Gabriel follows him. Manny shuts the door with the three girls, his biological children, still inside with him.

The whole motel stirs now. Gabriel's idea is for the two of them to go to Aunt Talia's. Orlando worries about their sisters in the room and their mom walking into the drunken chaos unaware. But his phone is still in the room somewhere. They hear Manny ranting at the girls and at the universe.

The brothers sit side by side on the curb a few doors down from their room. The night manager of the American, who does not like their family much, emerges from the office and tells them they can't sit there. Orlando makes a decision then—or maybe what he does is not a decision but rather the only option possible to a little boy in an unbearable sequence of motion. He uses the motel desk phone to call their mom.

◆　◆　◆

Evelyn holds her son's face in both hands, angling it toward the yellow parking lot lights. The intersection is busy with vehicles, and she experiences the indifference of the greater world carrying on undisturbed as her family's small space within it faces upheaval. Her eyes hover two inches away from Orlando's and she just stares at the redness of his cheekbone. Then she presses his head into the space beneath her chin.

After a time, she tells Orlando to stay there by the car. He clearly doesn't want her to let go of him, but he also doesn't argue.

Her arms and hands tremble as she unlocks the motel room door. She hears Marisol inside but nothing else. Manny is groggy and stumbling toward the door as she opens it.

"What the fuck?" he asks innocently.

Evelyn fights hard to control herself. Iris and Sofia sit at the table now with Orlando's cell phone, but they both appear tense, scared. Marisol is on the floor. Some poop has crept upward from her diaper and is smeared into the back of her shirt.

Evelyn bends down to pick her up off the floor, but Manny takes her shoulder firmly. He says again, "What the fuck?"

"I'm taking my kids."

Evelyn wrenches free from him and grabs stray clothes from around the bed and stuffs them in a backpack. Manny tries to justify what happened earlier—"That boy was talking shit! What did he tell you?"—while Evelyn focuses on packing more things. She tells Iris and Sofia to join the boys in the SUV. Manny blocks the doorway. He stinks. Evelyn tells him to move. He does not. She steps toward him, believing Manny will eventually relent to her like he always has. But he pushes her backward, hard. She thuds against the wall and he wraps his right hand around her throat. She can't breathe and her eyes lock on his other arm cocked back.

Evelyn has been beaten up by a few different men before. She has seen that terrible fury and fear commingling in a man's eyes before feeling a man's hand smash against some part of her body. Then as now, a part of her prepares for the possibility of being dead in a few moments; a drunk's anger always carries that potential. She has utterly no idea what would become of her children. A complicated powerlessness falls over her.

She doesn't know whether Manny releasing her has to do with the screaming girls, or Evelyn's own fists weakly pummeling his chest, or whatever expression might have passed through her bulging eyes, or Orlando entering the room and wrapping his arms around Manny's neck from behind, or maybe Manny himself deciding that life as he knew it a little while ago is over for him now. But the moment his grip eases, she rips herself away from him and half a second later has Marisol hoisted in one arm and Sofia's hand in the other. Iris and Orlando are close and the five of them leave the room and then are in the Highlander with Gabriel. All around the U of the motel, people have emerged to watch. Evelyn locks the doors. She breathes a few times but cannot slow down the hurtling progression of this night.

With little care, she maneuvers out of the lot and cuts into traffic heading southeast. At a safe distance from the motel, she glances back at her children. She cannot discern their expressions in the dark, but they are all abnormally quiet. She brought them here less than two months earlier simply for the prospect of attending a decent school. Now she takes flight with them into an urban wilderness.

She notices Marisol squirming in her car seat, craning her neck to try to peer out the rear window. Iris does the same. "Don't look back," Evelyn tells them all.

PART II

Los Robles Avenue

Wendi
1995–2006

WENDI GAINES DOES NOT FUNDAMENTALLY believe that marriage is meant to last for life. The separations of people she loved—her mother and her maternal grandparents, her mother and her father, siblings and stepsiblings, her children and her children's fathers—have steered the entire course of her childhood and young adulthood. When she herself marries in 1996, she is a twenty-six-year-old single mother of four who has been thoroughly taught that love and its accompanying promises of devotion are not solid enough to survive the stressors of poverty and of racism, wanderlust and interpersonal strife, selfishness and jealousy and anxiety. Yet she still permits herself to believe that her marriage, her love, and her promises will be.

◆ ◆ ◆

Before Wendi was born, her maternal grandparents severed ties with Wendi's mother and older brother. They had adamantly considered their white, rich, Christian daughter from Seattle having a baby out of wedlock with a Black man from inner-city Los Angeles to be an irresolvable social calculus worthy of estrangement. By the time Wendi was born in 1970, her parents were living in her paternal grandmother's home in Long Beach, California, before they found their own home in Compton two years later. When Wendi was five and had three more younger siblings, her family relocated north to Oakland, California, where her parents hoped jobs would be easier to find. They split up soon thereafter, and the arrangement held that her mother worked and raised the children while her father dropped off a white envelope containing child support payments once a month, which were for the most part the only times Wendi saw him.

Wendi's father didn't have much to do with his kids after that point; he didn't believe that men were meant to be involved with raising young children. Her mother had to work and kept a demanding, low-pay administrative job at IBM. Wendi was a half-white, half-Black child living on the Black side of one of the nation's symbolic centers of racial conflict. She herself had traversed the lines of that conflict.

Her maternal grandmother, though otherwise completely, voluntarily absent, sent Wendi a one-dollar bill in the mail every year on her birthday.

◆ ◆ ◆

Wendi bore her first four kids during and right after high school. The father of these kids became a violent partner as they tried to make their way through all of life's stresses. When this aspect of him emerged, she was thankful that he focused his physical abuse on her and not their children, and she thought that she could endure the layers of pain in order to keep their young family together. She never involved police or social services. Once the fear and risk became too great, she left him. She was twenty-four. Her mother was always taking in young children: she had five of her own and had legally adopted three of Wendi's childhood friends whose parents abandoned them. She informally parented many others for spates of time along the way. Wendi's own children, when they appeared at her apartment, were like new members joining this fatherless parade.

◆ ◆ ◆

The man who becomes her husband is ten years older than her, in his thirties, divorced with two young children. He mentions to her often how much he loves being a father. He has a regal affect that draws people toward him but he also exudes a mournful quality that Wendi feels only she sees and that is his most attractive aspect.

Their romance moves quickly, energizes each instant of her life, and leads to marriage less than a year after they meet, in 1996, at the city courthouse. Wendi is ecstatic to take his name and move into his apartment with her four kids and experience the economic stability of two incomes. She believes that an entirely new rhythm is being set for the rest of her life.

Their apartment is in a modern, no-frills building near downtown Oakland. His two children live with them. The three bedrooms are crowded with their blended family of six kids. Together, she and her husband have three more children over the next seven years. Their youngest, born in 2003, is named Emmanuel.

◆ ◆ ◆

Wendi knows that her seventh and last child is on the spectrum from early on. Emmanuel does not respond to stimuli in the same ways as his older siblings all had. As he grows into toddlerhood, his differences relative to other

61

kids become more pronounced and upsetting. His pain threshold is extraordinary. He doesn't grasp basic instructions—not because he is drawn to disobedience but rather because he doesn't cognitively process commands. Nor does he respond to affection or bribes. Instead of whining and groaning, he makes piercing screeching noises when he is confused or upset. He does not walk, graduate from diapers, or talk when others his age do. She cannot leave him even for two minutes in an adjacent room, because he is capable of truly hurting himself without even making any noise to alert her.

His needs require every ampere of her energy, every moment of her time. In this new reality, Wendi's relationships with her husband, children, and stepchildren all become secondary to the urgency of his complicated existence and the mysteries of the thoughts he cannot express to her. Over time, his physicality becomes severe and she is usually the focus of it, causing others—including her husband—to question what she is doing wrong.

And she figures that the remainder of her life will play out just like this, romantically complicated and thoroughly exhausting but with a meaningful purpose that only she can bear.

Wendi strives to sustain this existence for as long as she can, to keep these families together, to be a competent and cheerful wife, stepmother, mother, and caregiver to a child with special needs. She strives to be the source of her husband's happiness, his children's, hers. But what she finds in reality is that visions are not realized simply because the visionary is prayerful and earnest. People do not care genuinely for one another forever by virtue of sharing children and a marriage certificate. The more challenging symptoms of autism do not lessen because someone yearns for a loving, loved family.

Her husband struggles—he works hard, travels constantly, is ruled over by others. The money he earns on sales commissions does not always meet the money demanded of him by his first wife, his own kids, and life in California. Over time, he grows more and more dismissive and cutting toward her. Thankfully, given Wendi's past experiences, her husband is not a physical abuser. But he yells at and demeans her in ways that she can't recover from, that become a part of her sense of self.

For a few years after these patterns become ingrained, the dynamics bend and pull and strain them, but they all keep surviving. Wendi expends most of her spirit on Emmanuel's needs and the remainder on her six other sons and daughters.

During these years, her oldest son, who is seventeen, moves to Fresno on his own to escape their home; her second-oldest son, who is thirteen, gets in trouble a few times for minor infractions like fighting at school. Wendi hears about these instances but is too unmoored in her own inner life to really engage in the kind of intervention he needs. When he lands in the court system, Wendi can only sit helplessly in the benches for the couple of minutes he might have before a judge. Ultimately, he avoids imprisonment.

◆ ◆ ◆

In 2006, after ten years of marriage, her husband expels her and the kids from their home.

He has met another woman and, without warning, his mind has been set that he is leaving Wendi and Emmanuel and the others for a new and different life. His manner is cold. She pleads with him to let them stay and

to let her make their marriage function. But she knows that this arrangement, this dream, has been defunct for a while now. He is leaving again for
three days and instructs her to vacate before his return.

Those three days are frightening and exhausting as time elapses toward
losing her mooring in the world. She spends much of the first day lying in
bed while her eight-year-old son, Anthony, and her four-year-old daughter,
Tiara, fend for themselves within the apartment and Emmanuel clings to
her. She is wondering about how and why. She possibly experiences some
kind of nervous breakdown—rapid heartbeat, trouble breathing, numbness
in her hands and feet—but doesn't call anyone to seek help for it. Then she
realizes how pathetic she must appear even to her autistic four-year-old.
Beginning in the middle of that second night after the ultimatum, she starts
to think through this problem and her options.

She has no cash reserves but she does have a car and her last check from
work for $834. Her older children stay in Oakland with their father. She
takes her three youngest and drives a few hours south to where one of her
oldest friends lives, outside Los Angeles in the city of Arcadia. This friend
has been asking her to visit for years now, both before and during her marriage: leave behind the horrible experiences, the sour relationships, the
remnants of domestic abuse, and come to this warm place in Southern
California that has been a destination for people fleeing their problems for
generations.

The neighborhood where her friend is renting a small house is northeast
of downtown Los Angeles. Property is extremely valuable, which means
that tax revenues are high and thus schools and most other services are of
great quality. The trash trucks work efficiently on the designated days, as
do the street cleaners. The parks and public playing fields are well-kept and
watered. Wendi has known none of these flourishes in inner-city Oakland.

Her friend allows her to stay for a few weeks, to vent all her pent-up anger regarding the man she married and men in general, America and its broken health-care and education and juvenile justice systems and the costs she bears, children and how they grow up and forget what has been done for them and leave. Throughout her complaining, Wendi begins to understand that many of her problems reside in Oakland, and she comes to believe—a little too quickly, and with reliance on heavily biased advice from her friend—that a way to salvage her broken life is to relocate it here.

She has no current job, savings, or place to live; the stressors of her old life trail her in tattered strands.

She ultimately visits the Department of Children and Family Services. A line that long is not tenable for a child like Emmanuel. His mannerisms, especially his shrieking habit, upset people. She stands there prepared to defend him and argue with people who are themselves desperate enough to be standing in this line. What she encounters instead is a deep upwelling of kindness from other mothers and children and staff. Wendi and Emmanuel are shepherded to a city caseworker who hears out her story and doesn't rush her through even the irrelevant tributaries of how she has landed here. Then this worker prints for her a list of potential options for emergency housing.

Wendi leaves the office and calls the first entry, an organization called Door of Hope.

◆ ◆ ◆

The Los Robles Avenue home looks from the outside like many houses in Pasadena, a small, highly affluent city eight miles northeast of Los Angeles. It is Craftsman in style and quite large behind a pretty wooden fence. The windows are especially tall and wide to let in natural light because the home's construction predates the electric grid. Porches span the width of the first and second floors. All of these features leave Wendi confused while standing at the T made by the sidewalk and the walkway.

"This is a shelter?" she asks.

"This is your home," the woman who earlier introduced herself as Miss Abeba replies.

"This is a crazy house," Wendi states.

Miss Abeba laughs.

The intake process for the Door of Hope organization is straightforward and gentle, but providing both oral testimony and some documentation evidence of her needs concentrates a light on how little forethought is behind this existential decision she has made. Despite the fortune of having her own space here in this quaint home, on this wide and shady street in one of the region's most historically moneyed neighborhoods, her self-esteem has cratered. She is thirty-six years old and is entering a shelter for people experiencing homelessness. While receiving a tour of the house—simply referred to as Los Robles—she briefly meets two other residents in the common kids' playroom and the shared kitchen. Both of the women look to be no older than twenty, what seems to Wendi to be a much more forgivable age to be here.

Miss Abeba guides her, Anthony, Tiara, and Emmanuel into a one-bedroom suite on the second floor in the rear of the house, with windows overlooking a backyard that is safely enclosed and contains colorful tricycles and other toys for the very young.

Miss Abeba is in her forties, a dark-skinned Black woman of Ethiopian descent with a heavy Amharic accent, not that much older than Wendi but possessing a bearing that suggests a depth of wisdom to share. Her role in the Door of Hope organization is like that of a house mother. She is some combination of spiritual leader and chaperone and counselor. She does not let herself appear in any promotional photos or give public comments, preferring to work in the background, directly with families. In the apartment, she shows the boys their room. Emmanuel is calm today so Wendi lets them be.

Miss Abeba emerges a few minutes later and asks how Wendi feels.

"Relieved, grateful, but also like I might be sick."

"That's normal and to be expected."

◆ ◆ ◆

The organization that takes Wendi in far from home during those confusing days—a marriage's dissolution, the abrupt loss of a place to live for herself and three young children—saves her from perhaps ever having to experience homelessness herself. Her awareness that at the same time there must have been thousands of even more desperate mothers across the city means that Wendi will always feel a deeply spiritual gratefulness over the speed and graciousness with which shelter was provided to her.

The Los Robles house hosts nine families. The rules therein are mostly intuitive: no alcohol, no drugs, no male guests. Others are more nuanced, having to do with the shared spaces and the supervision of children, kitchen use and food storage. Wendi does not have trouble following along, though she can tell immediately that the young moms—which are all the other moms—are over-reactive and prone to friction with people. Wendi knows that Emmanuel, with his noises and gestures, is going to cause a stir. For her first few weeks in the house, she does her best to be polite and keep to herself, placing her gratitude above smaller territorial concerns such as someone using her refrigerator space or hoarding toys or side-eyeing her youngest.

Los Robles isn't a place where one can stay isolated. Residents are assigned days weekly to prepare meals for one another, and they have to eat together. Once she is settled, Door of Hope volunteers provide childcare while Wendi is obligated to attend nightly meetings that are split between job-centric presentations, personal finance classes, therapy, and Bible study. The former two types of classes are geared toward the mothers who have little experience with full-time jobs and managing an actual household. In the beginning, Wendi finds these hours to be rudimentary and boring with hypothetical questions that have obvious answers. She does not say anything overtly rude, but her opinions are obvious: a curt answer here, a half-veiled smirk there. Very quickly after being given shelter in the house, she gains a reputation for believing herself to be better than any of the other women there.

This assumption is not necessarily true, though Wendi does believe herself to be less disastrous than most of these younger women with no job experience and all their unruly children. Two weeks pass and Wendi is nearly reviled in the Los Robles house. She spends her free time shut in her room with her kids, afraid even to use the shared bathroom down the hall. She calls Miss Abeba.

"It's nice here but I don't belong," Wendi says. "I think I have to leave."

"You do belong here," Miss Abeba tells her succinctly. "Because you are here."

"I'm not like these other women," Wendi argues. "They all have these crazy, messy lives."

"You are here," Miss Abeba repeats. "You must finish well."

"I've been taking care of myself and others since I was practically a child myself."

"You are here. You must finish well."

Wendi's therapy begins with that concept.

◆ · ◆ · ◆

Wendi learns quickly that her childhood left more scars than she was ever willing to admit previously.

She did not grow up in a slightly hectic environment held together by her staid grandmother, hardworking mother, and a general faith in God, which is the story she has always told. She grew up in an environment of loss, bitterness, racism, and trauma.

She did not keep her mother and her siblings cohesive as a family throughout her childhood, as she warmly assures herself and her own children. Her family was in fact thoroughly fractured. She is one of the shards.

She does not have strong people skills. Her lack of these—more than the demands of Emmanuel's care, always at the center of her excuses—is the reason she has had trouble with her mother, friends, coworkers, and children as they grew up.

She can love Emmanuel wholeheartedly and unconditionally while still acknowledging the strain his needs cause her. If she does not reorganize her relationship with him and with his challenges, she will be in danger of blaming him later in life for her past and future troubles.

These are the most devastating of the many truths she learns about herself through counseling during the seven months she spends in the Los Robles shelter. She suspects that some of the discord among the other women might stem from all of them learning similar truths about themselves.

◆ ◆ ◆

The numbers associated with the homelessness all around them in the city are upsetting when the mothers talk about the issue in formal group training sessions on financial literacy, or during meals, or in the backyard with kids. Because she has never actually been without shelter, Wendi cannot collude with these women's anecdotes of sleeping in culverts, prostituting themselves, running with two children clutched to their chests as police pursued them through downtown shopping plazas where they may or may not have been thieving. Nor can she relate to the addictions that impelled some of these circumstances. She is a decade and a half older than some of these women—*almost* twice their age. A few of Wendi's children are older than several of these mothers. Her contributions often involve corrections of observations they make. But, as Miss Abeba has theatrically stated, *she is here.* Wendi is a part of this world. She is the head of one of the nine families being sheltered here on Los Robles Avenue in Pasadena. And she can commiserate in the anger and the sheer awe that surrounds the homeless count recorded in 2005: 65,287 people living outside on a given night in LA County. When those known as the "sheltered homeless" are added to this base figure of street dwellers, almost 120,000 humans are thought to be existing on the streets, in vehicles, or in emergency centers at this point in time. More than 35,000 of them are considered chronically homeless or to have been homeless for longer than one year. The revelatory snapshot suggests that over the course of the entire year of 2005, roughly 224,000 people would have at some point experienced homelessness.

"I think of that number and it's like, *fuck*," one of the moms comments while wiping grass stains from her toddler's kneecaps.

"It's like a full Rose Bowl," another very young mother named Yasmine says, in reference to the gigantic football stadium about a mile away.

"It's a bunch of full Rose Bowls."

What these conversations circle but never penetrate directly is the discomfort of being among the nine sheltered here. Much is demanded by Door of Hope while nothing is promised. They and their children have many deep needs and can offer very little as recompense. But the shelter and the food and the beds for the children and the many different serious people working on behalf of their well-being are costly gifts that appear almost absurd in the context of the hundreds of thousands of desperate souls seeking shelter in this land. Wendi herself is here only because there was space available at the exact moment that the exact social worker to whom she'd been assigned dialed the number—not a week earlier or later, maybe not five minutes earlier or later. A different social worker might have dialed a different number and landed her in a less ideal space. Something about the disparity between the kind of support that this organization is providing them and the support most women out there can access stirs a strange, uncentered confusion in the women regarding how they have been deemed deserving. But the kind of thinking that surrounds the word *deserve* can depress anyone, and the staff strongly urges the women to steer away from it.

The homeless count of 2005 is on everyone's mind in Wendi's new world. The county's fresh strategy to account for every person without shelter was one of the most ambitious and granular ever undertaken in the nation at that time. The last official count had been conducted ten years earlier and based on administrative records. Its results skewed low and were unverifiable, which meant that for the past decade those who oversaw budgeting for homeless services lacked an accurate estimate of how many homeless there actually were. During this new count, more than a thousand paid staff and volunteers canvassed 512 designated census tracts over three consecutive nights. Further in-person surveys tracked the turnover in the county's shelters, treatment facilities, jails, and hospitals. The results must have been about as close as a large county bureaucracy could come to assigning hard statistics to those subsisting outside the reach of any previous census.

Even though Los Angeles is considered the nation's homeless capital, the numbers are nevertheless breathtaking. The subject compels a few weeks' worth of sustained news coverage, much talk of reform, and much more talk of investing in affordable housing through construction, renovation, and repurposing. Then some time passes, the talk subsides, and the county's financial structure surrounding this issue remains functionally the same. Under new guidelines, handfuls of affordable-housing units—a few dozen overall, a comically low number—are set aside in new residential construction projects. No notable reforms are made beyond that.

The women at Los Robles stop talking about the numbers after a time. They need to focus on themselves and their children and their own uniquely hard paths forward. This countywide cycle will repeat itself every two years from now on: the LAHSA homeless count results are released, about three or four weeks' worth of public conversation follows, prominent stakeholders promise to take the crisis seriously and make resonant changes, and little actionable impact occurs.

◆　◆　◆

Yasmine is the most aggressively talkative of the other mothers. She has two children aged six and seven. The kids are older than someone as young as Yasmine ought to have. Wendi thinks that Yasmine must have been fourteen when she started bearing children. She has judgments about that—until she factors in the probability that Yasmine was raped while also reminding herself that she was sixteen when her oldest was born. Yasmine's kids are neither well-behaved nor well-looked-after, and these traits are easily explained by all the physical signs Yasmine bears of having been a serious drug user. Wendi strives to be patient with their situation because something that she has newly learned about herself at Los Robles—that truly surprises her—is not just how petty and hypocritical she can be but how little self-awareness she possesses. She's always considered herself to be accepting. But she is in fact not. Yasmine, at a high volume, lets Wendi know how she actually comes off: "You're mean on the inside," she says.

Yasmine likes to talk about her own experiences preceding shelter here: prostituting while her kids played in the nearest park, robbing people for money while her kids stood lookout, robbing people before prostituting, prostituting then robbing. She claims to be adept with a knife while using a knife to help with communal dinner in the kitchen. Wendi makes a point not to argue with her generally, even when she is directing withering criticism the older woman's way.

Most surreal is the way her interactions with Yasmine, even the ones that leave her low, occur while Yasmine interacts with Emmanuel. The young woman loves to play with all the kids in the house, but she grows a strong affection for Wendi's son. When Wendi has him outside, Yasmine will be on the ground with him, on his level, engaging with him like a child would but talking to him like she talks to adults, blunt and critical and profane. She imitates his movements and noises in a way that piques him. But when Emmanuel shrieks or lashes out physically, she raises her arms and mutters, "What the fuck did you do that for? I can beat your ass." Her reactions enrapture him and somehow calm his fits. Emmanuel does not really show affection or amusement, but Wendi knows some of the signs when complicated feelings are roiling around inside him. He really likes Yasmine. She gives him the nickname Momo.

◆ ◆ ◆

In addition to mental-health counseling, the organization provides both general life training and specific career services. This curriculum is geared toward women who have not finished high school or held a stable job. In Oakland, Wendi worked for ten years at the same hospital and so she zones out during much of the instruction. But over weeks she latches onto the most basic, vital advice couched within the classes, a tenet that has eluded her over the first three and a half decades of improvising her life: a person needs to have a plan, one that is thought through and can progress over time and is explainable.

◆　◆　◆

She finds a job at Huntington Memorial Hospital. Ringed by tall palm trees and characterized by art deco architecture, the grounds feel like Southern California distilled. The hospital is less than a ten-minute drive from Los Robles and services a predominantly affluent community. Compared to St. Rose Hospital, where she worked before and during her marriage, where the ER drew impoverished families without insurance checking in with everything from bronchitis to broken legs to gunshot wounds, the clientele she now spends her shifts processing do not bring stress with them beyond the medical variety—which can still be dramatic but makes them easy for Wendi to enter into the system. Her job is not peaceful or well paid. She and her colleagues are the people on staff who absorb the frustrations of both patients and medical personnel. But she is thankful for having it and the job also spares her more professional classes at the shelter. The fact that she does not currently have to pay for housing means that she is saving thousands of dollars per month and quickly building a safety net that she has never before in her life known.

The logistics of Emmanuel's needs remain her predominant challenge, because the only suitable care center she can find for him in the area is open only until 5 p.m. But her work does not end until 5:30 p.m. The Door of Hope staff and volunteer network provide robust childcare on the premises but for liability reasons cannot transport children around town.

Without being asked and without requesting any payment, Yasmine volunteers to plug this remaining hole in Wendi's day-to-day. Each afternoon Yasmine takes a bus to Emmanuel's day care and walks him the mile back to Los Robles. Wendi usually arrives home from work around the same time as they do, and even when Yasmine is in the midst of one of her tirades, Emmanuel is centered and at ease with her. He begins to appropriate some of her mannerisms in the concentrated way he has of imitation, including her loud cursing that Wendi won't admonish him for because she is laughing so hard. She doesn't understand this caliber of generosity from another human being at first—any human being, not just one who has been through what Yasmine has been through. Such grace from someone other than her own mother is not a part of Wendi's lived experience to this point. Even when she tries to ask Yasmine for an explanation, the girl doesn't tell her anything that Wendi can make sense of.

"I can do what I want," is what Yasmine says, with a tone of impatience, about choosing to spend part of her days walking with a nonverbal autistic boy.

During this time, Emmanuel becomes Momo not only to Yasmine but to them all.

◆ ◆ ◆

Miss Abeba bursts into their apartment early on a weekend morning while Wendi is still in her pajamas. Like a cyclone the woman begins gathering the craggy mountains of clothes and school supplies off the floor and stuffing everything in the closet. "He's coming, he's coming!" she urgently rasps. "Room check!"

She means that the man in charge of overall shelter operations is conducting room inspections. Being Momo's mother means that

Wendi does not devote much effort to cleaning. While she has been scolded a few times for the general cluttered state of their living space, she has never cared very much for the man or his standards. But Miss Abeba takes his directives very seriously. Wendi orders her kids to help with the emergency pickup while she changes clothes. When he knocks on the door, Miss Abeba is trying to jam the closet door shut with her shoulder against the weight of what is inside. Wendi stalls him until the latch clicks. He leans inside and if he is suspicious as to why Miss Abeba and the three children are all standing together in front of the closet, he doesn't show it. "Looks nice in here," he says. "Keep it up."

He moves on, and Miss Abeba exhales triumphantly. "Why do I always have to worry about you this way?" she asks.

"Why does anyone care about some clothes on the ground?" Wendi replies.

"Because how you do one thing is how you do everything."

After that, Wendi does make an effort to be neater.

Another Los Robles rule: during standard church hours on Sunday mornings, the families have to be out of the house. No one forces them to go to a specific church—no one forces them to go to church at all—but the rule is meant to steer them toward worship and Wendi complies. She has somewhat drifted from religion amid the years of stress in Oakland and her struggles in marriage and motherhood. Now, after having peered into one of life's deeper chasms, she chooses to reorient herself around the faith in which she was raised. Some burdens that she carries immediately lighten as a direct result. Others remain just as heavy as they have always been.

A wet winter passes over into a bright, temperate spring. Her son Anthony and her daughter Tiara progress through the school year with a growing sense of comfort that manifests in the stories they bring home. Her older son is released from his group-home sentence in Oakland, five hours from Pasadena, and she spends her days off commuting there to help him reenter school and the world. Her other older children who have been gradually moving to Fresno sometimes decide that they are on speaking terms with her and sometimes don't. Her mother in Oakland does the same, and Wendi accepts whatever dynamic they are in knowing now that there is a rhythm to these relationships, a music that isn't generated by her alone and doesn't always sound pleasing to her ears but is what she will always move to. She has some money set aside now to help them all—nothing lavish, but small gestures such as a countertop portable dishwasher to help her mother with her back problems, some decent clothes for her oldest son in Fresno to interview for a job, fees for youth sports leagues and other extracurriculars—expenditures that allow her to feel like a functional daughter and mother, interactions that begin to enable her to look backward and focus on aspects of her story besides the regret, besides the bad decisions, besides the constant predicament of coming up short on her and her kids' needs. Especially in the pews at church, she is newly able to identify moments of joy that have unfolded at different points over many strenuous years, and she can wrap her head around the possibility of such joy unfolding again in new ways in the years ahead.

Yasmine does not like the thanks or attention Wendi gives her, and she does not subscribe to the religious overtones.

"You're pretty fat, pretty old, pretty ugly, and pretty much on my nerves. So quit saying *blessed this* and *blessed that* and *blessed* all the other things. All right? Not everything has to be blessed all the time. Some things can just be what they are, like me and Momo walking home from school." The words are intended as a succinct summation, but maybe they also make for an absolution.

◆ ◆ ◆

Wendi and her children stay at Los Robles for seven months, during which she saves over $8,000 and qualifies to rent a unit in a nearby designated affordable-housing complex. In the shelter she has celebrated birthdays within her own family and in the larger group. She has witnessed her children cross milestones of youth. She has made friends. She has gained a church family. She has analyzed and isolated components of her life that subconsciously plagued her and lurked somewhere behind each of her most regretful choices. She has moved past—somewhat—the emotional brutality of her marriage. She has formulated a plan for the next stage of her life. She's also wept in sadness and frustration many times, engaged in some nasty verbal arguments, cursed other people's children under her breath, and compulsively wondered how she and her kids can possibly survive in the world beyond this shelter—even just a few blocks beyond this shelter, which is how far away her new apartment is.

Then, near the end of the year 2006, the staff and her housemates throw her family a modest but emotional party with cake and decorations in the yard. And a few days after that comes the time to move on. In the parlance of Miss Abeba, she has indeed finished well. Among all her pulsing worries and excitements, Wendi wonders what other mother might call the shelter at exactly this moment as Miss Abeba helps her and the boys vacate the room, cleaning the floor for the final time together; she wonders who will take shelter here after them; she visualizes other children inhabiting its spare but vital spaces, another mother recovering from her own singular time in the abyss. Wendi creates in her imagination an entire family that is about to go through what she has just gone through. And she realizes that there will be a family here after that one, and more after that, a succession of strangers who will land here at their lowest point because there is hardship and need without end in this city. In a modest refutation of that reality and the helplessness it casts upon people like her striving in its vastness, as part of her own worship that evening, she wishes all these unknown families healing and some cause for hope.

PART III

Mission Road

Evelyn

September–December 2018

THE BINDING OF HOME OWNERSHIP with power—whether that ownership is the result of hard work and saving, foresight and savvy, inheritance,
fraud and violence, racism, some combination of these—runs throughout
America's history and across its physical landscape. On that same scale,
the lack of ownership has been braided with instability and voiceless-
ness. From the moment a group of settlers built homesteads together on
an attractive plot of earth, the tension between the asset economy and
the service economy has been critical in determining any community's
social hierarchy.

In certain places and times, primarily in cities, the value of property has
risen far faster than the wages of those working in service of—and renting
living spaces from—property owners. As a result, in these climates housing itself has become an exclusive commodity and the number of people
without access to any kind of shelter has exceeded the capacity of whatever
services might be in place for them. Such individuals forced to survive in
public—whether in New York City in the mid-1800s or modern-day Los
Angeles—have crossed an important threshold; they have come to be considered by the wealthy, politically influential class not just as representatives of severe poverty but collectively as an expression of blight in their

communities, akin to excessive noise or smog: a demonstrative threat to quality of life.

The aspect of this cycle that is hard to reconcile with any ideals of humanism or mercy is that, historically, a homeless population is not deemed politically significant until it becomes widely visible, audible, smellable, and touchable—until its prevalence jeopardizes home values, deflating the worth of the precise commodity that the people considered problematic are guilty of being unable to afford. And it typically does not reach this level of alarm until the numbers have already overwhelmed the existing service infrastructure by a few orders of magnitude. At that point, the political solutions tend to resemble reactive triage more than comprehensive aid; they also tend to focus as much on removal as on ministration.

In 2017, after homelessness had been endemic for years, voters in Los Angeles approved a measure that applied an additional 0.25 percent sales tax to support homelessness prevention in the city—adding roughly $3.5 billion over ten years to what was already being spent on preventative programs. Many voices hailed the vote as a progressive triumph, but what the vote might actually have represented was a whole city quietly hoping that this investment would translate not necessarily into the elimination of homelessness but rather into the relocation of the dirty, the wandering, the sick, the unsightly individuals from its outdoor spaces. Over the following years, the number of homeless continued to rise. During this same time frame, the city commenced a stricter enforcement of minor vagrancy laws and trash removal, began placing newly funded emergency services in far-flung low-income neighborhoods, and started to lay cobblestone ground cover along freeway embankments and beneath overpasses. The latter effort was officially categorized and paid for as a transit beautification project. The stones also made sleeping on these surfaces untenable.

◆　◆　◆

On the night they flee the American Inn Motel after Manny's assault on his family, Evelyn takes the kids to Aunt Talia's. The woman is not pleased to be opening her door to them just after one in the morning, but she must sense the seriousness of the circumstances in Evelyn's voice and her face, even though Evelyn does not want to explain anything outright in front of the girls. They are so sleepy and so scared and so bewildered. Their foremost need is reprieve. Talia offers up her own bed to the three girls.

Evelyn will not remember what words the two women exchange, only that her aunt is kind and focuses on the older four kids while Evelyn deals with the separate but no less immediate mess that is Marisol's burst diaper. Poop has reached her face and her hair. By the time they finish with some deep scrubbing in the tub, 2 a.m. has passed. Iris and Sofia are still awake. Aunt Talia sits in the chair beside the bed telling them stories. Marisol falls asleep and Evelyn offers to braid Sofia's and Iris's hair. She takes her time with the interlacing strands and strives to focus on this task, only this task, the delicate and artful care that it demands if it is to be done well. Iris falls asleep as soon as her hair is finished. Sofia falls asleep mid-braid.

Evelyn wishes to lie down with them herself and drift off, but she has to check in on the boys. Orlando is pacing ovals around the small living room, which he has been doing since they arrived. Gabriel sits on the love seat in a sort of daze. Evelyn nestles beside him and ventures to put her arm around him. He lays his head on her shoulder in a way that breaks her heart for about the thousandth time tonight. Orlando raves about gathering his friends and returning to the motel to beat up Manny, his stream of consciousness a nonsensical madness. Evelyn permits him to go on for a while before she shushes him. In an instant Orlando becomes drained of all his energy. He collapses onto the remaining sliver of sofa opposite Gabriel, who is asleep. His head soon falls on her other shoulder and she curls her forearm so as to caress his bruised cheek. He begins breathing very deeply, then snoring. Orlando is nestled in her right arm, Gabriel in her left, as when they were small.

She wakes with a start in the slanted gloomy light of the early morning. She takes a moment to confirm the realization that this is where her life resides right now.

The first choice she needs to make is whether or not to send those children to school. This matter is not complicated for her because school is the direct driver of all their circumstances, school is the prize that will one day justify everything that is happening, and school therefore cannot ever be missed. She wakes and readies them all while ignoring Aunt Talia's expressed concerns and all the kids' complaints of tiredness.

"Being tired is not an excuse for anything," she says, clapping her hands to speed them. "I'm tired all the time."

◆ ◆ ◆

She drives past the motel and does not see his truck in the lot. The sight of the American is ominous on its own. Her neck is sore. She parks in a fast-food lot a few blocks away and sits for a time. Their belongings are a priority: clothes, school supplies, toothbrushes. Her phone ran out of power the night before, and the charger is in the room along with nearly all their stuff. Disconnected, she doesn't know if Manny has been trying to reach her. She doesn't know if he's been parked outside Aunt Talia's apartment this morning, or if he is passed out in the motel, or if he is following her right now.

In the end, she decides to trust the safety suggested by daylight. She parks and uses her room key. The room is empty. She somehow perceives the space as if she is entering it for the first time, as if she is coming upon the remnants of another family that has been dwelling here with dirty clothes mounded into the four corners, the wretched smell of sweat and beer and old diapers. She nearly cries then, knowing that this family is actually her own. As fast as she can, in no more than five minutes, she conveys armloads of their clothes, books, electronics, and toothbrushes into the back seat of the Highlander.

One of the motel managers confronts her right as she is leaving. He is an elderly Asian man and speaks in broken English about other tenants complaining. He declares that the police really should have been called last night. He is unpleasant and she is defensive. Together they create yet another loud scene of conflict in the parking lot of the American. In truth, she is grateful to all the passive bystanders that the police are not involved and that her kids are all in school today instead of separated and being asked questions and pitted against one another in isolated rooms, which is a scenario that might have come to be if one neighbor overhearing the conflict had been less apathetic, had worried enough for her children to punch three digits into a phone. There is no telling what family services would have made of the situation or what would have been done with her kids. She promises the manager that she will not be back.

About a mile away, she realizes that she forgot her phone charger of all things. She decides to buy a new one instead.

87

◆ ◆ ◆

The question coursing through all the fevered moments of the following days is how dangerous Manny might be. He sends her dozens of texts and leaves eight or nine voicemails. The content veers back and forth between sorrow and indignant rage. The mother in her has to consider the possibility that he might show up at Marisol's day care or the kids' school or her work. The wife in her believes deeply that he is too terrified a person to take even a remote risk of official trouble. His caution is one of the qualities that first drew her to him. Alcohol remains the unpredictable factor. Manny's fear of consequences does not mean that a six-pack will not have him pounding on the front gate of a school. His manic, unsolicited assurances via text messages that he is never going to drink again hold no functional meaning.

For the rest of that week, she does not work any shifts at Applebee's and makes sure to pick each of the kids up at their precise release times. She does not notify anyone at school of the upheaval within her family, and she instructs her children not to, either, despite the school's support resources. In their current situation, the imperative is that no one raise any questions at all regarding her family's well-being.

◆ ◆ ◆

Aunt Talia is apprehensive for her niece and the children, but she cannot shelter them for more than a few days. She senses that other tenants in her building are on alert, and a report to the management company would make all their lives very complicated. Talia has had an accurate sense of Evelyn's naivete from the beginning, the first night they had poured into the one-bedroom. She'd known that the following weeks and months would be much harder on them than they could fathom. But she'd also admired the way Evelyn had saved real money for this transition and spoke of the rental market like someone who had researched thoroughly. Manny struck her as a little dim and Evelyn somewhat hyper, but still Talia convinced herself then that this family—if nearly everything went right for them—would be capable of carving out a life here long enough for the kids to graduate from the school system into a world of greater potential than what they had been born into.

While doing her best now to attend to their immediate needs, in her heart Talia believes that the situation they are in—fractured, traumatized, broke— all but eliminates the possibility of entry into that better world. She'd encountered similar situations during her career in the school system, and those situations never turned out well without some strong intervention and good fortune. She does not see either of those elements occurring for Evelyn and the kids.

"You can stop by here sometimes for some food, a shower, short visits," Talia tells Evelyn before they leave again. "I wish I could do more."

"It's okay," Evelyn assures her.

What Talia thinks but doesn't say is that Evelyn should take the kids back to Lancaster.

What she does say is that she will call some friends from her church to see if anyone knows of any short-term housing options.

◆　◆　◆

"It's just us now," Evelyn says to the girls in the middle row of the Highlander before they drive away from Aunt Talia's. The words are meant as an assurance and also a deflection so that the girls won't ask questions about their father.

89

Though they all would have benefited from a quiet moment in which to talk together about how the violence they'd experienced was perceived by each of them, they cannot. The urgent need to locate shelter holds a new variety of fear, one that compounds exponentially with the lowering of the sun toward the horizon.

Dozens of places and people operate in the city with the sole purpose of supporting mothers and children experiencing what Evelyn and her children are experiencing. The civic, nonprofit, and private sectors have all long since recognized the braiding of domestic violence and housing instability. Shelters abound for this moment of peak crisis. Evelyn uses her phone to locate one that is close and rates well; websites such as Yahoo! and Yelp feature user ratings and star reviews and Evelyn peruses shelter rankings as she once did for schools. She takes her children to a six-story repurposed apartment complex on the edge of downtown. When they enter the lobby together, the act of pushing through big glass doors recalls their visit to the shopping mall before the school year began, except that this moment is nothing like that one. They don't brighten the energy of the space they enter here. They are six more bodies in a crowded room.

The staff is focused and attentive. Even though they do not have beds for the night, they begin the process of checking her in and promise to find them shelter space nearby. Evelyn senses her children watching her answer questions and fill out forms with a confused interest. The spaces asking for her current address throw her; she jots the info for the American Inn Motel, then erases it and replaces it with Aunt Talia's, erases that and replaces it with her mother's in Lancaster, erases that and leaves the box blank.

When the process is finished, she receives two addresses. The first is for a shelter where she can stay with Marisol, Sofia, Iris, and Gabriel tonight. The second is for a different shelter where Orlando will have to stay, because within the system, boys twelve and older are not allowed to cohabitate with girls.

Evelyn is moved to argue, but she is committed to causing no stir—to being unmemorable. At the moment, she believes that any misstep or misunderstanding could cause her children to be kicked out of school. She thanks everyone who has helped them and leaves the building with the paperwork and addresses. She throws all the paper away en route to the Highlander. Before any of the kids ask, she says, "We are not splitting up."

Because she still has a few hundred dollars remaining in her and Manny's bank account, she checks into another motel a few miles east of Monterey Park.

◆ ◆ ◆

Evelyn has not been working long enough at Applebee's to ask for big favors beyond occasionally switching a shift. She can't be late or absent for long stretches. She can't interrupt the clean lines between work and home by publicizing the turns of her life among staff. She can't make the job harder for anyone else. So she returns to her normally scheduled shifts two days after being choked by her husband and is contrite about the couple of shifts she has missed. She blames the flu but also emphasizes the fact that she almost never gets sick.

Despite the desperation of her housing search, she makes it a priority to fall in with the order of the restaurant, challenging no one, asking for nothing. Some of her coworkers are her age or younger with long-term aspirations far from mid-priced chain restaurants. About an equal number are older men and women who have possibly submitted to this job as being the best they can hold right now. Some have kids and some don't.

The kitchen staff performs harder work for less money but does not make noise about it because they are so easily replaceable. The managers have to express a level of impatience and disappointment all the time in order to run the place efficiently but seem like decent people with different pathways that have led here and different pathways that will lead away. Most everyone is civil with each other. They all seem to understand that their lives have converged here at Applebee's, all of them need the money, they might as well get along.

Evelyn is friendliest at this point with a server named Charlotte, who is in her late forties. They are not close confidantes but have reached a casual kindness and familiarity with each other. Evelyn knows that Charlotte has one grown daughter who lives with her a ways east of the restaurant—closer to San Bernardino than Los Angeles. The women have begun bonding noncommittally over stories of their children. Charlotte's commute is long for a service job but she has been here for years, has earned some freedom to choose her own hours and to speak her mind. She has been helpful to Evelyn in explaining some of the personality nuances of the staff, how to manage interactions smoothly, how the different managers like to run the floor.

In truth, Charlotte is not fond of Evelyn; she finds her to be self-involved, too often harried with some crisis that necessitates arriving late or leaving early. Because Evelyn is young and friendly and has healthy skin, the men in the restaurant—both customers and employees—are nicer to her than her performance merits. She also hears about Evelyn's life and is flummoxed by the notion of five kids under the age of twelve. Charlotte's daughter is not much younger than Evelyn. She attended Cal State's Los Angeles campus but is living with her mom now because the job market is so unforgiving. Charlotte can't understand why any non-rich person with any degree of foresight would bring more than one child into this world—maybe two within a stable relationship. Toward Evelyn she feels mainly pity. Yet she invests some effort in helping Evelyn avoid being fired within her first few weeks. The high turnover rate of serving staff makes Charlotte's life harder so, selfishly, Evelyn's continued employment benefits her.

On the Friday Evelyn returns to work, Charlotte asks her if anything is wrong.

"I was sick but I'm better now."

Charlotte looks at her the way she must look at her daughter when she knows her daughter is similarly lying. "For real?" she says.

"Things are hard," Evelyn says vaguely.

"If you need some more days—"

"I'm good," Evelyn says.

"If you're ever not good, you have to tell me if I'm here, so I can get you off the floor before you lose it on a customer."

"Do I seem like I might lose it?" Evelyn asks.

Charlotte waves both of her hands around her own head to denote the general messiness of the human mind. "People lose it all the time. It's Los Angeles."

◆　◆　◆

"Don't tell your teachers nothing," Evelyn instructs her children. They are gathered in the new motel room on a Sunday evening. She holds Marisol while addressing the other four sitting together on the room's double beds.

"Don't tell my teachers what?" Iris asks.

"About where we are or where your dad's at."

"Is this where we're going to live now?" Sofia asks.

"No," Evelyn replies. "This is just for a few days. I'm finding us a place to live—a really nice place."

"So where's that going to be?" Orlando asks. "This *really nice place*?" The way he challenges her like this in front of everyone infuriates her but also means that she needs some time to connect with him.

"I'm asking people."

The girls begin voicing the amenities they desire in the next place: their own rooms, bunk beds, a pool, a trampoline, an ice cream parlor, an aquarium. Evelyn feels herself growing angry, not just at Orlando, but at all her kids for having high expectations and at herself for nurturing exactly that.

◆ ◆ ◆

Through her close-knit church congregation, Talia finds them a living arrangement. Her pastor connects her with a pastor in the South LA neighborhood of Watts who rents rooms on the church property to needy families. Evelyn and her kids can stay there for $200 per week. They can do so without registering with the welfare system or being vetted by the city's Department of Children and Family Services or engaging any office that might notify the school district of changes. Since nearly being separated from Orlando at the crisis center, Evelyn lives in fear of all these entities, and Talia knows that. Having worked for a city bureaucracy, Talia cannot tell her with certainty that this fear isn't valid. The housing situation she refers is off the grid. She can only hope that it is safe.

The church is nineteen miles southeast of Monterey Park and will demand crushing commutes to school and work. But the space is available for immediate occupancy and affordable on a waitress's salary, just barely. They will be living with other families in similar predicaments. At the outset, the situation seems to Evelyn like the upper end of what they might permit themselves to hope for right now.

On a Sunday in mid-October they move into the apartment on 96th Street. The 10 a.m. service at the church on the other side of the large lot is in progress and the muted drift of hymnal singing seems to settle the nerves of the children. They have been hyper all weekend and tense during the drive from Monterey Park that traversed much of South LA. The boys have of course heard of the Watts neighborhood. Orlando has been making awful jokes about how they are all going to learn to walk crouched over in order to duck the drive-by gang shootings. The upsetting, unfounded talk confuses the girls and worries Gabriel and legitimately pisses Evelyn off.

"It's not like that," she explains. "It's, like, basically a suburb now." In truth, she does not know all that much about what Watts is like or how safe it is.

The awful violence in the motel, the quick move to Talia's, the confusion at the crisis center, the other motel, and now the long drive to this unknown apartment and neighborhood, sight unseen, is all tangling together and seeding within Evelyn and the children alike the nervous energy of transience. Evelyn has a difficult time focusing on the freeway leading them southward, on the narrower and more foot-trafficked streets of South LA, on stop signs and pedestrian crossings and double-parked cars.

The apartment comprises the top corner of a dilapidated, eight-unit structure. A bent metal gate guards the vestibule, and the interior stairway is wonky and dank-smelling. The unit itself is about twice the size of the motel rooms they've been in. They walk through a living room, two bedrooms, and a kitchenette. None of it has received much maintenance over many years, which means that the floorboards are warped in places and the walls split by long meandering cracks and there is discoloration from water pooling in places it shouldn't. The appliances are old and the bathroom is off-putting. But the rooms feel spacious to them and are outfitted with bunk beds and tables such that each person has a mattress on which to sleep and a desk on which to work, even if all these items are donated, mismatched, out of joint. The kids delight in being able to set down their bags of clothes and still have space to move around. They pass a few hours on that Sunday just being there and savoring that small freedom.

Since moving to Los Angeles and spending much more time in the car, the girls have developed a fondness for Taylor Swift songs on the radio. Evelyn has generally been opposed—she doesn't understand how the blond-haired, pale-skinned, very rich pop star can constantly cast herself as the world's victim—and in the evenings and during long drives she pushes Latin pop songs, even the bad Americanized versions. But the singer has a deep hold on all three girls, and Evelyn brings up a greatest-hits playlist on her phone that day so that all four of them—Evelyn and her daughters—can have an epic dance party. Moving and singing along with melodic narrations of the star's romances, they compete in resonance with the ongoing church service next door. To Evelyn it is absurdity of the very best kind.

"I've got to go," Orlando says in the early evening, after their first few hours in the place. Maybe it is the music and dancing that drive him away. The girls are exhausted now and watching a show on Evelyn's phone while she generates a grocery list. She hasn't been able to do this in over two months: contemplate buying and storing fresh produce and meat.

She pays close attention to every cent of family expenditure. At this time, she has a little over $500 left in her bank account and has been operating in the red by about $50 per week. The affordable rent here will theoretically equalize money coming in and going out, and a trip to the supermarket would be such a normal and cleansing activity that she marvels at the concept and composes her list meticulously. Orlando's declaration interrupts this trance she is in.

"You hate Taylor Swift that much?"

"I do but that's not why I have to go."

"You have to stay here," Evelyn tells him. "I'm going shopping."

He looks at her incredulously and it is as if the teenager within him is wrenching itself outward through his eyes like a gremlin.

"When can I go out?" he says.

"Go out where?"

"There's a park, like, six blocks."

"We don't know the neighborhood yet."

"I'm sure it's fine to go to the park."

"But you're the one who's been telling us all we're going to get lit up," she informs him, using his own colloquialism for being shot.

"You told us, like, fifteen times that it is safe!"

"Well, I don't know exactly. But you can't leave," she says.

"*Fuck,*" he mutters under his breath, and she lets the curse word go without consequence. She lets much of his coarser behavior go, because less than two weeks ago this boy's stepfather punched him in the face and her heart breaks for him.

She takes only Marisol with her to the nearest discount store. The aisles are narrow, crowded, and ordered in a way that doesn't make much sense. The produce appears old. But she lingers in that section with the toddler set in the cart seat. Marisol is delighted by the colors and shapes and the old ladies cooing in her direction. Evelyn navigates many overlapping loops through the rows of food while making funny faces and naming random items and emitting goofy sounds. She only half pays attention to her careful, spare list. The items from it barely cover the bottom of the cart, and she begins impulse buying bags of chips, vegetables, yogurt. She overspends her budget by twenty-five dollars, then an extra six dollars on top of that for a candy assortment for the kids. She finds this candy in a small rack surrounded by orange-and-black Halloween decorations, and she realizes how quickly the year is passing outside the context of her family unit, outside her mandate to protect her children.

She helps Marisol unwrap her Fruit Roll-Ups in the parking lot and then keeps the car in park, hiding out for as long as she can within this moment, listening to chewing sounds and happy coos and giggled exclamations.

◆　◆　◆

In this city, driving time does not depend so much on actual mileage between points as it does on direction and hour of day. Watts and Monterey Park are almost twenty miles apart. The conduit between them—I-110, which like many of the nation's freeways was cut through its city's poorest neighborhood—is the third-most-trafficked stretch of road in all of America. So the day after they move in and the five kids enjoy the most comfortable sleep situation they've had since leaving their home in Lancaster in July, Evelyn needs to wake and ready them an hour earlier than usual, which means she needs to wake and ready herself two hours earlier. She has always been a person who loves to sleep, who thinks about sleep constantly, who struggles to function ably without enough of it. These past two months of terrible, unhealthy sleeping patterns have exacted a toll.

She is an irritable wreck that Monday morning as she goads them all from bed and into their clothes and into the Highlander with a box of granola bars she bought yesterday that was off-list and that she couldn't afford. Her kids all think the bars taste weird and she regrets buying them and also wonders how her children have come to be such brats even while living with lack. The whole neighborhood is backed up with commuters like them all jockeying around narrow streets for the same freeway entrance ramp. Once on it, they jerk along a few feet at a time toward the hazy downtown skyline due north.

The HOV lane is usually an entitlement she takes for granted, but this specific freeway network uses a pay system by which license plate scanners charge money per distance traveled in the faster lanes. According to the digital billboards, her segment would cost $4.45 each way. Evelyn cannot pay that five or more times a week. So she and the kids battle out the distance in the band of slow traffic alongside all the other ten-plus-year-old SUVs, dented pickups, ailing sedans while the Teslas, Audis, and BMWs whoosh past on the far left—or so it seems to her.

◆ ◆ ◆

Each of her kids is enrolled in the school aftercare program, which keeps them there until 5 p.m. most days. This is a free, active, well-staffed program with art supplies and sports. Evelyn has a long-held theory that poor people in America are often forced to pay for worse versions of certain services that wealthy people can access for free, and the offerings of her kids' new afternoon care confirms it. The after-school program in Lancaster cost ten dollars per week per child and was chaos.

A normal afternoon shift at work lasts until 6 p.m., but Charlotte arranges coverage for her so she can leave an hour and twenty minutes early to pick the kids up in the evenings, and she is grateful even though the hours are ducked from her pay. The more lucrative night shifts are not an option in her life for the moment, either. Aunt Talia is able to help out with care along the edges—work emergencies and traffic jams and the like—but Evelyn is determined not to take advantage, a determination born less out of respect and humility than of a foreknowledge that she will continue to need her aunt's support in huge ways, and she would be unwise to wear the woman's kindness thin over minor needs now.

After pickup she and the kids then enter the evening's thickest traffic window toward the parish home in Watts. This transit takes about an hour. She might sometimes have Applebee's leftovers with her but she mostly tries to cook because this nightly act is cheaper and also represents an important return to semi-normalcy after their weeks in motels. Aside from giving over a full two hours of their lives each day to transit within the city, this new rhythm of life feels manageable.

Her kids continue to draw energy from school, teachers, and friends. To Evelyn, that is the paramount metric that justifies every excruciating minute in traffic, every horrid flashback to the American Inn Motel, every surge of anxiety that swamps her at unexpected moments throughout each day.

❖   ❖   ❖

Even in a well-funded, well-run school, a typical day of seventh grade is a frenzied block of time. So although Orlando treats seriously the fact that this school in Monterey Park is the best that he's ever attended—the most organized, the most focused, a place he desires to perform well in—it is still a public middle school in a dense urban space, and he is solving real or imagined social problems in pretty much every elapsing moment. Mostly, these problems involve girls: both those he likes and those he finds off-putting.

When he is not in school striving to catch up academically, he is with his family contending with the most urgent problem of all, which is his mother. She clings to new routines and chores with manic to-do lists, but beneath the unceasing activity and chatter he watches a human being he loves pull too hard, too often, against the fastenings of her spirit.

The atmosphere in the church apartment quickly proves itself to be neither very religious nor serene. Seven other single-parent families also live there. All of them begin with a somewhat low opinion of the newcomers due to the too-loud Taylor Swift tunes reverberating through the building on their first day. But noise is a problem for everyone. A constant din of mothers chastising children penetrates the walls and floors. Orlando's sisters are frightened by the anger that seems to permeate the air here, as if the yelling might turn toward them directly if they venture to play or even to creak a floorboard.

Whenever a crash occurs, which is periodic, it could be a kid knocking something over or a parent throwing something. At any given moment, someone young might be crying hysterically as someone older bemoans the crying. Then the crying ceases abruptly and then erupts again louder. The acoustics of the building seem to concentrate noise within their living room.

His mother never talks to him directly about the violence he suffered at the American. Neither of them seems willing to initiate a complicated conversation right now, and they are almost never alone together anyway. He revisits those moments constantly in his mind. Sometimes he imagines different, fantastical scenarios that could have played out, such as one in which he expertly evaded his stepfather's assault and then knocked the man out with one powerful, technically perfect punch. The sloppiness of the encounter and how scared he was and his inability to protect the girls and his mother haunt him—and what haunts him still further is an idea that gains traction in his repressed, unministered consciousness that what happened might have been his fault.

All the minutes of Orlando's typical day feel cramped with different tensions. He begins to visualize how much calmer his life would be if he could somehow place some distance between himself and all these other people's problems, if he could separate from his family's saga.

◆ ◆ ◆

"Hi," Evelyn murmurs to the woman silhouetted in her doorway around 2 a.m. on a Saturday night a few weeks after they moved in. This woman's hair is bound tight to her scalp. Her gray gums recede from her teeth and her eyes have a way of bulging and appearing very dim at the same time. She carries a toddler in one arm and an infant in the other arm, and a girl around Sofia's age stands groggily by the woman's leg.

"Can you take 'em now?"

"Take your kids?" Evelyn ventures.

"You said you can." The woman talks very fast and keeps checking the dark hallway behind her as if someone might have pursued her here. "When we talked this week, you said you can take 'em."

Evelyn struggles to recall an encounter they'd had outside, when the kids were playing together in that wary manner new acquaintances can have, and Evelyn unthinkingly, out of a pointless self-consciousness, offered to babysit sometime. "Um, okay, I did say that."

"It'll just be for, like, two hours. I'll come back for them."

And then the woman transfers the two younger kids into Evelyn's arms and shoves the other one forward across the doorway and disappears down the stairs. Evelyn brings the three kids inside. They sit in the living room.

She can hear some of her own kids waking up, but she doesn't want them to take part in this situation. She gives the kids each juice even though she can't really afford to be sharing food and drinks. Then she changes the infant's diaper, using one of Marisol's pull-ups, which are too big and which she also can't afford to share. They eventually sleep but Evelyn stays awake for the four hours before the mother returns to fetch them with a muttered thanks.

This interaction quickly becomes typical of living on 96th Street.

◆　◆　◆

They park near Aunt Talia's for Halloween in Monterey Park. The previous week, the girls brought some art supplies home from school to make their own costumes. Marisol is now plastered with orange doilies and supposed to be a pumpkin. Sofia colored and cut out a cardboard box to slip over her shoulders and resembles an old TV with a bunny-eared antenna. Iris carries a tote bag full of books and wears eyeglasses crafted out of pipe cleaners with her hair in a bun; she is a librarian. Gabriel's face is colored with red marker above his black sweatshirt and pants, a devil. Orlando decides he is too mature to dress up. They run into a few families from school and overall have a loud, late-night trick-or-treating in the neighborhood. Unless explicitly instructed to take one candy, the kids take handfuls and bring home a gigantic cache.

◆　◆　◆

As fall progresses toward the holidays, Orlando asks his mother if he can leave the school's aftercare program—which he likens to kindergarten—in order to spend afternoons with his two best friends at the skate park or at one of their homes. She agrees on the condition that he is never late to meet back at school when she picks up the others and that he tries to be a kinder person. The change gives him a block of time that is his own. He does enjoy his friends, but on some days he chooses to skate alone or wander around or just sit on walls in different places and observe the world passing. Other, larger groups of kids from school ricochet around the same few blocks of central Monterey Park. They cluster at Barnes Park picnic tables eating and drinking and vaping. Orlando gradually absorbs the dynamics of different groups, and he yearns a bit to become a part of the ones that include certain girls. But the nature of being their age and starting to gain some freedom presupposes the ability to buy things: clothes, accessories, food, tobacco products, smartphone apps. Orlando does not have that ability.

His lack of expendable money is already causing some tension with his friends; he has been given countless sodas and snacks from their homes and on occasion when they stop somewhere for food they will offer to pay for his, knowing he can't make an order otherwise. He begins to bear the weight of owing these boys and he resents them for it even while they overall seem unbothered. He starts pretending that he isn't hungry, which means that he spends more and more time hungry, which makes time around these friends harder to enjoy. He concocts reasons to not hang out with them. More and more afternoons he spends on his own, walking some laps around the neighborhood and usually landing at the park or one of the Asian shopping plazas near groups of teens and preteens, stalking around them at an unnoticeable distance, divining ways he might afford to join them.

His mother asks him to stop skateboarding. They are in the car, in traffic. She issues the command casually and he's taken aback.

"Stop how?"

"Just stop doing it."

"This is how I get around, the only way I get around."

Even though the cars around them are unmoving, she continues to stare straight ahead through the windshield as if the standstill requires concentration. "If you fall and break your arm or your leg or your head—I can't afford that."

"You have insurance, right?"

"There's still costs." Instead of trying to explain how Medicaid works—which she does not fully understand herself—his mother laughs at him in a way intended to make him feel little.

"I've never hurt myself barely at all."

"Orlando, come on. We all have to take care of ourselves better. Can you just not do the crazy stuff with the flips and taking videos?"

He turns away from her. Orlando can sense that his brother and sisters feel sorry for him and somehow this stirs more resentment. "I can still use my board on the street?"

"Would you consider wearing a helmet?" she ventures.

He groans at how unfair this all seems.

◆   ◆   ◆

Several of her new neighbors have mentioned being former drug users and victims of violence. The church property is open to adults in recovery, but there are no chaperones or support services on-site most of the time. So Evelyn figures out that at least some of the noise and much of the childcare she is asked to perform have to do with parties or men or both.

At this time in her life, Evelyn is not yet a person who will turn away someone's child. So within a couple weeks of living on 96th Street, the rare idle afternoon she comes by usually finds her with a bunch of little ones in her living room. The outdoor space in front of the building is unfenced, and watching toddlers there is too stressful. Sometimes she has the chance to talk with other mothers, commiserate a bit about their various travails, edge around the serious events that have landed them here. Women make broad references to bad men but no one really desires to enter the specifics of being abused. Evelyn's apartment becomes the primary play area because she has a job and a little money and she set a precedent of generosity before fully understanding the social landscape she is in.

Most of these kids might be a little unkempt but are clearly loved, like hers. A few suffer brazen signs of neglect like rashes and cruddy teeth. She sees in passing that two of the mothers are very rough with their children, yanking them by the forearm from one spot to another or side-slapping them across the top of the head. The longer Evelyn lives here and the better she comes to know the other residents, the less she desires to be involved with anyone else's problems.

On a Thursday evening, almost a month into their time on 96th Street, Evelyn is hosting two kids of two different mothers. These kids happen to both have clear mental-health conditions. One is completely self-contained. He remains wherever he is placed and focuses intently on a small, yellow toy truck that he always has with him. For hours at a time, he runs the truck backward in continuous circles and emits a soft but high-pitched whining noise to simulate the warnings that sound from big vehicles in reverse. The other, a girl, exhibits some sort of compulsive disorder. She reacts sensationally to physical and verbal affronts, some of which seem to occur only in her mind.

Evelyn carefully referees these two kids, along with Iris and Sofia, while Marisol naps. At a certain point the compulsive girl decides to take issue with the quiet boy.

"What are you, some kind of psychopath?" she shrieks all of a sudden. This is a refrain of hers. The girl is six years old and Evelyn suspects she hears the word at home used demeaningly and interprets it as a blanket expression of annoyance. Evelyn isn't keen on her own kids picking it up and deploying it in their classrooms at school.

The quiet boy does not appear to clock the question or the person asking it. He continues circling his truck with the piercing *reeee-reeee-reeee* sound. The girl sets herself in the truck's path such that it lightly bumps her. She screams in fake pain, then pushes the boy backward and has a loud fit. He is not injured and merely resumes circling the truck in an adjacent space. The girl grows infuriated. Evelyn attempts to calm her or at least divert her attention, but the girl is intent. She smacks the boy hard on the top of his head and moves to strike him again but now Iris enters their orbit.

"He didn't do nothing!" Evelyn's older daughter shouts too loud and too close to the girl's face.

"That psychopath hit me with his truck!"

The disaster continues to unfold at this volume and with this inanity. Evelyn and Gabriel, who are both overly sensitive to loud noises, try to quell them together but end up shouting as well.

The girl's mother then enters the room without knocking and at the precise nadir of the situation. From her perspective the scene appears as Evelyn and her kids yelling at and physically restraining her helpless child. She whirls into an elevated rage. Evelyn defends herself. Uninvolved families emerge from their rooms and begin commenting from the hallway. The mother suddenly claims that Evelyn hit her kid. Sides are taken. Threats are issued. The woman storms around and at one point backs Evelyn— who is much shorter than her—against a wall. "I'm going to fuck you up," the woman says. And then, turning to leave: "You wait for it, you bunch of psychopaths."

"*Psychopaths,*" her daughter repeats in a low mutter from her mother's arms.

The word resonates through the space and through Evelyn's fragile soul. Stress keeps her alert for the duration of that night. Even after the drama subsides and the building is quiet, she feels surrounded by enemies. She knows when she wakes from another bad sleep and goes about waking her kids from their bad sleeps that this place cannot remain their living place for much longer—no more than a few months, once she saves enough money— though in actuality she has yet to save much at all, because she has been spending surplus income on all the extra gas burned commuting as well as on nice, small things like ice cream and mangoes, nonfrozen chicken breasts and stew meat, milk, and decent hygiene items like shampoo and toothpaste so that her kids' health doesn't deteriorate like some of the others here.

◆   ◆   ◆

Iris, the middle child, can feel overlooked much of the time even though she is by far the loudest, most attention-seeking member of the siblings. Perhaps because of her extroverted nature—the constant singing and dancing and laughing—she is assumed to be happy most of the time while her quieter younger sister and older brother seem to need more tending. Her mother turns to her most often when she herself seeks a quick raising of the spirit, and Iris at age seven assumes that role: the well of limitless good cheer and positivity.

But she is also at an age when permanently imprinted memories begin to form, and so when her day collides with other kids who have different ways of unloading their own terrible experiences onto her, and when she has to stand quietly behind her mom as other moms scream insults at their family, Iris carries those moments with her—the moments to which she is able to apply the least amount of reason.

She still fixates on the instant when her father struck her brother and the time afterward while her brothers were outside the motel room and she remained inside with her sisters listening to their father assure them that everything was fine. He gave them water and checked his phone and kept muttering bad words. And then they were driving away and she hasn't seen her father since.

No one will directly answer her questions about why that is and when she might see him again. Iris thinks of her father as the person in her life who does give her small doses of extra attention and she misses that. She knows he hurt her brother and her mother and this has a lot to do with all the moving around, all the worry that has affected her mom's behavior and appearance. But Iris at this time still expects her father to rejoin the family pretty soon, because no one has told her any differently.

In the meantime, although her family is annoying her with all the prevailing bad moods and pouting—which are inescapable because they spend so much of each day driving together to and from school—the hours of the school day have a beautiful way of resetting all the confusion that characterizes this time in her childhood.

Her second-grade teacher's name is Ms. Tsao and she is at once nurturing and also unassailably rigid. Iris did not know what to make of these contrasting traits at first, and during the first weeks of school she found herself in trouble constantly. But she quickly grew accustomed to the orderliness of her school days. As long as Iris engages herself with each parcel of the schedule—the worksheets, singalongs, quiet time—then Ms. Tsao is pleased with her and she has predictable, rewarding days. She loves now to exit the complicated atmosphere of her mom's car, leave behind all the unanswered questions—questions she has learned not to even ask anymore—and cross the schoolyard and enter into her teacher's orderly, controlled space. Comfortably enclosed by the four walls and ceiling of her classroom, Iris knows in advance exactly what challenges her time will entail—simple arithmetic, short written paragraphs with creative prompts—and how to do well at these challenges and thus earn praise from her teacher and her classmates. Family continues to be the center of her life, but school leavens the fraught process of making her own sense out of events that no one seems willing to explain to her—events that she is warned over and over never to mention to Ms. Tsao.

◆　◆　◆

As she did at the American Inn Motel, Evelyn decorates the apartment with flowers. She is inspired by recent events in the complex to hoard money as quickly as she can so that they can move as soon as possible. She stops buying fresh fruit and vegetables and brings home only the cheapest prepackaged meat. She downgrades her cell phone plan. Yet every week or so, she spends $3.99 on a cellophane-wrapped bunch of orange chrysanthemums or goldenrods. She splits the stems up among drinking glasses and sets them around the sills of the apartment's three spaces. Evelyn is fastidious about caring for them: gradually snipping the stems on a diagonal and trimming away the brown edges of leaves, replacing the water, forestalling their eventual wilting declines. What Evelyn begins to want very badly is an outdoor space, even a few square feet of patio, even a metal fire escape grate outside a window, on which to raise bulbs from dirt.

◆　◆　◆

Manny withdraws $400 from their Citibank checking account, a nearly ruinous figure that leaves her short on food and rent money for November. For some reason during the weeks since she and the kids fled the American, in spite of his sporadic flurries of text messages, the thought that he would take money without warning never occurred to her. Because Manny for the most part was paid in cash for his work and she has been the only one making bank deposits, she has treated the account like her own but not yet taken measures to block his access.

Manny makes this withdrawal not long after Evelyn confirms a growing, secret awareness that she is pregnant again. Over the previous three months she'd attributed the signs—the missed periods and deep fatigue, the bad moods and sporadic nausea—to stress and anxiety, which had made sense for a while. But at a certain threshold they no longer made sense and she knew that she was growing a sixth child in the late fall of 2018, at age twenty-nine. Then the two blue lines gradually coalescing on the cheapest home pregnancy test available prove her right. Some rough math dates the conception back to the beginning of August, sometime during their last weeks before leaving Lancaster for Los Angeles, when she and Manny were filled with anticipation and hope.

When she finishes her work shift that day and picks up her kids from school she mentions nothing about Manny's draining of their bank account to anyone. She continues to keep the pregnancy to herself as well. To the extent possible she places a full mental barricade against these irreversible developments and the new urgency they wedge into her life and its every decision.

◆　◆　◆

The celebration of her cousin's daughter's fifteenth birthday party—her quinceañera—is in Lancaster on a Saturday in late November. The gathering is colorful and loud and replete with people who haven't heard much from Evelyn since she left. They want to know how life in Los Angeles is going for them. She has prepared her kids to deflect the details the same way they've been doing at school. They've all grown excellent at this style of evasion, and for about half an hour Evelyn is able to enjoy the sensation of homecoming and welcome and belonging. Her mom, siblings, cousins, and the rest of her extended family act genuinely thrilled to see her and the kids.

But after that half hour, the huge amounts of alcohol being imbibed begin to glaze the eyes and mush the words around her, and some of the uglier aspects of her family inevitably manifest. Uncles carry on decades-old disagreements. Two of her cousins actually have to be separated from throwing punches. The girl they are celebrating keeps weeping and then pulling herself together, weeping and pulling herself together. One of Evelyn's sisters is cold to her because of a local rumor that she left Manny for another guy. Another accuses her of abandoning the family, which is not untrue. Her brother asks her if he can borrow money. Her mother stoically watches everyone.

The hardest person to be near is an older man who had been part of her late father's orbit, always very close to the family's goings on, who now holds court by the table with all the bottles, regaling younger family members with his best anecdotes they have all heard before. He is a large, red-faced, balding man, the sight of whom now makes her physically ill. This person began molesting her when she was seven, Iris's age, both touching and demanding to be touched. After a few years he stopped, probably knowing that at a certain point she would fight back or find people who would. But she could still read his thoughts in the way he looked at her then and onward into adulthood. Secretly, one of her deepest reliefs in being away from Lancaster is being away from him.

Everyone wants to know where Manny is. Evelyn's story is that he is not feeling well. Her children, particularly her daughters, are thrown by her easy lying. She understands what a horrible example she is setting as well as the expanding breadth of the deception in which she asks them to collude, but she doesn't know any other way right now. Her family being made aware of the downturn of her life is not going to ease matters; it will only make for a lot of phone calls.

On her worst nights on 96th Street, Evelyn misses her family—and everything she misses about them is present here: the effortless familiarity, the shared history, the food, the jokes still funny after hundreds of tellings, the revolving door and tight embraces.

But on those same nights she tries to remember why she so decisively moved away, and all those reasons still reside here as well.

The music and dancing tonight in the yard are beautiful, though. Her eyes tear up three separate times. Yet she cannot help paying attention to all the young people here from around Lancaster, observing closely their antics and overhearing their conversations, and reaffirming to herself that her kids are on a brighter path than anyone else in this yard. Guilt accompanies but does not undermine this reflection. Her life has flung apart in many ways since deciding to leave, but she has to believe that the children are better off there than they would be here.

◆ ◆ ◆

Back in Los Angeles after the Lancaster party, she takes them to a park in the Hollywood neighborhood, where a nonprofit offers free art lessons using found items. Marisol and Sofia immediately take a seat and make messes of themselves with leaves and glue. Iris and Gabriel hang farther back trying to seem old and disinterested. But they eventually have their turns and craft nice pictures. Gabriel's is quite beautiful, a miniature three-dimensional cityscape rendered from pine cones. The volunteers are kind and give the girls a great deal of attention. The park is small but is situated on a hill that is taller than the apartment buildings around it and thus offers a somewhat grand 360-degree view of the city.

Orlando stands with his mother. They both watch Marisol closely to make sure she does not run away anywhere and also that she doesn't poop her pants and isn't too rough with the other kids. This job keeps them very busy. But he and his mother still have a few minutes in which the other four are occupied and they can marvel at the skyscrapers to the south of them and the mountains to the north and millions of people in between. The farther, higher mountains have snow crowns around the peaks. At street level, Orlando finds the city to be unattractive. But here, maybe sixty feet above it, the sprawl astonishes him.

Orlando has just recently grown taller than his mother. When he stands beside her, he feels somehow adult. The way they are situated as two people sharing the responsibility for younger kids can give him the sense of being a partner as much as he is a son. His mother has never liked him trying to posture as older or more mature than his age—she actually becomes mad—but ever since Manny ceased to factor into their nuclear family and Orlando has been increasingly responsible as the kids' caretaker, his mother in subtle, perhaps subconscious ways encourages him to assume this role.

"Marisol is starting to get a little . . ." He raises his eyes to imply that the toddler is losing her mind a bit. "She's probably going to hit someone soon."

"She'll probably just hit Sofia," his mother predicts. A moment later, Marisol proves her right.

"Should I go talk to her?" Orlando asks, already taking steps in the direction of the art table.

His mother pauses him gently. "They'll figure it out."

Orlando is skeptical but obeys, and they watch side by side as Iris slides a container of acorns toward the toddler to distract her while talking Sofia out of retaliation. Soon the girls are admiring one another's artwork. Orlando feels an actual pride just then in being part of their upbringing. The sun is bright and the event is not yet crowded. He looks at his mother.

"Maybe I can get a job," he says. "Help you out so we can move places."

Evelyn tells him, "You do have a job, or actually more like two jobs: school and taking care of all them."

"I mean one that gets paid."

"That's nice," she says, "but you're not old enough yet. You can't drive."

"I can skate."

"I told you to stop doing that!"

"Just to get around, you said."

She reaches her arm up in order to sling it over his shoulder and draw him closer.

"Really, you are helping me a huge amount," she tells him. "Way more than any other man I've ever known has helped me."

The kids keep generating more artwork until the event fills up and they are asked to make room for others. The girls do their best to clean up and then they descend the hill to an area where food trucks congregate. They eat at the cheapest one—tacos—and Orlando can tell that each exchange of money causes his mother some pain. But the girls then beg and beg to try a Hawaiian shaved-ice treat that is expensive. He watches closely the way his mother pulls the expression on her face from one of irritated aversion to one of authentic excitement; he is attuned to her ability to manipulate skin and muscle to project exactly what she desires the little ones to see.

◆   ◆   ◆

"You're gorgeous," a woman informs her as if Evelyn needs this confirmation from a stranger. Evelyn is delivering a third round of drink orders to a table of girls in their late twenties—her age—who are out at Applebee's on some kind of girls' night that involves many skinny margaritas and bursts of obnoxious profanity. She carries a visceral dislike for groups like this, the blithe lack of obligation that courses through their conversation and their jokes.

"Thanks," she replies.

"Are you in a relationship?" the woman asks.

The rest of them are snickering in fits that Evelyn considers unbearable. She finishes setting their drinks out while thinking of a common scene in many movies in which a character in her situation dumps the drinks on the heads of the customers. Evelyn refrains from doing this.

"Definitely not."

◆ ◆ ◆

After Thanksgiving, she tells the church members who help manage the apartment property that she doesn't have enough money to pay the $200 for the month of November, but she will absolutely have it in full in a week. A woman sent by the church then visits without warning on a weekend afternoon. The apartment is messier than usual after one of the crowded playdates she hosts here and Evelyn is embarrassed. The woman is maybe in her sixties.

"We think it would be a good time for you to register with CalWORKs and CalFresh."

These are the primary state welfare programs for cash aid and food assistance. Evelyn has researched them online and disqualified herself because she works more than the one-hundred-hours-per-month threshold and because registration requires an in-person meeting and address that she fears could redetermine her kids' school district.

"But I have a job," Evelyn replies. "I'm at work almost every day."

"That doesn't disqualify you from receiving some support. Especially food support. Especially with your kids."

"I definitely read that it did."

"There are programs within CalWORKs to help make sure the kids are fed, the kids have clothes. The kids can see a doctor."

"But I do feed my kids. They look nice for school. They're healthy. They're housed here. I work almost every day." She adds: "The city doesn't need to be involved in our situation."

Evelyn keeps repeating that she works. The patient woman keeps replying with her own script about existent programs. Evelyn infers that if she doesn't register with county welfare, she won't be able to live here anymore.

Aunt Talia takes the kids during the day when Evelyn's CalFresh appointment for food aid is scheduled the following week. The office is drab but not too drab, the wait long but not too long, the men and women and children around her beaten down but not too beaten down, the office workers curt but not too curt. The place and people together make for an apparatus that is efficient and good-intentioned but overwhelmed by the math of the city's collective need. One of the reasons Evelyn holds aversion to such structures is the reminder that she and her kids have become a variable within that math problem.

Evelyn brings most of the documents required—her license, pay stubs—but she intentionally lacks some as well like a utility bill or any document that would list an address. The person registering her is a middle-aged, competent man. He is patient with her and makes eye contact. As she did with the woman from the church, she assures him that she really isn't in the same category with mothers who need welfare assistance. She wants above all to establish that her children do not need checking up on, do not need to be brought into this process, do not need anyone at their school to be contacted.

He frames the matter this way: "Does your employer withhold taxes?"

"Yes, some," she replies.

"Do you buy groceries, pay sales taxes on those?"

"I guess."

"Then you don't have to think of this as a handout."

Despite the sensitivity of this one person, the process of receiving aid even in the most basic form of a debit card for groceries proves thorny for a whole mess of reasons: not just because of the kids' school registration bearing Talia's apartment address but also because of her own somewhat off-the-books housing situation and because she has not yet undergone the whole DMV ordeal required to change her license and registration from Lancaster to Los Angeles, which will be expensive. Her marital status is also an issue because according to the state Manny still needs to be accounted for in terms of total household income. The boxes on the form keep ramming her into walls. She stammers and backtracks and strives to avoid anyone knowing that she was beaten up, that one of her kids was beaten up.

The caseworker is savvy enough to sense that something subsurface is bringing her to dodge every question about marriage and school. He understands what matters and what does not, and he spares her much hassling about these points. But still she will need to figure out with the DMV how to register as a city resident in order for him to complete her file and greenlight some benefits that might supplement her job. He places digital markers in her file so that, once she is straight with the DMV, whomever she sits with next in this office can pick up where he left off without delay. He is overall so easy with her that even though the appointment is not successful—she doesn't actually receive any assistance before she leaves—she still manages not to feel like a broke and depressed person. This exoneration she experiences is one that many other men and women meeting at other workstations, judging by their expressions, do not share.

She goes online that evening to schedule a DMV appointment and learns that changing her license and re-registering the Highlander will altogether cost $385. She will not be able to pay anything close to that amount right now, so she effectively defers the progress brought by the good fortune of meeting a truly helpful caseworker.

◆   ◆   ◆   ·

The weather turns from hot and windless to gray and gusty with some rains. The end of the first school trimester passes. While the kids' lives outside the campus are in continual disarray, their lives in school—as captured by the thin snapshots that are academic progress reports—appear galvanized.

Though Marisol had a rough first few months in the Head Start preschool program in Monterey Park—the delayed potty training did not help—she has lately earned praise for creativity with art supplies, her sense of rhythm when music is playing, and sharing.

Sofia is an anxious kindergartner who places an absurd amount of pressure on herself to perform well; Evelyn once watched her take a full three minutes to write her name above a scribbled drawing. But she is the self-proclaimed friendliest kid in elementary school.

Iris has trouble socially because she is self-confident and stubborn and those traits are intimidating to second-graders, but the wariness others display toward her does not make her unhappy, and in the meantime her fall report card shows her at or ahead of grade level in every area except reading.

Gabriel tends to exhibit no strong feelings about fifth grade, but when Evelyn prods him gently during a rare quiet moment he will suddenly bury her beneath great mounds of social-emotional learning, relationship curiosities regarding both girls and boys, and lofty aspirations of academic excellence and a baseball career.

And while Orlando is almost satirically evasive about his day-to-day life, he receives three As and two Bs along with fawning admiration from his subject teachers regarding his positive attitude even though he is behind his classmates in most subjects.

Each of these children understands that consistency in school is their mother's absolute priority over all the family's other needs and that performing well in school is the most genuine way to give her some joy.

◆　◆　◆

As if out of some sixth sense attuned to the most damaging timing possible, Manny becomes unhinged during this precise moment of her life. First, he learns their address on 96th Street when one of the girls, while playing a game on Evelyn's phone in the apartment, responds to a location ping he sends. Then he parks outside one night and drunkenly screams for her and for his children. Evelyn, scared and mortified and concerned for her kids, stays inside while some other moms in the building curse him loudly from the windows and threaten to call the police. He eventually leaves.

When Evelyn buys her weekly flower arrangement the following day, she brings some extra for these mothers as thanks. In the hallways and other interactions, the women console her and commiserate.

The second night Manny does this, someone actually calls the police. He flees before the black-and-whites arrive. But this means that Evelyn has to resolve this with the police before they become too concerned or curious about her situation. Standing on the curb in the middle of the night, she tells them that Manny has been behaving badly lately, but she is not in danger and cannot stomach the prospect of spending a whole night at a Watts police precinct filing a report and initiating the process of a restraining order.

She is aware that women die all the time as an indirect result of just these sorts of decisions.

The third time Manny comes, he is intercepted by police and arrested for disorderly conduct. Again, the idea of filing for a restraining order and all the logistics and invasiveness that entails seems overwhelming, and Evelyn demurs. A restraining order is a legal proceeding anyway, which means time and money, lost work shifts, kids involved, probably some visits to her residence, probably school administrators contacted. Her understanding is that Manny will be released with a disturbance fine the following morning.

She takes her kids to school the next day even though they are not in any kind of emotional state for it. She does not have a work shift today and, since it is cool outside, lies back in the driver's seat of her car and sleeps for much of the morning. She walks a few laps around Barnes Park, somewhat in awe of a group of elderly Asian men and women performing elegant motion exercises in unison to the sound of string instruments on an old boom box. She thinks about her life, cries a bit, remains afraid. But the solitude, the physicality of walking, and the long deep breaths of cool outdoor air help.

That evening, upon returning to the 96th Street complex with the kids, she sees a group of women congregated in the small parking area. Whatever combination of chemicals that causes the sensation of fear surges through her head and her chest to her fingertips wrapping the steering wheel. She finds herself hoping that Manny is hurt, and not that he hurt someone else. But once she parks and these women step around the Highlander, she sees the hostility in their faces and understands that Manny is not here. Clearly, these women have prearranged a confrontation with her. In front of her children, they take turns cursing her and cursing her situation. Even though

122

Manny's first incident a week ago had elicited kindness in her building, the women are now all scared, tired, and pissed.

Out of patience herself, Evelyn escalates the confrontation. She calls each of them horrible names and cites the ways in which they have taken advantage of her and generally made living here miserable. Then she commits the cardinal crime of letting them know how difficult their children are.

In the cool, gray atmosphere of that late-November evening in the parking lot on 96th Street, in the center of a maelstrom of angry humans, swollen with her own anger, Evelyn's life reaches a new, dangerous level of tension. She separates herself from the women and hurries upstairs. Within twenty minutes, their belongings and food are packed into the Highlander. Marisol is crying; Sofia and Iris are in a state of shocked, disbelieving silence; Gabriel is self-contained; and Orlando is antsy, as if looking for a clear passage from them all. And without a place to sleep that night or any spare money left to afford one, with dusk quickly turning over into darkness, Evelyn drives her family away from the trouble that seems to trail them through this city.

On I-110 she retraces the long drive back toward the striking downtown skyline and then straight through the city and past it: forty-five minutes farther east to the Applebee's where she works.

"For real, Mom?" Orlando asks when she tells them where she is driving them.

"I get a discount," she says.

"Can we get the nachos?" Iris asks.

"Yes, we'll get nachos," Evelyn replies.

"And french fries?" Sofia blurts.

They walk into the restaurant together after 8 p.m. She has called ahead

123

to secure the large corner booth in the rear of the space, where the kids can spread out and feel comfy for a time.

◆ ◆ ◆

Charlotte serves the table and marvels at the family. The boys look strong and they sit straight. The girls are polite and wear perfectly plaited hair. They are kids who appear loved.

She has heard Evelyn carry on often about what a good mother she herself is; Evelyn is not a humble person in this regard. Charlotte has always found that people who speak frequently about one particular quality they possess don't usually possess that quality—are more likely in fact to embody its opposite. She has never been invested enough in Evelyn's existence outside the restaurant to care much about the veracity of her claims, and Charlotte humored her. Tonight, she tends to the family and suspects that Evelyn might have been telling the truth all this time. Charlotte has a sense that part of why Evelyn brought them here has to do with needing someone to see her and her kids exactly as she wants them to be seen.

◆ ◆ ◆

What Evelyn likes about the restaurant's atmosphere is the way that each table hosts its own isolated emotional ecosystem that supports only the people sitting at it. They are just one island in a cluster of many, and this helps her cast a momentary illusion that their most pressing concern is to parse the extensive menu and decide what to eat. Evelyn knows what the best meals and values are. She over-orders and prompts the kids to do the same.

"We'll have leftovers," she says when she feels the older kids questioning her indulgences.

"In what refrigerator?" Orlando mutters.

She glares at him, employs the silent language a mother uses to tell a child to shut up. Then she smiles toward Charlotte, who has returned and may or may not have overheard the exchange. Very quickly they are spilling lemonades with abandon and competing over who has snatched the cheesiest tortilla chip, who's opened the ooziest fried cheese stick. They talk about the food and nothing else the whole meal: ordering it, waiting for it, eating it, feeling it settle. Anytime the conversation angles elsewhere, Evelyn swerves it back. Food is about the easiest and simplest thing in the world for a family to talk about.

After they eat, she tours the kids through the kitchen. The staff is wonderful to them; the poofs of fire bursting over the bourbon steaks in the sauté pans amaze them. Charlotte is able to comp all their drinks and desserts and gives Evelyn a 15 percent employee discount on appetizers and entrees. While they linger there over a few brownie sundaes, Marisol falls asleep slung between Gabriel's and Evelyn's laps.

Then the warm and generous reprieve ends. They are outside in the huge parking lot. Most of the other businesses are closed, yet a surprising number of vehicles still remain. In an isolated thought, Evelyn wonders how many people sleep in their cars here on a given night.

On behalf of everyone, Orlando asks what they are doing now.

She shrugs. She has purposely spent these last two hours not parsing that very question. None of them finished a full meal, and so Gabriel and Iris have take-home boxes stacked in plastic bags dangling from each of their four arms.

"We'll go to Aunt Talia's," she decides with resignation. She hasn't wanted to do this to her aunt again, has been hoping some creative, self-sufficient alternative would occur to her during dinner. But her mind remains a blankness of ideas. Maybe the hour is late enough that they can squirrel in and out of Talia's without neighbors registering them, but she knows that the number of times they can use this privilege is dwindling to absolute zero.

◆ ◆ ◆

"You should go back home," Talia tells her niece the morning after taking them in once more. She is talking about Lancaster. "Go back with the family and get yourself together again."

It is a little after 9 a.m. Evelyn has returned to the apartment after the round of school drop-offs in order to clean their things from the floor, organize bags, make their footprint as small as possible. She is acting tremendously gracious and sheepish, but from Talia's vantage her face looks sunken, sallow. Her mannerisms are twitchy. Talia can tell that Evelyn hopes to earn another night or two, which Talia is unable to give.

"The schools are no good there," Evelyn replies.

Talia motions her hand across the kids' balled-up blankets and pillows on the floor. "What good is any school if you don't have any beds?"

"I'm sorry we had to leave the last place. It wasn't a bad place. Maybe we can go back in a couple days."

"I don't want you to apologize about places that aren't safe. But coming back here is no good. I still get a lot of complaints about the last time. Neighbors are watching, landlord is watching." They've had this part of the conversation before.

Evelyn sits on the worn love seat on which she slept last night. Talia sees a person for whom the world is falling away in chunks; she sees before her all the worries that were seeded on the family's first overwhelming night in Los Angeles plus new, graver concerns she hadn't imagined then.

"I'll find a place for tonight."

"Okay," Talia says. "And what about the next night?"

"I'll find a place for the next night."

"Okay. And what about the night after that?"

"I'll find a place for that night. I have to keep my kids in their school." Now she is pleading. "Please don't tell anyone back home what's going on."

"What's the harm in telling?"

"It'll be a mess."

Talia shakes her head. Evelyn carries all their things except the leftover takeout food from last night to the Highlander and heads to work.

◆　◆　◆

All afternoon at the restaurant she is on her phone as much as she can be without causing trouble with that day's manager. Using Google to find short-term solutions for housing instability in one of the world's most expensive cities is depressing on many levels but mainly because the list of options is effectively endless but none of the options is easy or good.

The women on 96th Street—at least those who were generally nice to her and seemed competent—referenced often the city's 211 line as a number they called when in a serious plight. This recollection occurs to her during a quick lull between some entrees being ordered and served, and she sits in a bathroom stall to look up the service: 211 is a general line intended to categorize and coordinate all the many scenarios in which sudden housing instability arises for individuals. Evelyn is still having a difficult time labeling herself as homeless or in crisis; she remains convinced that because she works and is not dependent upon any substances and loves her children, she can manage their challenges.

What stands out from a quick scan of the city's website, below various emergency services and health services that Evelyn remains fearful of after their first visit to a family shelter, is a separate link for hotel vouchers. This link does not elaborate much on the service beyond a rote description: *After regular business hours, 211 LA can provide crisis housing motel vouchers for any eligible family (dependent on motel capacity/availability).*

With these few bytes of information and a semi-plan in mind, she is able to go about the remainder of her shift.

At five fifteen that evening, she has all the kids save Orlando gathered in the Highlander from their after-school programs. Pulled over on a side street near the elementary school, she shushes them and dials the three digits then spends ten minutes giving touch-tone responses to a series of automated questions. Boredom quickly replaces her anxiety. Frustration replaces boredom. At first the automation asks her to give yes and no answers. The system fails to pick up her voice no matter how clearly she annunciates the monosyllables. This might have to do with one of the kids piping up with an exasperated complaint always at the precise moment she is trying to speak. But at any rate she needs to resort to using her keypad. The system doesn't do much better with that method, maybe because her Samsung is a few years old, the touch screen cracked and glitchy from letting the kids watch videos on it. Soon Evelyn is pounding the tip of her finger against the display of numbers. Iris and Sofia think this is hilarious, like a great comedy routine conceived just for them.

After some time, Evelyn establishes in the system that she is physically within the county, she has five children, she is not in immediate physical danger, she does not need transportation.

When the recorded voice inquires if Evelyn is currently pregnant, she is unsure whether or not to be truthful. She suspects that being pregnant might bump forward her priority level. She also fears that the condition might land them in a medical center or another strict environment where questions are asked. So she keeps pressing the "8" button, knowing the system won't recognize it, until finally she is put on hold for the next available human.

The kids are antsy now. They've grown into great passengers during the past weeks of long commutes, but something about being in the SUV without moving anywhere agitates them. Meanwhile Evelyn considers the sheer vastness of the city they are in and all the tens of thousands of people around them who also need help. She figures that she will be on hold for a while. So she drives them to Barnes Park playground and tells the kids to run free but not far. She finds a bench and settles in with the phone to her ear. Without needing to be told, Gabriel watches Marisol on the playground.

This park is one of those places that can be very busy but still feel peaceful, perhaps because there are just as many old people there walking slow laps and playing at the game tables as there are young people using the structures and sports fields. Humanity appears balanced here. Her kids join other kids in hurling themselves over and under the swing set. The time is six o'clock and then six thirty. The sky has long since gone dark, though the playground is well lit. Most families have headed to their homes. She begins to worry about the battery on her phone as it falls below 20 percent.

Then a woman comes on the 211 line. Evelyn tells herself to speak slowly and calmly so as to be understood and not categorized immediately as frantic—but not so slowly and calmly as to seem undeserving of help or high on something.

The woman—who identifies herself as a community resource advisor—is warm but to the point. She begins by asking most of the questions that Evelyn already answered for the automated system. Once they speak for a few minutes, she assesses that Evelyn and her family qualify for a voucher, which she will send electronically along with an address to a hotel or motel somewhere in greater Los Angeles that has room. The whole process is at once frighteningly vague and a kind of salvation.

When she hangs up, she sits on the bench by herself for a few moments refreshing her email. She watches her children play, and in a poignant touch of grace within these difficult hours, she sees Orlando on the playground, having somehow found the family on his own. He is running and swinging around while his three sisters chase after him.

◆　◆　◆

The email from city services guides them to a motel in Huntington Park, in South LA, in the direction of the church apartment but not quite that far. They stop for fast food on the way—Del Taco—and eat while driving. The building is on a commercial stretch and from the outside appears more upscale than the American Inn Motel. The clerk at the check-in desk has clearly seen these vouchers before, and without any delay they have a room with instructions to be out before 8 a.m., which is no problem anyway since they need to be at school in Monterey Park before then.

They transport inside only what they need to sleep. Evelyn lies flat on her back on one of the beds and closes her eyes for a few idle minutes. She asks all her children to think about how wonderful it is that they are here.

But then comes the business of bathing and teeth and general hygiene. Then come fits of tired cantankerousness. Then come preteenage boys vying for space where there is very little. Then come manic pleas for TV and screens while she implores them to finish homework. Then come protest and outrage at the prospect of bedtime. Then come all the relentless challenges of motherhood.

In the early morning they wake together, groggy but motivated. They gather what they brought upstairs and pack it all in the Highlander in just two trips. Checkout is easy. The drive isn't too bad. Everyone enters school on time.

The 211 line is designed for emergencies: people in the city who have nowhere to stay and don't know where to go. Each of the seven sectors of the county has its network of established shelters and crisis centers and the majority of 211 calls result in a transfer to the most appropriate organization that can shepherd a given person or family through one night or more. In part because the region holds about three times as many homeless people as shelter accommodations, the motel voucher program was conceived primarily to help families who experience a sudden loss of housing after shelters are filled or closed for the day. Many of these situations occur because of domestic violence, runaway children, or often both. A free night in a motel with late check-in and early checkout is a temporary, relatively inexpensive, triage-like solution meant to provide safety until morning, when trained service providers open again and families can seek oversight for their survival. The voucher program is an emergency resort and is not meant to be sustainable for more than a few nights in succession.

Yet no legal cutoffs exist by which the city can deny this service to a family after a certain number of uses, probably because that is the sort of regulation that can appear inhumane, and practically no callers would opt for the hassle of nightly holds and unknown destinations over other transitional options.

In Evelyn's mind this specific emergency service that asks very few questions and records no permanent information becomes the fulcrum of her plan for the near future.

◆   ◆   ◆

At school, Iris is just becoming curious about popularity and what it means and to whom it is awarded. A classmate who was very welcoming to her during the first weeks of second grade before later turning cold and seeming to align a group of her other friends against Iris—snorting when she ventures to answer a question in class, or getting her legs tangled in the long jump rope on purpose at recess—is definitely the most popular girl in her class. She is not the most well-liked, but her opinions seem to steer others. Iris is not a very restrained child already and her attempts to be heard more often only draw reprimands from the teacher. She is in a state of tentative confusion now, desiring neither to be in constant trouble nor to quietly blend into the walls of the classroom.

The transition from fall to winter in late 2018 finds her vised between this pressure at school and all the pressures at home—including the image of her father as a ranting drunkard outside the 96th Street apartment and all the angry women there chasing them away. One evening at Barnes Park while her mother talks to city services and Orlando pushes her on a swing, she asks her older brother about school: how to navigate the girl who everyone else follows.

Orlando laughs, not the mean kind, more of a commiseration. It is cold outside. The sun went down a while ago but the lower western horizon is still afire. He tells her that this sort of problem changes shape as kids grow older but never really goes away, and he tells her that over a longer arc of time the kids who know who they are inside, who don't adapt their personalities to suit others, are the ones who have the truest friendships.

"I'm pretty sure I know who I am," she says.

"I'm pretty sure of that, too," he replies.

Then he changes the subject to a flyer on the window of the park's main office advertising a youth dance class program: eight classes for ten dollars, the prospect of which makes Iris very excited.

◆ ◆ ◆

Math class is destroying Orlando. He never had an attentive math teacher before, never enjoyed the subject, and never really tried to understand it. He received decent scores at school in Lancaster but on state standardized testing always ranked around the fiftieth percentile. Until this year he had always felt fine about coasting through school this way, the only way he and his friends ever had.

Four months into seventh grade and now officially lacking a home, he is still acclimating to an environment in which classmates pay attention to one another's test scores and teachers needle him about small errors and the social hierarchy is largely based on grades. Also new is the way in which math and science hold a greater value than writing or social studies. Once Orlando registered this importance a few weeks into the year, he assumed that some extra focus on the STEM subjects would even things out. But the conceptual gap between the arithmetic he'd been learning in sixth grade in Lancaster and the algebra taught in seventh grade here is wide and the boundaries of his thinking remain limited. He just doesn't understand much of what is being spoken or drawn on the screen in the front of the classroom. On quizzes and tests he receives Cs for the first time in his life. He has largely hidden these grades from his mother so far, praying that his teachers don't contact her.

His math teacher—whom he really appreciates and is fond of—has been attuned to his struggle and begun checking in. A few times this teacher has asked offhand the question most dreaded by Orlando's mother: "Is everything all right at home?"

◆   ◆   ◆

During the days when her kids are in school and she doesn't have an Applebee's shift, Evelyn searches for a second job, also in food service, because that's what she knows and where she has references. But between her family and her existing job and the mandate to be on the phone with 211 services at exactly 5:01 p.m. each evening or risk being on hold for an hour or more, she does not have the flexibility that even the greasiest, cheapest over-the-counter taco joint demands.

She realizes that the job search is costing her too much gas in addition to being exhausting and depressing. She gives up after a few days.

◆   ◆   ◆

Alameda Street takes them over a few freeways, past a few parks, within sight of the iconic and cinematic city hall building and the gleaming glass-paneled police headquarters, closer to the geographic center of downtown Los Angeles. Their route skirts the edge of Little Tokyo with its busy manga

stores and the Arts District with its galleries and outdoor modern sculp-
ture installations. They pass dim sum restaurants and craft breweries with
lines out the door. The large windows of converted loft buildings glow
warmly above the streetscape. Modern luxury condo buildings that have
just opened advertise vacancies with expensive signage.

Then they intersect on Alameda with Main Street. This juncture is
where the tents begin: a continuous line of mostly blue and gray and green
tarps slung from crude plywood lean-tos that are themselves tied to metal
gates and fencing along the south side of this block, and the next block, and
the block after that, disappearing over a swell of road.

Skid Row is a surreal sector not just of Los Angeles but of America: an
area where the width of a city street separates a fully developed, twenty-
first-century urban center from concentrated, government-sanctioned destitution, addiction, and suffering in which physically surviving one day to
the next is an actual uncertainty for many of the thousands encamped.

From the Highlander Evelyn sees—and she can't prevent her kids
from seeing—the dozens of shirtless, shoeless people shuffling along the
outskirts of the shantytown. Most are Black and most are men. Some are
so filthy that race and gender are unclear from a distance. Many look to
be scanning the ground as if for a quarter or some lost trinket. Others sit
hunched over in wheelchairs or on the curb. One elderly, bearded person
vomits between his legs as they pass but doesn't bother to move his bare
feet from the forming puddle. A woman who might have been late-term
pregnant or might just have a midsection distended from malnourishment
stalks around screaming at a man who ignores her.

"*Fuck*," Orlando says. He's been saying this word often as a general com-
ment on life.

Evelyn sees on her phone map that she is supposed to turn left, directly into this zone, toward the motel they've been assigned by the 211 system tonight.

Driving toward downtown from the east, the view was dominated by a handful of glassy skyscrapers looming over older, blockish buildings, with multiple huge high-rise development projects in progress. From that distance, the city was luminous and inviting and in a state of rapid vertical growth powered by untold investment. The sun was low, ricocheting a deep orange sheen off the tens of thousands of windows just so. Even though Evelyn was driving there in order to obtain another free motel room—they are almost two weeks into this new nightly voucher routine and exhausted by it—the sight stirred her just as it had when they'd first rounded a bend in the interstate on arrival here in August, when it had all seemed to exist just for her and her family.

Now she is directly underneath that skyline on streets unseen from afar and the city appears very different here: at once scary and heartbreaking. She has heard of this part of downtown Los Angeles her whole life and has probably seen photos in a newspaper or on a website at some point. But even in her less-than-privileged upbringing, she has never actually had to wrap her head around such a horrid nexus of human lack.

Evelyn follows the map program's directions and makes the left turn. The tents that cover the one side of Main Street also dominate both sides of Sixth Street as well as the streets branching off perpendicularly in either direction. A tense line of people forms around the Union Rescue Mission, one of the two largest shelters in the city. In this line, Evelyn sees at least twenty children who are her kids' ages. Their own assigned motel room for the night is two blocks farther.

"Are we safe here?" Gabriel asks once they are in their room on the second floor, looking down on the dark street.

"For tonight," Evelyn assures him. But she makes a mental note to avoid this motel in the future if they are sent here again.

Shouts, arguments, and wails rise sharply outside throughout the night.

The family has little awareness of the history above which they are sleeping, the half a square mile called Skid Row that since 1976 has officially been recognized by the city government as a "containment zone," as if poverty and homelessness were virally contagious. They don't know about the poor seasonal workers and low-wage railroad laborers once drawn to this area due to its proximity to the train depot and the density of cheap short-stay hotels, the rezoning laws of the 1950s that intentionally made workers' housing structures cheaper to demolish than to refurbish, the proliferation of people sleeping on the local streets instead, the erratic approaches to this open-air poverty that included anti-camping laws, raids, mass-arrest events, the depositing of mentally ill patients from closed-down health facilities. They don't know much at all about the city's homeless epicenter—which in its uniqueness and household name recognition is also very much the nation's homeless epicenter—because the general populace's attitude toward this place has remained across all these decades remarkably constant in its apathy and avoidance. Now, the residential development of downtown high-rises and loft conversions has proliferated all around the perimeter of these fifty square blocks, practically blotting them from view unless, like Evelyn, one is taken through them inadvertently by a phone navigator. This place is officially stated to be home to between four and five thousand people who have no home. But social workers and service providers argue over this number, which might be as high as ten thousand, might be higher.

◆　◆　◆

In their new iteration of family survival, which hinges daily upon the 211 service, the weekends prove hardest to endure. They still need to check out of whatever motel they are staying in as soon as they wake up, hustle the younger ones into the car, and then confront a full day with no destination and no money with which to create one. The city contains few indoor spaces in which six people can occupy a significant amount of time without spending money to be there.

On a Saturday a few weeks after the motel voucher cycle begins, Evelyn takes everyone to the beach. The Pacific Ocean is stunning, a bowed edge of the city she has experienced only a few times in her life. She packs some cheap snacks and finds free parking. They stand together atop a bluff eighty feet high and peer down across the off-white expanse of a wide beach. Far below them people ride bikes along a concrete strip that meanders through the scene. They descend a stairway and cross a footbridge over a busy oceanside road called the Pacific Coast Highway. The kids all run fifty yards through the dry sand, past a volleyball game and sunbathers and a dirty man breaking down the tent he slept in last night. They reach the ocean's edge. The water is annihilatingly cold, but the boys swim in the shallows. Evelyn feels they both look too bony. None of them are experienced swimmers and the girls are scared to go in above their ankles.

They situate their things amid many other families, and her kids play with other kids. Evelyn is certain that here and now they don't seem like they are homeless to anyone else. For a few hours that morning as the air grows warm, she feels like this will be the place that they always can afford to come to—the place that will make this passage in life not just bearable but memorable.

Then the kids one by one grow chilly and sandy. Marisol has a diaper situation that has to be dealt with in a public bathroom. The bathroom is built as part of a long wall on the bikeway, and along the wall in both directions perhaps thirty or forty grungy homeless people sit and crouch and lie, people of all races and ages and states of health. The bathroom is nasty from being overused and undermaintained.

The beach isn't actually an ideal place once the novelty fades and they have nowhere to retreat for warmth or shade. Everyone is exhausted by the early afternoon, and they still have hours before she can call for a hotel space and drive to wherever that might be so they can clean off and rest.

She asks her kids for patience multiple times that afternoon and on many subsequent afternoons as days and weeks accumulate and the family searches for places to spend time.

The California Science Center museum is free and includes being able to walk around a retired space shuttle, which is awesome in its scale. But the entire museum really takes up only about two hours. A few of the city's art museums are free; they try those and find that the girls cannot last long before one starts trying to grab at the installations or trace a finger across a painted canvas.

Some public libraries have weekend hours and special events where they can pass a part of a day now and again. Evelyn becomes an intrepid explorer of picnic spaces and playgrounds. Depending on what area of the city they awake in on a given morning and how much gas she can afford, they sample different parks and collectively become experts of the city's recreational landscape.

She signs Iris up for dance classes at the Barnes Park rec center and these are wonderful for an hour a week. Gabriel enrolls in the basketball program, which also costs only ten dollars for the season; he loves the concept of being on a team and having a uniform but is scared of the coach, uncoordinated, and rarely passed to. At both the dance classes and the basketball practices, the kids have a cheering section hollering for them wildly. Even though Evelyn obsessively worries about injury, she has learned that urgent care centers in the area are decent and that her kids are nearly indestructible. The joy and physicality feel worth the risk.

All afternoons pass on into evenings with the apprehension of Evelyn's 211 calls to learn if they will have a motel room and where that room might be in the city. Sometimes that room is a ten-minute drive and sometimes an hour and a half; Los Angeles is vast. They find relief in that room for a night's sleep and then together submit to another day of the same uncertainty. Because she cares so much about where her kids are able to attend school, this mode of existence remains preferable to enrolling with a short-term housing organization or signing up for any of the region's long-term housing programs—most all of which, like Section 8, have months- or years-long waiting lists. Their lives revolve around leaving places.

Evelyn is just beginning to show her pregnancy.

Between the holidays oncoming and the weather worsening, more people call 211 each evening. The hold times are longer. The possibility of being denied a motel voucher is increasingly real.

◆ ◆ ◆

In an outdoor corridor in between classes, Orlando finds himself walking alongside a boy he's been paired with a few times in science. They exchange nods and male niceties: "What's up?" "Nothing." "All right." "Cool." The kid mentions something about a new edition of an Xbox game he just picked up. Orlando spontaneously invites himself over that evening. Tactically, he adds that because of his mom's work schedule he won't have a ride home after six.

"Just stay over if you want," the kid offers, as Orlando hoped he would. "We have a ton of space."

"That's cool with your parents or whoever?" Orlando checks. "On a school night?"

"They don't even care."

"Cool."

Not until later in the afternoon, shortly before he would normally be meeting up with his family at Barnes Park, does he text his mom that he has another place to stay that night. He uses exclamation points to present this as a net positive: one less mouth to feed, one less body crowding the motel room. Within the tonal limitations of texting, he does his best to hide the fact that even if only for one random Thursday night he is glad to be free of their situation.

In a wordy back-and-forth she asks who this boy is, why she's never heard of him, where he lives, what his family is like, how Orlando is going to get to school on time the next day: a litany of neurotic questions through which he interprets her hurt.

I'll probably see you at the park tomorrow, he writes in reference to the spot by the playground where they always come together while she waits on 211.

Orlando has a wonderful time at his classmate's house, which is in a hillside neighborhood of curving streets south of the commercial district where the schools and park are. The house is not large but still has a distinct dining room, kitchen, living room, and TV room. Orlando spends most of the evening watching the kid play the Xbox game. He enjoys the idleness of it, the complete pointlessness and lack of urgency, the emotional extremes his friend experiences with the flow of the game even though it holds no bearing at all in the world they inhabit. The family is originally from some area of China—Orlando immediately forgets which one it is—and the boy's parents do not speak much English, but his mother is sweet and serves them gigantic plates of the most delicious noodles Orlando has ever eaten. He scoops and sucks these into his mouth with a level of rudeness that reflects how weary he is of the Vienna sausage cans, waterlogged beans, and stale tortillas that have lately composed his dinners.

As the sky darkens, he spends much of the evening staring out the window, which provides a view directly north along Garfield Avenue, lit with a steady flow of tiny headlights. He sees school in the twilight. He sees Barnes Park. He sees the area of Aunt Talia's apartment. He sees the distant freeway and the city's distinct low-rise sprawl in all directions. What he can't see—because he doesn't know—is where his family is bedding down within that sprawl, and this absence stirs him with discomfort but not enough to reach out to his mom and ask if they are all right.

◆　◆　◆

Dozens of wide doorways surround the vast indoor space. Within each abounds a kaleidoscope of color: hues of purple, orange, and blue that seem transposed from rare night skies. The city's wholesale flower market is always crowded and roaring loud. She comes here all the time now when the kids are in school and she isn't working. Sometimes she spends a full morning browsing and emerges having bought just two or three stems. Some of the ladies who run the stalls have her marked as a serial flower-gazer; they glare and mutter to one another. Evelyn still takes her time. As desperation becomes a central mood of her life, she cares less and less how strangers perceive her.

She first noticed the flower market on a night when they were assigned a room in another of the Skid Row–adjacent pockets of downtown. The building was closed but she registered all the vans lined up and the carts loaded with blossoms being wedged into them. She made a mental note to visit, and the mall soon became her only real place of contentment in the city, the only place she could locate some fleeting calmness. Roses, carnations, lilies, and other standards pack entire stores. She also finds rarer varieties from the Mediterranean and from Pacific Island nations: grevillea, agapanthus, plumeria, amaryllis, bromeliad. These are flowers she's never seen or heard of before. The market is muggy and smells worse than one would suspect—more like stagnant algae-lined water than fresh blossoms. But she loves it here and has to restrain herself from spending too much money: maybe ten dollars per week on a mishmash bouquet that she keeps in coffee cups in the Highlander's drink holders.

Each night at the new motel, once their clothes, bath items, and school supplies are in the room, Evelyn makes a special trip back to the SUV in order to transport the bouquet to the room's bedside table. The boys don't seem to notice. Iris thinks she is silly for being so precious. Sofia and Marisol, though, love that she makes this effort.

◆ ◆ ◆

Her engine splutters and fails to catch after a shift at work. Some forceful key turns eventually start the SUV, but the same sequence happens a few times in a row: the pause in the mechanism, the upwelling of nervousness, the eventual successful rumble of metal parts spinning. She chooses not to take the Highlander to a garage since even a minor problem could potentially bankrupt her. Instead, she figures out through trial and error how to pump the gas pedal a certain number of times with a certain pressure before ignition. The issue abates for now.

◆　◆　◆

Like many highly rated public schools, theirs depends on parent volunteers for many of the environmental aspects that make for a pleasing place in which to learn. Parents tend to the large planters filled with both edible and aesthetic plants that surround its outdoor spaces, and they staff the library so that it is open throughout the week, and they decorate the hallways with student artwork and giant posters promoting school spirit. Beautification days are devoted to deep cleans inside the buildings and extra flourishes outside like painting cement and hanging shade sails.

In the beginning, Evelyn found herself at once intimidated and excluded by the school's constant calls for unpaid time and labor. Back in late August and early September she was searching for a job and a place to live. Then she was working and still searching for a place to live. Then she was fleeing domestic violence while working and searching for a place to live, then commuting from Watts, then searching again. All the while she was delivering children to and from school daily with positive mindsets. She could not contribute more than that. But when she overheard other mothers talk about their volunteer groups and the hours they invested in the school, she nevertheless experienced some guilt. Anytime these mothers tried to loop her into their conversations, she could only shrug and make real excuses that must have sounded like fake excuses.

Since leaving the 96th Street apartment, she has begun volunteering all the time—most often for library shifts during the week when she has days off from Applebee's. The library gives her not just a place to be but people to be with. The work is easy, the space is peaceful, the moms are pleasant, and the feeling of connection to her kids' learning is indescribable—her attempts to describe it actually bring her to tears. Otherwise she would be alone at the flower market or drifting around the city dwelling on her problems. She also signs up for weekend campus projects like painting and planting that mean her kids can spend all day playing around a place they know and enjoy while Evelyn meets other parents—mostly women—and occupies her mind with small tasks. Almost always, people bring coolers filled with cold drinks, sandwich trays, large spreads of chips and desserts.

At the ends of such days she and the kids are tired but never hungry. The most satiating element of this new pattern has to do with the gratitude she receives—not just during volunteer shifts but now throughout each week while waiting outside of school and in widely spread emails from the principal's office thanking helpers. Strangers, acquaintances, and people who are becoming her friends constantly tell her how grateful they are that she and her kids have joined the community. She has never before known the receiving end of this sentiment.

◆　◆　◆

In late December of 2018, the days are cold and short. The Barnes Park playground grows dark now before Evelyn can even call 211 at 5 p.m. and so this playtime takes on a melancholic quality. They usually retreat to the Highlander for warmth while she is still on hold. The hold times continue to lengthen, the kids acting more self-pitying during these waits.

One early evening on the playground, a girl of about Iris's age approaches her carrying a cardboard tray of chocolate bars and other candy. The girl is slightly aggressive as she explains that she is raising money for her cheer-leading squad.

Evelyn notices now two other children, the girl's siblings, canvassing the playground's parents with their own trays. She asks how much the candy costs. The girl replies, "Six dollars."

Evelyn can't afford six dollars for a package of M&M's, but she can't say no, either. She gives the girl a one-dollar bill and apologizes for not having more and tells her good luck with her cheer squad.

Later, she sees the children one by one returning to their mother, who has been watching inconspicuously from a picnic table on the periphery of the playground. From a distance, the woman appears snappish with her children, as if they aren't earning enough.

Once Evelyn is off the phone and gathering her own kids, she finds the girl and gives her another dollar. Night has fallen now and the two desperate families diverge beyond the playground's overhead lights, Evelyn ushering her brood to their 211-assigned motel and the candy vendors disappearing to wherever they are for the moment surviving. Evelyn never sees them at Barnes Park again.

◆　◆　◆

"Everything feeling okay?"

The doctor is a young Asian man and is so attentive and friendly that Evelyn almost feels suspicious of him.

"I think so," Evelyn replies. "I've had some cramping the last few days so I just wanted to make sure."

She is reclined beside the ultrasound machine, not actually worried about the pregnancy because after five healthy ones she has not considered the possibility of anything going wrong. Recently, she has felt a powerful urge simply to see the baby inside her. Then a midweek morning to herself arose and she ventured to this urgent care center to find out if that could be possible without having to be entered into any systems or speak to any social workers. The young woman checking people in assured her that her privacy was safe here, and clearly Evelyn was not the first woman that morning to ask. The process is efficient and unintrusive. The spaces are clean and everyone here is kind.

The movements on the screen do not at first form shapes that she can discern, just gray and black blobs and weblike imagery. Then the doctor finds the correct spot and angle against her lower abdomen and she sees her child curled within its slightly bent obloid. The head is delicately tucked against the body. For a moment the image has near-pristine clarity and she sees the curve of cranium, dignified brow, the beginnings of a prominent nose. She sees jaw, spine, and ribs above what resembles a long tail that she knows is a normal feature at this stage. The doctor points out the heart, a tiny, incredibly fast dilation a few pixels wide. She listens to it beating while the doctor uses the cursor to make a few rough measurements. He tells her the baby appears to be developing wonderfully. Evelyn knows this already, even if during her weakest, most doubtful moments she finds herself wondering how life might be much easier—or at least incrementally less difficult—if this conception had never happened or had naturally, harmlessly expired. Yet while gazing at what is to come, she experiences only pure wonder.

Then she moves, or the baby moves, and the image distorts back into a mush. The doctor is unable to capture it as well, and maybe he has realized that she did not come here for any real emergency. She thanks him and tells herself that she will not take advantage of this resource more than once every two months or so during the remainder of the pregnancy. The small copay makes her feel selfish.

◆ ◆ ◆

The winter holiday approaches with its requisite school events: Marisol's preschool class has an art show; Sofia has a singing concert; Iris is part of a talent show; Gabriel is also supposed to be singing, though he is so mortified that he won't talk about it, won't even name the songs. Orlando does not mention anything involving the seventh grade.

Each evening in December, once they arrive in the assigned motel, Sofia and Iris perform for the rest of them. Evelyn sits upright in the center of the bed with Marisol in her lap. She exhorts Gabriel and Orlando, if he is with them, also to form an audience. The focus of Sofia's class's set list is multiculturalism. One of the songs is a Spanish ballad, another is in Chinese, the last is an American pop song by Pharrell Williams called "Happy." Each afternoon at the park she proclaims to have memorized all the various lyrics, and each night in the motel she forgets them all anew and her performance becomes one of nervous humming and dancing. Being the most shy child even in this intimate space of family, Sofia unravels and ends up curled in her mother's arms, wailing that she is going to die if she has to be in the concert, she is actually going to cease to exist—or at least never be able to attend school again. These meltdowns are overwhelmingly adorable, and each time Sofia practices, Evelyn secretly hopes that she loses composure and balls up. Because in those moments no space exists really beyond their two bodies. Whatever motel takes them in on a given night, whatever the condition of the room is, above Skid Row or above an upscale shopping mall in a suburb—those seconds wrapped up together transport them from the world.

At the same time Iris, being much more daring in general, has undertaken the choreography of a Hula-Hoop routine with two friends for their portion of the second-grade talent show. She doesn't seem to be worried that she has never really picked up a Hula-Hoop before in her childhood. Evelyn has the sense that her daughter glommed on to two other girls whom she talks about often—girls who back her up versus the popular bullies—and this is more of a strategic social ploy than an earnest segment of entertainment. Iris is a child who does not care to see more than one move ahead of any given decision she makes; that she is similar to her mother in this regard is lost on Evelyn but no one else in the family. In keeping with this trait, even as the date of the show nears and it becomes clear that the girls' makeshift recess rehearsals are going disastrously, Iris seems confident that once the show begins she will suddenly become a master of the craft; she will shift the hoop in unison with the others from her waist to her neck to her arms and all the way down to her ankles; her glorious performance will cement a lifelong friendship with her two favorite girls in her class. Altogether her projections make for an astonishing display of self-advocacy.

Evelyn cannot help but to play out mentally some of the worst-case scenarios on Iris's behalf: she sees her daughter fumbling painfully through even the most basic moves, her hoop clattering to the wooden stage floor again and again, sad moans of sympathy interspersed with laughter from parents in the auditorium, humiliation, tears, ostracism.

A little more than a week before the date, Evelyn buys a hoop at the 99 Cents Only Store and carefully wedges it in the Highlander with their bags so as not to kink the flimsy plastic. Then every afternoon after school in Barnes Park while she waits on hold with 211, and every night in the motel parking lots around the city, she forces Iris to practice. During the nights when their motel is located in areas where the parking lot does not feel safe, they wedge all the room furniture into the corners and she practices inside.

Iris is neither graceful nor fluid in the way that this particular brand of athleticism requires. There is absolutely no world in which she will acquire the ability to manipulate the hoop around her limbs the way the others can. Evelyn's hope is that she might simply be able to keep it moving around her waist for a minute or two.

Concurrently, Evelyn works with Marisol on an elaborate preschool cardboard project meant to signify being grateful during this time of year. The goal is a sort of three-dimensional depiction of their family. Evelyn is not an artistic sort but together they cut out six stick figures and glue them upright around some squares meant to represent the Barnes Park play structure. The hardest question that arises is whether or not to include her father.

"Daddy here?" She plants her finger in a spot right next to the figure of Evelyn. She has arranged the family tallest to shortest. She points to the other end of the line, next to herself. "Or here?"

Evelyn says, "But Daddy is never at the park with us."

Marisol replies, "But we can invite him to come." She adds with some longing, "When he's not too busy."

That's what Evelyn tells her daughters sometimes now, as memories of the American Inn Motel soften with distance and they seem to forget why they all had to leave him: their father is too busy working to be with them.

"It looks like there isn't enough room for Daddy on your cardboard," Evelyn says. "I think it's okay if, in the picture, Daddy is still at work."

◆　◆　◆

On the morning of the concert for the lower grades of the elementary school, Evelyn signs in and fills out a sticker name tag for herself at the front desk. With the purple Sharpie marker she draws tiny hearts around her name. Then she stands with some parents she knows from volunteering and awaits entry into the auditorium. They chat together and Evelyn joins their talk of the pride they are experiencing right now and relief for the break from school. Their talk moves toward holiday plans and Evelyn idly envies the trips that some have planned, the home decorations they still need to put up, the gift cards they are presenting to favorite teachers. Soon Sofia's class files past. Sofia is rigid, her eyes stoic and fixed on the back of the head of the boy in front of her. She is probably terrified. Evelyn at first resists shouting out to her, but then she shouts anyway: "You got this, girl!"

The assembly begins with the youngest classes working through some songs and dances. When Sofia's class enters the stage and begins, Evelyn can tell even from far away that Sofia has predictably blanked on all the lyrics but is doing an admirable job of faking them, opening and closing her lips in an exaggerated imitation of singing. And then the Pharrell Williams song, which involves some dancing, sweeps her up and she shakes her shoulders and hips alongside her classmates, and other parents stand and dance, and Evelyn does the same, physically giddy.

"Which one is your student?" the woman beside her whispers.

"She's the one in the middle row, second from the left," Evelyn replies.

"Mine is the boy right behind her, the tall one."

"He did so great!" Evelyn says, though honestly she did not pay an iota of attention to any kids besides her own.

Once Sofia's class finishes, Evelyn's experience at the show grows more tense as the schedule runs further and further behind and it becomes clear that seeing Iris perform will mean being significantly late for work. She surreptitiously texts Charlotte, who is unable to fill in. She texts a few other servers from the restaurant whom she doesn't know as well. No one can help; each person has his or her own crazy life and family and school holiday concerts. Parents around her stare judgmentally at her on her phone, even though they all have their phones out to record their kids. Each class's performance is budgeted in the program as five minutes but keeps taking ten or more when factoring in the time required to transition kids on and off the stage.

Just as Evelyn is about to hurry out in a disconsolate fit, Charlotte texts back that she can in fact move some things around and cover for her. Another forty-five minutes of kids singing and dancing pass before the second-grade talent show commences. A few kids perform magic. Some others tap-dance. A troupe of kids wearing sunglasses and shiny sweat suits raps. A Latino kid attempts a card trick that doesn't pan out. Each is underwhelming to all but the parents of the children onstage, and that is the point of it, that is the ritual they are all a part of within the vast constellation of the school system and the city and the world. Evelyn has never really occupied this rite of passage, neither as a student nor as a parent, and she is fully immersed in it—captivated in a way she did not at all anticipate.

For Iris's segment, the team at the last minute has adapted its choreography to accommodate Iris's shortcomings such that she stands behind the other two girls, moving back and forth from one side of the stage to the other, doing a standard waist-level Hula-Hoop for as long as she can sustain it, then snatching the hoop and starting again. All the while the more talented girls in front of her do their tricks in time to a hip-hop beat. Somehow, the act works, and in Evelyn's estimation the three girls draw the very loudest applause. Evelyn feels as if her soul is exploding in a massive burst of stardust.

❖   ❖   ❖

Onstage upon finishing, Iris and her friends huddle together in a three-person hug. Together they are quivering and giggling and her known world is reduced to this closed space between their bodies and the currents between their smiling faces.

Her friends, named Mia and Lucia, found her this morning crying at her desk. A portion of the morning was allotted to practice for the different acts and they asked her to come into the hallway to run through their routine a few more times. Iris told them that she didn't feel well. They did not believe her and she confided that she knew she was not skilled enough to be in their routine and did not want to ruin it. She told them to practice while she did word puzzles with the small number of classmates who had chosen not to perform.

Her friends laughed and did not seem to register quite how miserable she was feeling, how exhausted Iris was from sustaining this act of over-confidence both at school and at home—all the while knowing that she did not belong onstage with these friends who truly were incredible Hula-Hoopers. Together they grabbed her by the arms and pulled her into the hallway. With just a few run-throughs of the song, they figured out how Iris could do what she was capable of—about fifteen seconds of spinning at a time—and still be a part of the group.

Now the applause goes on and on. To Iris the noise sounds actually thunderous. She breathes hard and the nervousness remains still active in her chest. She hugs her friends tightly until their teacher gently pulls them apart and ushers them toward the side stairs. At some point the clapping has stopped and the next group now waits for them to clear the stage. While walking off, Iris looks for her mother, but the lights are bright and all the faces blend together. Then she sees two arms near the back of the auditorium waving much more frantically than any of the others. Her mother's wide eyes connect to hers and Iris holds her Hula-Hoop above her head like a gigantic halo.

◆　◆　◆

The school's upper-grade show occurs the following evening at 6 p.m., which poses a different problem in that Evelyn will likely need to be waiting on hold with 211 at that time. At work throughout the afternoon she thinks through the dilemma. In the best-case scenario, she picks up the girls, calls at 5 p.m., is quickly transferred to a caseworker, and is granted a motel room within an hour. In the worst case, the call goes on and on interminably, forcing her to pace exasperated in the lobby during Gabriel's concert. She can potentially hold on to the call while seated in the way back of the auditorium—but she knows that such a move would invite withering stares from other parents and, worse, might lead to her dropping the call somehow and losing a room for the night.

She picks up the girls as usual, takes them to the park, gives them snacks. She anticipates the timing of her call with the instant the clock flips from 4:59 to 5:00 but apparently dials too early, because she receives the automated 211 menu for business hours, which is different from the recording given after hours. She hangs up and dials again, but the mishap punts her backward in line. While still on the phone, she loads the girls into the car again and drives two blocks to school. She cannot find street parking anywhere close and ends up returning to Barnes Park for a spot and walking with the girls to campus while still on the phone. As is very often the case in her most stressful moments, neither her seamless imagining nor her worst fear actually comes to pass, but rather some previously unconsidered trouble: her phone charger somehow wasn't plugged in the right way that afternoon and so the battery turns red. The hold time continues. They reach school and join the line of parents entering. Six o'clock passes and the show is starting late, so she stays in the lobby. Her phone beeps with 5 percent power remaining.

Iris then salvages the family's evening by noticing another mom also on her phone, the same kind of cheap Samsung model Evelyn has. Evelyn borrows a charger and plugs into a wall outlet. She sends the girls into the auditorium to save seats.

She speaks with a human only about eight minutes later, but she also is aware that Gabriel's fifth grade is performing first. By now she knows what questions the caseworker will ask and how best to answer them in order to preempt further questions and speed the whole process along. She receives a room in a motel very far to the northwest in the San Fernando Valley, and then immediately bursts into the auditorium in the middle of a song. She has missed Gabriel's group and is crestfallen, consoled slightly that at least the girls were able to see him.

She thinks they can leave early but the girls have noticed that Orlando is sitting with the seventh-grade chorus in one of the front rows; for some reason he has been lying to them about not being involved in the concert. Confused, Evelyn settles in and waits. Orlando is onstage less than an hour later. They sing a Billy Joel song called "And So It Goes," followed by a faster pop song called "Despacito," which has been on the radio all the time, followed by an unmemorable classical song. Orlando is not one of the kids granted a solo but Evelyn feels that she can hear his voice apart from all the others. She is angry with him for lying but grateful to prolong this brief, wonderful point near the end of their tumultuous year.

Later, while driving them all toward the motel an hour away, she has

"Despacito" playing over and over on her phone. "You did not tell me you joined the chorus!" She shouts this both in accusation and in exultation.

"I didn't *join*," Orlando explains. "It's, like, mandatory. We all have to do chorus or band."

"But you didn't tell us!"

"I didn't want to make a big deal out of it like you are now."

Even in the darkness of the car, she sees in the streetlight glancing across his face that maybe he is blushing. At the same time, she notices in the rearview mirror that Gabriel is pouting somewhat, and so she bends her attention and her mood toward him. "Gabriel, I'm sorry. I really tried so hard to be there. I wanted to be there more than anything else in the world. I must have missed it by two minutes, or one minute even."

"It's okay," he murmurs.

A standing truth of having a large family—one that does not become apparent until the kids age, one that can't really be prepared for emotionally—is that almost never can everyone be happy at the same time. Someone invariably has cause, legitimate or not, for the kind of downcast expression that Gabriel wears now. Evelyn spends the remainder of the drive fixated on propping up his spirit and feeling lousy because what she really wants to do is give Orlando more praise—and Marisol and Sofia and Iris, too—but there simply isn't enough of her to provide them each what they deserve.

◆　◆　◆

The first day of the winter holiday break, the Friday at the end of that week, is also the first time that the county fails to provide them with space to sleep. Because of a diaper situation with Marisol, Evelyn is a few minutes later than usual to dial 211. When she learns that no available rooms remain, she argues uselessly for a minute. The caseworker that evening offers her connection with a crisis center as well as multiple other shelter options. Evelyn declines.

She can afford a cheap motel room for one night; she tends to have now between $100 and $300 available depending on the time of the month and day of the week. Right now, on this night, she has $143. In the context of her current, precarious financial rhythm, losing a chunk of $60 or $70 for a room is not ideal but can be managed; the kind of poverty they are in warps the value of money, making a dollar simultaneously precious and expendable. Alternately, she can drive to her mother's in Lancaster for the night but that will cost her about the same amount in gas that she saves in room fees and also no doubt inflict on her many questions and an emotional toll.

Her issue is psychological in nature: half of her accessible income spent on one night in what will no doubt be a derelict place means that then the whole break from school will become an exercise in stretching each dollar even further than usual for food before she receives her next paycheck at the month's end. She will then begin the next pay cycle significantly behind in her normal financial calculations. In addition, Christmas is very near. She is devoted to the idea of giving each of her kids one very thoughtful gift before they gain another sibling and another human life to sustain in the upcoming year.

And so Evelyn almost casually turns over the idea of sleeping in the Highlander that night. This is not the first time the possibility has occurred to her, but it is the first time in which it has struck her as a practical choice rather than an abstract scenario, one in which the pros rationally outweigh the cons, one that can be framed in her mind now as sensible.

Iris catches on first to the fact that tonight is different from other nights.

They are all in the Highlander and Evelyn is aimlessly driving while she ruminates.

"How far to the room tonight?" she asks.

"There's no room tonight," Evelyn says plainly, as if she has observed a distant cloud that might signal rain, or a lane closure ahead.

"So we have to go to Aunt Talia's?" Orlando asks. Evelyn circles the picturesque blocks that border Barnes Park. The fields and knolls and play structures there have really become the center of their family life.

"We can't do that to Aunt Talia anymore," she says. "Maybe one or two of us, but not all, and not without notice. I'm thinking we just sleep here."

"In the park?" Iris goes bug-eyed with equal parts incredulity and excitement.

"The car. There's a lot of room. It's not cold out. Then we don't have to go through the whole process of finding a motel, paying for it, checking in, dealing with all our stuff." Maybe the kids are stunned or maybe they are just thinking this through, like Evelyn is. "It seems like the easiest way."

"You just park anywhere?" Orlando is pensive and unexpectedly soft.

"You can stay with a friend," she suggests to him.

"I should be with you," he says. She feels warmly toward him then.

"Let's eat somewhere and then decide."

They have food at a Yoshinoya, which is no one's favorite fast food but has something everyone likes. Dinner is quiet. Evelyn keeps assuring them all that this is just a simplified way to pass one night before they resume their usual routine tomorrow. But her children behave as if a fundamental shift is occurring or has already occurred.

She fools with her map application for a few minutes but knows this is moronic. Not even Google can tell her where the ideal spot is for a family to sleep in a car. The city has recently begun establishing safe parking zones—lots with gates and some security presence—but Evelyn does not know much about these and she definitely can't let a security guard see five kids sharing a medium-sized SUV.

She contends directly for the first time with a sweeping contradiction of homelessness: having people around means safety; having people around means suspicion and potential reportage.

She knows of a street parallel to I-10 that she uses on the way to work sometimes when the interstate is jammed. Certain spurs of it dead-end, so there is not much traffic. Segments are residential but bordered on one side by a barrier wall. This thin knowledge gives Evelyn an idea that Mission Road might make for a safe but discreet area in which to spend just one night.

◆　◆　◆

So they do this: find a quiet block that seems suited to their needs, crack the windows, cover them from the inside with clothes on hangers, fold the back seats down, shove their bags of clothes around in order to fashion pillows and mattresses, and try to sleep. Evelyn puts the small clutch of flowers she bought earlier in the week in a plastic cup on the dashboard. The kids have brushed their teeth at Yoshinoya but no one wants to change into pajamas in the tight space. At first they laugh about elbowing for room, debate who is hogging the most blanket, predict who will snore. Evelyn does not have any material with which to cover the windshield, but she parks close against a large van ahead of her, intentionally leaving only a couple inches so that no one can walk directly across the front of the car. Then she wedges herself next to Marisol's car seat and nestles against the toddler, lets Sofia press against her other side. Iris, Gabriel, and Orlando make sardines in the back, with Gabriel's legs propped up on the middle-seat headrest. No one is tired. Evelyn has an idea to put a family movie on her cell phone before retracting the thought because someone outside might see the light or hear the sound. They whisper a bit with one another, each of them nervous in different ways. An hour passes and nothing eventful seems to occur outside—maybe six or eight vehicles pass without slowing—and Evelyn strives to downgrade her terror to a lower tier of unease. The atmosphere gradually loosens. They marvel some more together about how well the performances at school were, and how cute Marisol's preschool artwork was. The bigger kids complain about space, but in a farcical way such as when Orlando silently sneaks his foot to within an inch of Evelyn's face and she smells the dirty sock. An hour or more passes like this. Then they are actually tired and the kids begin falling asleep: Marisol first of course, then Iris, then Gabriel, then Sofia. Evelyn and Orlando remain the last two awake.

"Really, it's only for tonight," Evelyn reaffirms, most likely without conviction.

"It's okay," Orlando says. He yawns. Then he is pretending to sleep. Then he is asleep; she can tell by the rhythm of his breathing just as she had been able to tell when he was a baby crossing over from waking life to dreaming life.

Evelyn is thankful to be the only one left alert when midnight comes, when the night becomes real and seems to scratch at the window. That precise instant separating 11:59:59 p.m. from 12:00:00 a.m. holds its own psychology. Before then Evelyn can in a certain way believe that they are camping out, sleeping in this space as some poorly conceived but escapable family adventure; she can perceive nearby footsteps as belonging to a harried night-shift worker on the way to a factory or a harmless bar patron shuffling home rather than transients, dealers, human traffickers, police, or other real threats; she can believe that morning will bring not just light and warmth but a return to a life that is simple, comfortable, perhaps even normal.

Once midnight passes, none of those illusions props her psyche anymore. That is when their situation grows truly frightening and begins to hollow her inside.

PART IV

Agape Court

Wendi
November 2019–July 2021

THE HUNTINGTON HOSPITAL EMERGENCY ROOM administrative center is quieter at night. Parents, spouses, and other guardians bring in their loved ones facing sudden, scary health situations such as premature labor, sharp chest pains, high fevers, trouble breathing. The ambulance crews come and go. But the overall pulse is less frantic than during the day. Wendi enjoys these shifts. The draw isn't so much that she has less work to do but rather that more emotional space exists in which she can establish reassuring connections with incoming patients as she guides them through the intake steps. There is more time for pauses between words, meaningful eye contact, and listening within her interactions.

During her half century of living a difficult life in America, she has experienced nearly the full spectrum of causes to panic: expulsion from home more than once, teenage pregnancies, abuse at the hands of multiple men, poverty, a child with autism, a child in the juvenile justice system, children who wouldn't speak to her for years at a time, children who themselves faced many of the same hardships that she had, cycles that seem cosmic in their capacity to repeat—cycles that seem almost sentient in desiring to repeat. Wendi is a grandmother now and has had grandchildren sick enough to be admitted to the ERs of cities all over California,

165

and she's made those drives through the night in order to ask harried doctors the right questions.

In the meantime she has been doing this same job at the same hospital in Pasadena for fifteen years. While she is at work—even when she is making insurance inquiries on behalf of families who don't have insurance and other such unpleasant forays into the American health-care system—she sees her primary purpose as using gentle good humor, highly relevant anecdotes, well-timed laughter, and a few reliable Scripture passages to shepherd people through their hardest days and nights.

◆ ◆ ◆

Back in the year 2006, just a few weeks after Wendi had graduated from Door of Hope, Miss Abeba called her and said that an emergency had come up and she needed an experienced leader for that night's Bible study. Wendi was not experienced and she didn't see herself as a leader, but she agreed assuming this would be a one-off assignment. She was nervous, nearly sick. The study went well aside from a few gripes regarding the laundry machine and other shelter dynamics that had nothing to do with the Bible. She focused that first evening on a line she loved from Psalms: *He is the lifter of my head.* Those gathered came up with different interpretations and the hour passed quickly. Afterward, Miss Abeba asked when she would be arriving the following week to do it again, causing Wendi to wonder if there had actually been any emergency the first time or if Miss Abeba had planned this low-level, unpaid position beforehand. Miss Abeba, for all her altruism and virtue, was shifty that way.

Wendi became Sister Wendi within the organization's sphere and came to devote an hour each Thursday evening. She has done this for nearly fifteen years now while working hospital shifts, raising Momo and Anthony and Tiara, and volunteering as often as she could in her church.

In this manner she has remained modestly connected with the organization and has worked closely with hundreds of families passing through the shelter, seen hundreds of versions of absolute poverty in the city. Most of these families graduated and moved on into permanent housing like Wendi herself did. Some could not handle the shelter's restrictions and left too soon with their children, usually in abrupt fashion in the middle of the night so as not to be tracked or made to feel guilt. Wendi was a part of Door of Hope throughout the Great Recession, when the topic of homelessness was temporarily at the forefront of city media and politics. And she was there weekly when it wasn't mentioned anymore even as the number of homeless continued rising. She witnessed the nonprofit expand and convert two more local properties into transitional housing.

Her adult children ask her now and again why she remains so committed to a small charity that, from their perspective, helped her a little bit during a rough stretch a long time ago. In response, Wendi speaks broadly of gratitude and faith, to which her kids in turn roll their eyes and say that she doesn't owe anyone that much.

◆　◆　◆

Momo is in high school now. If his trajectory continues on its current course, he will graduate from a special education program in two years. Her older son, Anthony, and daughter, Tiara, both graduated from a well-rated public school in Pasadena. They still live with her in the Agape Court apartment complex. Anthony works as an Uber driver for the most part. He talks often about applying to community college without as yet applying. Tiara also speaks of higher pursuits. Both help significantly with Momo's transportation and care—they always have, though Anthony more so because being with Momo requires a measure of physicality, not for discipline necessarily but simply to guide him through environments, keep him from wandering off or being rough with people unintentionally. Momo has become tall and heavy. His strength is tremendous.

Her apartment is not usually a peaceful place to be, with his constant noises and someone always listening to loud music and someone else watching the TV—plus neighbors and thin walls. The tenor of the place is another reason she likes the night shifts at the hospital. And yet even fourteen years after moving from the Los Robles shelter to Agape Court, Wendi constantly marvels at the fact that she possesses this apartment in a wonderful neighborhood, she's raised three kids on her own here, she's worked nearby while those kids progressed through area schools that they liked. This unit is small but has been her stable home. Many of the families she's worked with through the years at Door of Hope, even with all the support given by the organization, failed to establish that most fundamental and most elusive of necessities. Some of those mothers and children didn't survive.

Wendi doesn't know if Yasmine survived. After graduating from Door of Hope shortly after Wendi did, she and her daughter left Los Angeles with a drug-addicted man and lost touch with everyone there who cared about them. In her daily prayers, Wendi touches upon the memory of that girl and the gifts she gave. She hopes Yasmine is alive somewhere.

◆ ◆ ◆

Not quite two years earlier, in 2018, Wendi was diagnosed with peripheral neuropathy. The disease is no less painful for being fairly common. Basically, progressive nerve damage that has accrued over a long period of time reaches a tipping point within the body's pain alert system, on the other side of which daily activity causes substantial numbness and discomfort in her feet. Her doctor guessed that her case might have had something to do with stress and with sugar intake. The cause seemed to matter a great deal to her when she was first diagnosed, as if a minor change could reverse a massive system failure, and it gave her the motivation to eat fewer dessert foods to ease the symptoms. But that effort cost her some small pleasure and didn't help with her pain, so she returned to eating what she wanted. Now she is in her early fifties and her feet hurt all the time and that is the way of things.

The hardest challenges at this point are not the physical ones. Her daily responsibilities at the hospital require some walking to guide patients and family members to different areas, conveying physical copies of administrative forms, covering colleagues' desks during high-volume shifts. Those efforts cause pain. But Huntington Hospital is a functional, easy-to-navigate building. Her superiors like her and they also do not want to be sued over labor violations so they are accommodating to her need to rest often.

By far the greater aggravation is social and comes from her younger coworkers. In the low-key political framework of her workplace, Wendi is a senior figure. But in the parameters of her administrative work, what her years of experience tend to gain her is resentment from younger, newer staff who do the same tasks but are paid a little less and expected to work a little harder.

As situations arise more frequently in which Wendi's friends on the staff might run an errand on her behalf while she elevates her feet in the break room for a few minutes, chatter begins to sound that she is lazy; she is entitled; she doesn't do any work. Wendi is not a passive person in late middle age like she was as a younger woman trying in vain to please her husband, and she begins engaging in daily skirmishes with her colleagues. These interactions can be loud and profane. They are always exhausting and they make work unpleasant and sad.

She sometimes entertains the idea of moving on from Huntington Hospital. She has looked for a similar job in the less demanding environment of a private practice; she has considered pursuing a certificate to be a supervisor; she has daydreamed about starting her own small business-management office.

Wendi talks through these and other notions aloud to Momo while she oversees his bathing or watches him exercise on the bolted-down weight equipment in public parks. But just like her two older children do, she expounds frequently upon her future without making any tangible motions to actualize change. After all, her job at Huntington might be difficult, low-paid, and socially tiresome—but it also provides solid family medical insurance, a 401(k), and a pension.

She has felt strange during these years at the end of the 2010s: someone who has every reason to be thankful for the many fulfilling aspects of her life and for the unlikely durability of her independence but who is increasingly discontent.

◆　◆　◆

"Enough already, woman," Miss Abeba says, exasperated, on the front walkway of the Los Robles shelter property where Wendi has been complaining generally about work, children, health, life. "Sister Wendi's good, Sister Wendi's bad, Sister Wendi's happy, Sister Wendi's sad." She makes wide gesticulations with her arms, swaying side to side like a tree heaving in big wind while forming a face that is at once sour and still affectionate. "Choose however it is you feel and then *act* on it!"

"Why can't I be all of it?" Wendi asks back, also animated. Miss Abeba over time has become something like a volunteer work-wife. Their relationship is definitely not immune to egocentric tiffs like this. "Why can't I be what I feel one day and the next?"

"Because you are driving me bananas with your sad-mad faces," Miss Abeba replies. Then, more seriously: "And the parents need to be able to look at you and feel inspired themselves. You are not giving them much right now."

"I can't be inspiring all the time."

"Wrong word," Miss Abeba amends. "They just have to see you as someone they can become one day *if they follow through on the promises they make to themselves now*. That is all."

This conversation happens in November 2019 and leaves Wendi indignant. "I think I probably look like I'm doing okay!"

Miss Abeba then cocks her head slightly and speaks with thorough earnestness. "You've looked better in your life."

"I'm in my fifties!"

"And you're walking funny."

"I have neuropathy and you know that!"

Miss Abeba hugs her and holds on for a while. "What you have is not going to change. *You* need a change."

◆　◆　◆

Wendi is committed to taking care of Momo for all the rest of her life. She might have had other aspirations, once—both grand acts of service and places she wanted to see—but those plans dissolved over time into his need for her. The alternative is to place him somewhere affordable with Medicaid, but she has seen the spareness and inertia of such facilities and sworn never to do that so long as she is physically capable of keeping him fed, exercised, stimulated, and loved. But the pain and numbness in her feet frighten her for this reason, too. Her body is failing her too soon.

Over the course of Momo's life thus far, some doctors and family members have tried to convince her that other options exist beyond her committing her middle and old age entirely to him. The cruelest interactions occurred when those people posited that she was selfishly being a martyr, or that Momo wouldn't even necessarily feel the difference between her care and the kind of professional care provided in an assisted-living home. He did not show love the way normal people showed love, they reasoned, so he must not feel love that way, either—through hugs and declarations, meaningful eye contact, and the like. Wendi could never explain to these people the degree to which she remains certain that Momo would absolutely wither without her. She no longer tries to explain. She just ignores their voices and carries on.

When she has the conversation with Miss Abeba about the vague, hypothetical life changes she needs, COVID-19 is already in the news, has made its way to America, and is thought to be working its way around the city they live in.

A few months later the hospital is madness. Very often Wendi and her colleagues wear used N95 masks or tripled-up blue surgical masks while working face-to-face with incoming patients who can barely breathe in between their dry, sometimes fatal coughs.

Over her years in the ER, Wendi has on occasion worked with patients who are in very dangerous situations. She's seen dead bodies and witnessed a few human beings actually die, which is always a profound experience. The frequency of death around her with the advent of the coronavirus does nothing to dilute the unfathomable weight of a soul passing. It does leave her less able to rely on her religion to interpret the passings with lines of Scripture. And it stretches the relationships between coworkers to an untenable point of tension.

They are all accustomed to working in an environment that surges into stressful longitudes with any sudden random burst of trauma intakes: a bad car accident, for instance, or a building fire. They all know how to choreograph one another's responsibilities on a rolling basis, keeping their interpersonal gripes on a simmer so as not to logjam the lifesaving performed by nurses and doctors. But the pandemic makes many moments of each day feel life-threatening to *them*—low-skilled, low-wage hospital administrative staff—and this stress intensifies the typical irritation of their workplace. Their work puts them in a strange position of being necessary frontline workers but not the ones who actually provide care that can be celebrated as heroic. At the hospital, where most gestures of graciousness have disappeared into the life-and-death frenzy, Wendi spends huge portions of each day being yelled at by patients, superiors, and coworkers. People are afraid and people are angry now—deep in their hearts and almost all the time.

Wendi continues to work because she needs to earn paychecks. She spends a solid half hour at the end of each shift physically on her knees praying that none of those nasty little spike-ball molecules have gained purchase within her lungs during the previous eight hours surrounded by people spraying them into the atmosphere. She begs her God to permit her to survive this place and time for Momo's sake.

Families argue throughout the Agape Court apartment complex, which is composed of forty-four small one- and two-bedroom apartments squared around an interior courtyard. The apartments do not have balconies. The windows are small and do not offer much ventilation, so many residents generally keep their front doors open. Most of them, like Wendi, live pay-check to paycheck working difficult jobs that they do not have control over. All the stress and negativity and fear building within each living unit during the pandemic pours from the doorways and seems to pool thickly in the inner courtyard. Under the stress of the time, Wendi and her family contribute plenty of their own energy and noise. The negativity that characterizes life now feels total.

To center herself, she takes walks with Momo around the wide sidewalks and consistently clean streets of their neighborhood. They walk slowly together, sometimes only covering a mile or two in the span of an hour. She narrates their small loops.

"That is a brown bird," she says.

"That's a brown bird," he affirms.

"That is a blue bird."

"That's a blue bird. I think it's actually called a bluebird!"

She points: "That's an orange bus."

Then he points: "That's an orange cat."

"Yes. I hope it finds its way home."

Once in a while they encounter a flock of parrots based in Pasadena. These birds are locally famous. It is thought that many years ago, some irresponsible pet owners lost or abandoned some birds, and these birds found one another through their mating shrieks, and they did what animals do in the wild—and now in the present day hundreds of these birds bandy noisily about the area's lush treetops. Wendi and Momo hear them from afar, and this is one of the few encounters that can motivate him to run, which due to his girth and weight is more of a waddle. But the motion fully expresses his joy and transmutes a dose of it into his mother. Upon seeing the parrots, he remains in a placid state for hours afterward, sitting on the sofa and emitting soft murmurs of residual awe. When this happens, the day is good. But that is rare and her neuropathy makes walking with him harder and harder to bear.

As the year 2020 progresses, the pandemic removes her church and Bible commitments from daily life. Wendi's consciousness is whirling, kicking up anew all the dust and debris of her past. Rarely, when she is home sitting in a sort of coffee nook that she has fashioned from a side table pressed beneath one of the kitchenette windows, she hears the parrots somewhere outside in the environs of Agape Court. They might even happen by close enough to be seen swooping with their wide green wings, yellow flanks, and long purple-tipped tails. They really are stunning. She shouts for Momo to come and they press their heads together at the small window to watch. She looked up the word for a group of parrots once and learned that they can be called a *pandemonium*. So when she and her son see them now, they both point and shout together, "It's pandemonium out there."

◆　◆　◆

In July 2021, over a year deep in the pandemic and a few months after vaccinations have become universally available, Wendi is just beginning to catch glimpses of her working life returning to a less harrowing pitch. The situation at home is easier. Momo is in school again, and church services resume. Wendi's feet are always either numb or burning on a low flame from the inside but otherwise she feels all right, like she can live this way for more years.

On a Tuesday evening after Bible study at Los Robles, which Wendi has been conducting outdoors, Miss Abeba asks her to stay and sit with her in the yard. Thin stilts of light pass through the oak foliage over their heads. A group of children from different families currently sheltered here come down to play a game that involves batting a ball back and forth across a trampoline-like net on the ground.

Miss Abeba explains in an uncharacteristically lecture-like voice how their expanded transitional housing system continues to help dozens of families each year extract themselves from situations of homelessness. New prevention programs are helping dozens more avoid homelessness entirely. The leadership of the organization is smart and the supporters are generous. She says that Door of Hope is thriving even during this stretch of unforeseen volatility in which widespread tent communities across the city and state have become a symbol of society's failings.

Wendi knows all this and wonders what purpose this conversation serves since she does not need to be sold or resold on the organization's merits.

"Where we lack impact is in the *after*," Miss Abeba says. "Once people graduate and are placed—not everyone ends up well like you did."

"Oh, but I *struggled*," Wendi says. And she adds: "I still struggle. You know all about it."

"But more and more people cannot overcome the struggle the way you have," Miss Abeba sermonizes. "They leave here with some savings and a place and a job, and suddenly it is back to big birthday presents for the kiddies and getting nails and hair done because it has been so long without looking pretty. And then, well, you know how fast it goes back to the street."

"I do."

"So we would like to extend some new programming to alumni to continue teaching them and also continue being in touch with them and *seeing* them. The *seeing* is oh-so important."

Wendi now believes that she understands the tack that this dialogue is taking: Miss Abeba is going to ask her to volunteer more hours by doing home-visit Bible studies or some new service like that.

"I can't give more than I'm giving, Miss Abeba," she begins. "My job, my kids, my feet . . ."

Miss Abeba is already sweeping her hands back and forth. "I will not ask you to give more," she says.

"Then what is it?" Wendi is weary and her feet really do hurt.

"You will come work with us."

Wendi laughs. She is flattered of course, but the immediate thought of relinquishing a hospital employment in which she has layers of insurance and a pension for some newly created nonprofit position strikes her as being quite stupid—and also contradictory to all she's been taught by the staff of this very organization about smart, thoughtful, professional decision-making.

"That's sweet," she says. "But it's not for me right now. I'll help the program out however I can with what time I've got, but I can't do nothing, like, *official*. I can't give up my real job."

Miss Abeba smiles at her because she already knows the outcome of Wendi's denials.

◆ ◆ ◆

Wendi begins the new job at Door of Hope about two months later. Even after her official interview and much discussion with over a dozen stakeholders regarding what this new endeavor of alumni support can be, Wendi still considers herself unprepared for real social work. She is leaving a position she has held for over fifteen years—one that is chaotic and socially miserable but of which she understands every single nuance—for a role that has never existed before, that has a broad and dignified purpose but not yet any sort of day-to-day structure.

During her first morning in the Door of Hope office, she organizes her cubicle desk. Meanwhile, the young people in their twenties who do most of the outreach and coordinating work for the organization whirl busily around the space talking to each other in a shorthand language while thumbing their devices. When they are sitting, they seem to be typing on their keyboards at dozens of words per minute. With a pen and paper, Wendi works on a basic to-do list for her day.

Miss Abeba does not spend much of her time in the office, but she comes to check on Wendi.

"How are you today?" she asks.

"I'm a little scared," Wendi replies. "I'm not too sure I decided right."

"You should be relieved. You're here now, not there."

Wendi assumes that she is referring to the hospital. "It isn't *so* bad there."

Miss Abeba's eyes become two very serious points of focus. "You were dying there," she says. "I have been watching it happen. And here you can live. It is that simple." Then she makes a skittering motion with her fingers toward the thinly forming to-do list on Wendi's desk while backing away. "Now go, go, shoo, get your work done."

◆　◆　◆

The organization's new program of alumni support is an enhancement intended to ensure that individuals who have managed to reclaim some housing stability hold on to it in the face of myriad socioeconomic forces running counter—not just the terrible arithmetic of the city but also PTSD, vindictive exes, opportunistic family and friends, childcare logistics, questions of capability and self-worth, depression. Wendi's efforts here operate in the realm of life and death. Her new post is part of a major expansion of services the Door of Hope organization strives to offer at the turn of the decade as the greater surrounding cityscape is overrun by the physical bodies and layers of need of almost a hundred thousand people without homes.

Back in 2005, when the structure of her life dissolved, the magnitude of the task of simply saving herself and her children felt titanic and barely endurable. Now in the summer of 2021, she finds herself spearheading the same task on behalf of thirty or more families at a time. She starts out in this work with virtually no idea what she is doing.

As she begins making the rounds of the shelter facilities to acquaint herself with her first graduating class of alumni that she will support, Wendi immediately begins hearing warnings from some of the mothers.

They tell her to be on alert for the woman named Evelyn and her many children. Apparently this family has been in one of the shelters for almost a year now and their mention prompts low whistles and flurries of hard-to-believe anecdotes. Wendi does not accept everything she hears, but she understands that they are going to graduate soon from Door of Hope transitional housing to become part of her responsibility—and that she needs to steel herself and be wary, because this mother is wildly protective of her kids.

PART V

The Villas

Evelyn
April 2019–July 2021

SURVIVAL IS NOT CLEAN OR elegant; there is no music to it, no pageantry, no accolades; it does not follow straight pathways or hold pauses for rest or reflection; it does not feel fulfilling or noble, strengthening or cleansing, spiritual or redemptive. There is no immediate reward, no effortless landing on the other side. Survival is a scary, humiliating, ugly threshing of the body and the soul.

On a Friday night in the spring of 2019, about six months into their true homelessness and just a few weeks before the baby will be born, Evelyn and the kids are assigned to a motel off the freeway in Calabasas, which is a monied community in the western end of the San Fernando Valley known for its prep schools and celebrity mansions. The room is decent and they sleep well. After their 8 a.m. checkout on Saturday, Evelyn drives the family on a curvy road that traverses the Santa Monica Mountains along steep edges and switchbacks and through tunnels cut in the rock. After fifteen miles and with the kids growing carsick from the curves and the heights, this route drops them down into the center of Malibu, California. The beach isn't crowded yet, just some walkers and a few old men with long silver hair who look like they haven't risen from their beach chairs in decades, have just been sitting there talking idly this whole time. They park easily and for

183

free on the Pacific Coast Highway and sit beside the pier watching surf-
ers take long rides. The light is gorgeous and not yet too bright, the water
soothing on their feet. Herons forage in an adjacent marshy area. Gigantic cantilevered homes line the hills above the beach. The Pacific Ocean is
blue, serene, deep, glassy, reserved in its power. Evelyn rests on the sand
with her hands folded over her pregnant stomach. The kids fan outward to
climb over rocks and to marvel at urchins and starfish in the tidal pools.

"This is a perfect place," Sofia declares, and everyone else, including
Orlando, concurs.

Two days later, on the Monday morning following that lovely adventure,
they are hustling out of a downtown motel just south of Skid Row in order
to make their way to school drop-off. Marisol sees the lights first: police
cars and ambulances. Half a block away, officers use yellow tape to cordon
off an area. Within it, a body lies on the filthy sidewalk. Evelyn does not let
her eyes linger there and she tries to turn the younger kids away before anyone notices details, but the person who died during the night is definitely
a woman and ragged in the way that people who have been without shelter
for a long stretch tend to be.

"Someone got killed," Iris observes without much emotion.

"We don't know what happened," Evelyn replies sharply. "Maybe it was
an accident. We don't know. Let's get to the car."

◆　◆　◆

The nights when they don't receive a room and must resort instead to over-
nighting in the Highlander somewhere along Mission Road do not become
less fitful or scary or depressing with experience. Throughout each of these

dozens of nights, especially as she grows hugely pregnant, she wills herself to believe that this one—*this one*—will be the last.

They have refined a system, somewhat. A crinkled light reflector stretches across the Toyota Highlander's windshield, and coats arranged on hangers fully cover the side windows. A makeshift clothesline blocks the rear window with T-shirts and blouses, even though the glass is tinted, because Evelyn once witnessed some scavenger trying to peer in with his fingers as a visor. Behind these various thin veils, six human bodies vie for sufficient space to sleep.

Orlando always reclines in the front passenger seat with Marisol directly behind him curled in a car seat that is tilted slightly backward by a duffel bag jammed under the front. The remainder of the second- and third-row seats are folded down to make a platform on which the other three kids lie parallel to one another with stray feet and arms propped on cup holders, with pillows made from trash bags filled with clothes. Evelyn remains in the driver's seat, which is awful because she cannot lean it back far enough to clear her pregnant stomach from the steering wheel. The wheel tends to press against a specific spot on her abdomen that makes her need to pee all night. She constantly must resist the longing to slither back among her children and pass the night holding them, because she has to remain in the driver's seat in the event that the car is approached by a predator or police officer or concerned citizen and she needs to peel out quickly. She prefers to lie angled a few degrees on her left side, facing toward the secondhand gray windbreaker mostly covering the street-side window, pulling the fabric aside slightly to peer outward from time to time.

They always park adjacent to the ten-foot-tall cinder-block barrier wall, painted beige in arbitrary patches, that separates the working-class residential neighborhood from the twelve-lane I-10 freeway east of Los Angeles. Its sheer uninterrupted face serves as a kind of protective rampart for the family such that she needs to worry about noise and motion on only one side of the car. The reverberant, constant rushing of high-speed traffic on the other side of the wall, just a few yards away, sounds distant and can almost—*almost*—be imagined by a weary, willing mind such as Evelyn's as waves on a coast or wind through a valley. She keeps the windows cracked a few inches for ventilation. The air quality outside is poor but their breath needs an exit or they can all actually suffocate.

The kids sleep fitfully in the Highlander. At any given moment one of them might be awake. When they are, Evelyn speaks and even laughs with them in faint whispers: about work and school, and the various people who populate their days, and the shenanigans and absurdities. They talk of events that have already occurred and also those to come. Evelyn strives to keep these conversations positive and very, very quiet—which is hard with the littlest ones laughing and the older ones groaning for them to stop laughing. Sometimes they are all awake during some early-morning hour and having a delightful time together, the heat of their bodies warming one another, the reality of the space receding for short stretches.

But there are also points throughout each of these nights during which Evelyn is the only one awake. These moments are filled instead with fear, sadness, longing, self-criticism, rage, regret. Above all, while listening to the wheezy snores of the kids since one or more of them always has a cold, she projects a possible future life in which her children—including the not-yet-born one—are forcibly taken from her by the city's massive, powerful foster system and assigned to adults who don't sleep in cars. She wonders if she herself could survive that potential outcome, which with each night spent on the street feels like more of a probability, an event that has not yet occurred but has unfolded so many times in her mind that it is somehow already a part of her lived experience.

◆ ◆ ◆

In April 2019, Evelyn goes into labor prematurely at a motel in North Hollywood. She is too far from Aunt Talia's and in too much birth pain to take the kids there first, so they all go to the nearest emergency room together. The hospital is large and well-staffed. The doctor and nurses are all kind to her. No one asks her many nonmedical questions until after her baby is in the world. The boy is slightly underweight but strong and healthy, and sleeping well in her arms. His name is Devian, quickly shortened to Dev by his older siblings. Talia takes her older kids back to Monterey Park and Evelyn cherishes the hours alone in the quiet with her baby. She has regretted the circumstances of her pregnancy for the majority of the last seven months since confirming it, but she is incapable of regretting this preciousness now.

The social worker appears during the first evening while Dev is under observation in the nursery and Evelyn tries to enjoy having her own bed and attending nurse for one night—to wish away just for these hours the anxieties of insurance and the hidden costs that this childbirth will entail. The knock on the door is gentle. The social worker is an older woman with a polite but businesslike demeanor. She asks questions about the other children who were in the hospital waiting room together unsupervised during much of the labor and about Evelyn's lack of her own OB/GYN or pediatrician, her state of employment, maternity leave and childcare situation, insurance, and other details. For some, Evelyn has quick answers. For others, she stammers—such as when she tries to explain how anytime during the course of the pregnancy that she felt the need to check on the baby's devel-opment, she went to urgent care for an ultrasound. But the woman seems satisfied for the moment with the explanation that Evelyn is fairly new to Los Angeles, lives with her aunt in Monterey Park, she has Medicaid cover-age and some family support in Lancaster, and Dev's father is not currently involved in her life. Evelyn hopes that she has stirred some sympathy and that the sympathy will gain her some time. She then calls Talia to ask her to help check her and the baby out as soon as she can, before any more official people can ask any more questions and before billing representatives can start dropping off complicated forms. She has the sense that while they have her here, administrators will try to drain as much information and money from her as they can, but once she is out then she will be able to sort through the ramifications and costs of childbirth somewhat on her own time frame. Medicaid will cover nearly all the costs of Dev's delivery, but the couple of percentage points that she is responsible for will be ruinous if she is made to pay in a lump sum.

Thankfully, Talia appears and uses the skill set developed over a career in a public school system to alternately argue and stonewall Evelyn and Dev's path through the bureaucracy and out of the hospital less than forty-eight hours after the birth. The old woman's performance is captivating.

◆　◆　◆

On weekends during Dev's first months of life they give in to family pres-sure and drive to Lancaster and stay with Evelyn's mother or one of her sisters.

She is grateful for the nights and days of shelter as the weather grows hotter, but she hates the time there for all the same reasons that caused her to leave. At this point, Evelyn has proven that she really does not intend to return ever, which in Lancaster is the same as stating that she feels she is better than the others who remain there. Everyone also has awareness that she is struggling severely but refusing to admit how much or express remorse or ask for help. Questions and concerns and some consternation continue to encircle the fact that Evelyn has gone and had another baby without Manny seeming to be a part of her life; she's been deflecting questions asked over the phone about Manny for months. She deflects in person now. Pride and privacy are well-understood traits in her family, perhaps over-appreciated, but they combine to give most of the time here a tiring edginess.

But Dev's cuteness has a way of smoothing enough moments with everyone to give the time meaning, and the baby care is terrific. She can for the first time in nine months take naps. And when she is awake, all the cousins playing with her children permit her some sustained hours with Dev— those absurdly valuable hours of encasing his chest fully with her hands and gazing for long periods of time into his light blue eyes, hours that are worth all the demons still residing here.

"He looks like his grandfather," her mother states multiple times, meaning Evelyn's late father. Evelyn does not agree with the observation. She finds in her boy a close semblance to Manny.

As much as she wants these weekends to be a simple exchange of her children having a place to sleep and company and her extended family having some time with the baby, Evelyn's life no longer seems able to situate simplicity within it. The man who ruined her childhood and haunts her adulthood, although he is increasingly infirm as a result of a punishing lifestyle, is still around. He seems often to be where they are in the homes of various cousins around Lancaster, sitting in chairs in corners, drinking and maybe cracking a joke in Spanish now and again but mostly quiet. She does not believe he is capable of hurting anyone anymore, but even projecting whatever thoughts might be knocking around in his head when Iris or Sofia is near makes her queasy. Yet now, just as when she was young, saying anything aloud risks upsetting the already uneasy equilibriums she tries to maintain with her mother and siblings.

She also tires of absorbing the travails of her many extended family members: relationship and job drama to be sure as well as growing problems related to cost-of-living imbalances that have by now migrated from the city all the way to the desert. An average two-bedroom apartment in Lancaster—where she and Manny once rented a stand-alone house for $1,675—currently rents for over $2,000.

Throughout that late spring and early summer, on Sunday evenings after a generous dinner, they drive back around the mountain range and dogleg into the city so that the kids can all be rested and on time for school Monday morning. She plans their departures so that she can call 211 and be on hold for a room while they drive. Once school lets out for summer, they spend some extra nights in Lancaster but still keep mostly to their back-and-forth routine so that Evelyn can work as many shifts as possible and the kids can enroll in free summer camp programs.

◆　◆　◆

When school resumes in the fall, she begins taking her kids to Aunt Talia's church—a modest Catholic congregation in Boyle Heights, which is a historically Latino neighborhood sandwiched between the city center downtown and Monterey Park. The two-story pale yellow Spanish-mission-style church on East Cesar E. Chavez Avenue seems to exist either in opposition to or in hiding from the tense, inexorable process of gentrification that has been altering the neighborhood: high rents even in dilapidated buildings; old bungalows being torn down and replaced with boxy town houses that maximize square footage relative to lot size; multigenerational households and small family businesses being not-so-gradually edged out by young white people and coffeehouses precious about the rate and angle at which hot water is poured over the grinds.

The worship is traditional—and usually excruciatingly boring to the kids—with a cadre of old men leading endless prayers in English and Spanish. The initial draw for Evelyn herself is threefold. She enjoys the time with Aunt Talia, and joining her in the pews feels like an act of goodwill. Church is also a physical place to go for a block of time on weekend mornings after their motel checkouts, with homemade food served buffet-style to congregants afterward. In both of those senses, church attendance is practical and maybe a little self-serving. The third component of the pull feels wholly original to Evelyn upon experiencing it but—she will learn later, in therapy—is a common effect of homelessness and domestic-violence survival on mothers in particular: the search within a panicked mind for some abstract purpose behind her suffering, because the concrete reasons tend to feel horrifically arbitrary.

For Evelyn and for almost every person she has encountered in her homelessness who has faced struggles even vaguely parallel to hers, that search leads to religion. The alternative is to believe that they are simply unlucky or, worse, they did something to deserve what is happening to them.

Evelyn's mother was deeply religious, and church services throughout the week were a part of growing up. Neither her mother nor the services offered any solace or grace when she was being abused as a child; the abuser was often in the pews chanting prayers near them. So her teenage revolt against Catholicism and her draw toward the community offered by a

Lancaster gang was maybe not so much a frivolous, childish matter but one of strong self-determination. Her persistent opposition to her mother's faith and way of life played a role in everything from the boys to whom she was attracted in her teens to her rocky familial relationships to the rhythms and tenets by which she raised her children and the directions her mind turned during hopeless moments late at night.

Now, in the midst of her life's most punishing travails, she becomes adamant that the family not miss Sunday service with Aunt Talia—even if they are placed at a motel in the far northern valley of the city, even if they have to pick up Orlando from a friend's home farther east, even if Dev is in a feral tantrum. Evelyn needs to feel as if the entire world has not abandoned her—a need met not only by the sermons but by the fact that seemingly everyone in the congregation believes in the value of large families and adores Dev during the potluck afterward, tells her how beautiful he is, tells her that she is amazing for having him and all her children.

◆　◆　◆

The kids continue to thrive at school and Evelyn finds a succession of short-term housing options: garages, church groups, below-board offerings. There are many days spent at Aunt Talia's, evenings spent at Barnes Park, nights spent in all manner of motels spread throughout the massive county, and increasingly more nights on Mission Road, where a baby's soft cries can sound like a blaring alarm. For the most part they spend the months avoiding official people and their official concerns.

Evelyn's body hurts from her difficult job and all the hours spent driving the car or sitting in the car or sleeping in the car, nursing and carrying a baby, holding a toddler, sitting in bleachers at Gabriel's and Iris's Little

League baseball games, arguing with older children, continuing to volunteer at school, striving to be in many different places for many different people every day. Time operates in strange ways as life carries onward, passing slowly and quickly, feeling within her control and beyond it.

In January 2020, Evelyn is promoted to one of the manager positions at Applebee's. After a full year of homelessness, including seven months with an infant in her care, Evelyn believes that she will at last have a sufficient income stream to rent their own place in the spring. She likes the job, which entails more responsibility but less work. Her kids are all proud of her. For a time she is so happy that she entertains being like Charlotte and staking out a career there at Applebee's—not the grandest of careers but one that can eventually provide benefits and see her children each to college. That was all Evelyn wanted in coming to the city.

During the two months before the pandemic seizes much of the earth, she sees a clear passage through for her family.

◆　◆　◆

After the virus closes work and school that March, instead of touring legitimate rentals like she hoped, Evelyn resorts to another temporary living arrangement in Temple City, which is a suburb farther east of Monterey Park. She is connected to the new place through a dishwasher she befriended at work: a friend of a cousin of his, or something like that, who leads her to believe that some kind of garage conversion is available short-term. Desperate as ever, she agrees sight unseen. But for a hundred dollars per week in Los Angeles, Evelyn should have known better. The garage is not a guest quarters but an actual one-car garage with a paint-stained concrete floor, uninsulated walls, and a single electricity outlet. She has already paid for two weeks before seeing the place. Still, the structure stands separate from the house and has a wedge of private outdoor space. Evelyn thinks that with a hot plate and space heater and two mattresses, it can be nice for the family to sleep in the same location for a while and have some remove from the virus. The city's emergency shelter system and 211 options have become overburdened during the pandemic and are no longer reliable on any given night. They've been sleeping in the car probably a third of the time. The streets themselves have become more dangerous, the homeless population truly sprawling across all neighborhoods and a fair portion of this population keeping nocturnal hours.

They are living off aid from the CalWORKs welfare program, which has taken her over a year to register for, and which for the seven of them provides $600 per month. Evelyn qualifies for more support but she purposefully fails to report the existence of Dev, Marisol, or Sofia to CalWORKs because she does not want to be swept up in a whorl of social workers deciding that she has too many kids. She receives $200 each for Iris, Gabriel, and Orlando.

To access their school's improvised, evolving system of online education, her kids share her one cell phone in order to each attend thirty or so minutes of class time per day. The school district offered laptops and Wi-Fi hot spot devices on loan to families at the onset of the closure, but Evelyn was certain that these would be stolen or broken or spilled on or otherwise ruined in short order, so she didn't sign up.

For reasons she can't wrap her head around, the school resumes taking attendance and her kids begin to rack up absences. Only when schools are closed down and dependent on screen access does Evelyn fail to deliver her kids to their classes. Still, for a few weeks the kids huddle around the phone on floor mattresses in this garage most of each day while Evelyn feeds and entertains Dev outside on the hot driveway. They subsist on their usual fare of rice and canned ingredients. They make do and they reason that they are better off stationed here than they would be roving around, and maybe this garage can at least see them through the summer when Evelyn assumes the world will be reopening. Then a nervous neighbor reports the housing code violation and they have to clear out quickly.

◆　◆　◆

Weeks later, after the school year ends, Evelyn and her six children are stirred from trying to fall asleep by a horrible pounding on their motel room door. Even with the protections granted by the 211 emergency shelter program, this happens to them sometimes—maybe because Dev is crying during the night or because many of the people staying in the dingier spots in the Skid Row area are clinically unwell. This time, the disturbance occurs because someone reported domestic violence after Iris threw an uncapped marker at Gabriel, who retaliated by pounding on her shoulder, which resulted in her piercing screams and some banging around that must have reverberated through the walls before Evelyn yelled at everyone.

As the kids have grown older and bigger over the years, and as their needs have expanded while their circumstances and physical spaces remain narrow, the tension between them bursts from time to time. The venting can be horribly loud and draw the dangerous kind of attention. But Evelyn has lost the foresight and fortitude required to avert these blowups in advance. Nowadays, she usually just lets the kids have at one another until they tire out. She does not like this about herself—but she thinks that she is managing the volatile dynamics between them adequately.

At any rate, on that night they are not only kicked out of the motel just before midnight but some meddling stranger also takes the liberty to call family services. This has happened to them a few times before, too. Evelyn has two options: pack the kids into the car as fast as she can and sleep on Mission Road—or meet whatever weary social worker arrives on-site, prove that no abuse occurred, and hopefully be allowed back into the motel room with a warning and the impassive expression that most social workers need to wear in order to perform their jobs night after night.

Evelyn opts for the latter because she is too tired for the former. This decision will alter their lives.

The social workers arrive and perform the belabored process of confirming that the noise and screaming were due to a typical conflict between children. One of them, a young guy, mentions that he works closely with a church-based shelter in a good neighborhood in Pasadena and he happens to know that an apartment space is opening up. He asks Evelyn if she would like to be referred there; behind his protective mask, he appears to be deeply affected by the number of kids she has and the state of the motel they are sheltering in that night.

She does not think much of that last part of their interaction. She has received many referrals to many different shelters and none of them have ever been able to take a family of seven without placing the two boys elsewhere. She asks him if this would be the case at the shelter he mentions. He replies that he doesn't know, but he can ask, and he takes her number.

The following afternoon they are in downtown Pasadena—a district in which Lululemon and Williams Sonoma stores flourish in between old libraries and post offices bearing original artisan masonry. The kids are bunched together on a small couch in the Door of Hope office waiting room, beneath three watercolor paintings of large ornate houses. The kids share a cell phone screen while Evelyn and the baby sit in the large meeting room with a staff group who promise repeatedly that they aren't vetting her in any way even though they must be doing just that. She doesn't know these people or very much about their organization. They are mostly white women, overtly gracious and well-dressed. She feels cornered. Everyone's face is half-hidden behind patterned masks and the effect is unnerving despite the kindness in their eyes and their voices.

This group plays for her a short video describing the organization, a montage of scenes in which mothers push children on outdoor swings, do arts and crafts on outdoor tables, eat meals family-style from large bowls set upon a long table, sit together on the wide front steps of a large and dignified home, do homework together. In all the scenes, everyone involved appears happy and engaged with the world before them. Gentle background music plays. Then some women give testimonies about their experiences being homeless and taken in by Door of Hope and given some stability, a chance to both save money and train for a job. They weep with sadness and joy and hug tightly the toddlers in their laps. They thank God repeatedly.

In the video, one light-skinned Black woman who is much older than the rest—maybe in her fifties—speaks of being a domestic-violence survivor and the parent of a special needs child. This woman cries as she predicts that without Door of Hope housing and support services, she would have lost her children and most likely her mind; she would have become one of those people wandering the streets talking to invisible antagonists. Instead, now she is a devout church member and Door of Hope Bible-study volunteer, with a career in hospital administration. The video ends soon after that woman speaks.

Evelyn smiles and nods to indicate her shared experience with these testimonies, but she is unmoved by them.

Over the year and a half since she and her family spent their first night sleeping in the Highlander, she has encountered a lot of different people who assured her that they cared about what happened to her. She has watched a few emotional videos in meeting rooms. Most of those people were not as genuine as these ones seem to be, most of the videos not as well edited, most of the offices not as comfortable. Regardless, none of those meetings ever ultimately resulted in real help for her and her kids. A few nearly resulted in relocation and separation before she gathered the kids and fled.

Evelyn is hardened now. She does not trust anyone to do what they claim they can or will do. She is suspicious of the uplifting stories given by others. Whatever softness of spirit she still has, she angles inward and reserves for her children.

◆　◆　◆

They park outside Door of Hope's newest shelter, which looks nothing at all like a shelter. Evelyn actually recognizes it from one of the watercolor paintings in the waiting room earlier that day. The large Craftsman home has been retrofitted to accommodate nine families. The sprawling structure is on East Villa Street in Pasadena. The walls are of slatted wood painted light green with a thick band of exposed-brick foundation at the base. A wide second-floor deck faces direct sunlight; the porch beneath it is pleasantly shaded. Stately homes with huge quarter-acre front yards like this one's line the street for blocks in both directions. Evelyn peers forward and back from her parking space. A few houses farther along, an older lady is in the midst of some light yard work. Past her, a construction crew reshingles a garage. A young couple pushes a stroller with a black Lab walking beside the baby. A few cars pass but not many. The street is peaceful and very, very safe. Evelyn and her kids haven't known what peaceful and safe feel like for almost two years now.

On the walkway, a young woman with sheeny brown hair and a casual outfit that has been put together with some care waves as she approaches the Highlander.

"Evelyn?" she calls while making a scrunched, silly face toward Marisol, who is peering out of the rear window.

"Yeah. I'm Evelyn and these are my kids."

"You're right on time—welcome to the Villas!"

The girl's enthusiasm only heightens Evelyn's underlying nervousness.

"Am I okay to park here?" Evelyn asks. She nods toward the street sign demarcating a permit zone. For Evelyn, parking tickets are life altering; the couple of instances in which she has received them over the past months wrecked her careful expense calculus.

The girl has a permit placard at the ready, which she passes through the window for Evelyn to hang from the rearview. In the Highlander, her five older children stare at the house with a blend of curiosity, skepticism, and wonder that Evelyn finds off-putting for some reason. Dev still rides in a backward-facing car seat and can only stare up at Iris in the seat next to him.

"Put your masks on and be nice," Evelyn tells them.

◆　◆　◆

Their mother is more snappish than usual on the day they are set to move into what is pitched to them as a "fancy shelter." She keeps assuring them that this morning will be their last time packing up a motel room in a hurry like this. She desperately wants them all to look "like nice kids," and that means she is busy with the girls' hair and simultaneously feeding the baby while deciding that any shirt Orlando dons is gross, which is basically true

because he tends to go through his shirts two or three times between opportunities to do laundry.

Orlando completed eighth grade less than a month ago, in mid-June
2020. Sadly for him, he could not log onto the graduation ceremony on
Zoom. His own cell phone plan was cut off by his mother last year to save
money, so he couldn't even text with classmates during that hour. Over the
course of seventh and eighth grade, most of his friends' parents deduced at
least something of the nature of his family's transience. While none of these
adults pried much, during the pandemic in the spring they did designate
Orlando as someone unsafe to see or have over.

By the end of eighth grade he has become almost completely disconnected from the social circle that he so successfully widened in seventh
grade—the people who with casual generosity and little inquiry saved
him. Instead, he has been spending all his time with his family. Since the
pandemic began, they have hardly ever been placed in decent rooms or
calm neighborhoods. All their motel assignments over the past three or
four months have been dilapidated places on gritty stretches of the city,
motels that are not prescreening for the virus or presumably deep cleaning rooms in between guests. These days, the nights they are relegated to
the Highlander on Mission Road seem safer sometimes. Overall, the last
few months have been grueling—their most brutal and fearful months
of homelessness.

The new Door of Hope apartment promises some form of renewal
in Orlando's estimation, which is why he obeys his mother's commands
during their entry into the Villas shelter property for him to smile even
from behind the mask, to stay with everyone, to nod politely, say *please*
and *thank you*.

His mother has never cared so much about appearances as she seems to on this day. Her obsessiveness is annoying to be sure, but for Orlando it is probably the most normative behavior she's exhibited in a while. He is fairly sure at this point that his mother is going crazy—that their long stretch of existing on the very precipice of disaster has eroded her capacity to generate calmness, reason, and joy. His unselfish hope surrounding the Villas is that a few months of staying in an apartment like this on a street like this will rebuild these parts of her so that she resembles again an earnest person with a bright spirit and valid dreams.

He hopes also that the new space will reset his own perspective such that he is able to enjoy his family again. In their current mode of life, which accommodates little emotional space, he has found that blaming different members of his family for different symptoms of his overall unhappiness is the least complicated way to live.

Before school was shut down, his peers there had free time, clean clothes, some disposable cash, sports practices and tournaments, babysitters who took care of younger siblings, extra food that meant they didn't have to subsist off school-district lunches and that they often tossed in the trash at the end of lunch period anyway. Over the fall and winter of eighth grade, as his state of homelessness crossed its one-year anniversary, Orlando became increasingly fixated on what he saw all around him that he did not have himself. As a somewhat natural recourse he grew angry: at classmates for what they had, at his mother and siblings for what they did not.

He has enough sensitivity to understand that his anger is not just unfair but supremely unhelpful to anyone. Yet over the past year and a half its hold has tightened, two wide hands clutching the full breadth of his skull. And he is at the mercy of this psychic vise when Door of Hope ushers them in.

✦ ✦ ✦

The children immediately fan out across the yard. Iris carries Dev—she loves to carry Dev, whom she's taken on as her primary responsibility—to a picnic table. Orlando finds a squishy football near the porch and begins tossing it with Gabriel. Sofia chases Marisol in wide circles in some kind of spontaneous, indeterminate tag game.

Evelyn watches them while standing with an older, dark-skinned lady who is smiling but reserved. Her name is Miss Abeba and she is helping them settle before other support staff come tomorrow to sit with Evelyn and more formally go through what the next months are meant to look like for her: what she can expect and what will be expected of her. The latter aspect of that meeting roots her perturbation. Evelyn knows vaguely that a prerequisite for staying at the Villas is having a steady job, which she does not at the moment see any viable plan to obtain with most area restaurants either shut down or operating with pickup service only. Her mind is spinning. It always is now, really; she hasn't had a casual conversation with another adult human probably in months. The school and her volunteer work there had kept her time filled, her relationships sustained, and her soul grounded. Church had been helping, too. Without them, her thoughts have had a tendency to spiral outward into the realm of disaster scenarios.

But this person, Miss Abeba, provides a calming presence and asks her only superficial, easy questions about her children and their interests and how she braids her daughters' hair each so differently and perfectly— incidentally one of her favorite subjects. Evelyn can barely reply to these comments without stammering, and she has no idea how tomorrow she is going to be the subject of a meeting of actual substance, in which she likely will be expected to explain how she is going to provide for these six children moving forward.

Miss Abeba keeps talking about how delightful the children are as if without worries for any of them, so Evelyn tries to emulate. She also notices that from the windows along the second floor of the home, the faces of children discreetly peer downward into the yard to study the new family sharing their space. After a while her own kids begin gravitating back to her and they all file inside to see the apartment.

By most any standards, the unit at the top of a wide stairway and down a long hall is modest: a living room attached to three small bedrooms and a bathroom. The room they had on 96th Street was actually larger. But the space has qualities that the family hasn't experienced in a very long time: tall wide windows that let in bountiful natural light, well-finished hardwood floors without any warped sections or upthrust nail heads, no visible dust or cobwebs even in the corners of windowsills, sturdy and matching furniture, multiple deep closets, no unpleasant odors emanating from odd places, a separate bathtub and shower. Basically, the apartment has been cared for and that care is immediately evident in a way that transfers a sense of profound worth onto the family—and that effect is by design.

The rooms are all the same size but one has been furnished as the master bedroom with a queen bed, and the other two each have a full bed and a bunk bed. A wooden crib is set against a recessed wall in the living room and Miss Abeba tells them that they weren't sure which room Dev would sleep in so they left it in the middle.

"We usually sort of all sleep together," Evelyn says.

"You can arrange it however you want, child."

Miss Abeba has been doing this habitually all afternoon: calling her *child*. Evelyn finally ventures to make a joke. "Miss Abeba, I don't feel much like a child. I don't know if you've counted, but I've got six of my own."

The woman smiles and replies, "To me, you are still very young, yes. But you keep the *aura* of a child. And that is a good thing. That will see you through the other side. Because a lot of women, by the time they get here, they've lost that. They've seen too much, done too much, and it is very sad."

Evelyn grows quickly self-conscious and asks about food and cooking. She knows this was explained to her at some point during her first interview at the Door of Hope office but she didn't retain much.

"So that's one of our rules: food and food prep all stay in the kitchen downstairs. We have supplies and families organize a rotation to cook for each other. But it's a nice kitchen with everything you need. I'll show you that next. Importantly: no food of any kind in the rooms."

With the last bit of warning, Evelyn picks up her first sense of Miss Abeba's authority here. She doesn't process the rule as easily as she should because nearly all their meals for two years have been eaten together in the car or in the park or on a bed or on the floor. The idea of cooking and sitting formally at a table outside their living space strikes her now as strange.

"It's partly so we don't have issues with mice and other critters and especially *roaches*," Miss Abeba adds, visibly shuddering at the mention of the insects. "These houses are old and that was a problem back when Door of Hope first started, with people leaving food and trash around. You see the rooms are pretty nice and clean and that's partly because of no food allowed."

"So nice! So clean!" Marisol echoes.

Miss Abeba concludes: "But the main reason for the rule is so that families here spend time together. I don't know your full experience with shelters and different kinds of shelters—"

"We mostly stayed away from shelters till now," Evelyn says. "Because they didn't want to let the boys stay with us."

Miss Abeba replies, "You will all be together here, child."

◆ ◆ ◆

They are served dinner outside at a picnic table that evening: bowls full of pasta Bolognese with salad, pitchers of milk and lemonade, homemade bread steaming with a napkin folded over it. The food donor, a gracious older man who frequently volunteers to feed families on their first night, chats with them for only a few minutes and lets them know about the chocolate cake he has in the oven. But he otherwise leaves them alone outside, knowing that right now on the front end of the first comfort they've had in recent memory they don't need intrusions. This first meal is designed around the understanding that families landing here have usually been arguing all the time, because they are living scared and under stress and loaded with guilt and blame, fear and unmet need. A spectacular food spread, prepared and served with care, softens tension like few other commodities can, even money. Evelyn's kids hardly speak to her or one another except to agree over and over that this is the best dinner they've had in memory.

Later, on washed sheets and each on his or her own mattress, all the kids including Dev sleep for over ten hours that night. Evelyn doesn't. Though she moves the crib into her bedroom—that is actually the very first thing she does in the new apartment—and is soothed by Dev's faint snores, she tosses from her right side to her left side and cannot find comfort or summon tiredness. She is wide awake the entire night. This is the sort of awakeness that feels as if a low-level electric current hums on the underside of her skull. She suspects that the reason has to do with her other children feeling far, far away in their rooms. Perhaps she is saddened by the way they themselves fell asleep easily without her. Perhaps the sudden and drastic level of the change they are experiencing—even if it is thoroughly positive change—unnerves her, and she is worried about the meetings tomorrow. She also considers that she hasn't experienced deep sleep in so long that the state itself has become like a faraway place that looks wonderful from a distance but that she will probably never be able to visit.

◆ ◆ ◆

"It's important that you use this time wisely."

She's been nodding at everything said to her for a while now; she nods again.

The social worker who specializes in job training is here with Miss Abeba and a few other people who work for Door of Hope. They are having their first of what will be many, many conversations regarding how Evelyn plans to proceed in her life following the grace period that this shelter provides. A primary decision in that regard involves how she aims to earn a living. She describes with enthusiasm her experience working in the service industry in Lancaster and her year and a half working at Applebee's. She brags about her promotion to manager right before the pandemic. No one here seems impressed by that part of her life. In this group-wide non-reaction, the hundreds of hours she has spent rushing to and from work, the tens of thousands of pounds of plates and glasses conveyed across the crowded floor space, the thousands of human interactions in which she's taken part with the main goal of pleasing others, the sheer intensity of the effort required in order to not lose her job and her family's ability to survive are converted to an afterthought, a bullet point on a résumé that might read: *2018–2020, server, Applebee's.*

"What is something you've always wanted to do?" the social worker asks her. "Think back to being in school yourself, even if you didn't finish school. What is something you thought about then like, *I can spend my life doing that*?"

"I didn't really have one," Evelyn says cluelessly and feeling a little bit of irritation.

"Even when you were really young, like middle school or even younger?"

Evelyn pauses as if she is concentrating hard even though she isn't. "I really didn't think about it except, like, what can pay my rent, buy food, buy some clothes, get me out of my parents' place. That is how my family is, how my friends' families are."

Evelyn keeps glancing toward Miss Abeba in a kind of panic, and Miss Abeba steers the conversation toward skills Evelyn already possesses. As a server, she developed social intelligence, and she needed to mentally organize multiple orders at a time, and she dynamically adapted to others in a hectic environment. They all talk seriously for an hour. What she cannot adequately explain is that at the moment she does not care at all about what she pursues. Her job is to raise her children and not permit them to be hurt or taken away from her or drop out of school. Whatever she might do to earn money is in her eyes supplementary to that. She no longer carries any expectation or even conceptual thinking of experiencing happiness or fulfillment in the workplace in a manner that doesn't encompass her kids.

The people in the room strive to coax some personal aspiration out of her. If they are concerned about the lack of one, they hide it well. She says a few different times: "I didn't come here for me." But the sentiment doesn't land the way she means it.

◆　◆　◆

All the other kids in the Villas—fifteen in addition to Evelyn's, living in eight other apartments—are younger than Orlando. He and Gabriel, once they quarantine for a few days and pass a COVID-19 test, become their unofficial overseers while other parents are busy with job training, financial literacy classes, computer tutorials, cooking, church. During idle mornings and afternoons Orlando sits at the picnic tables and makes sure none of the older kids—the nine- and ten-year-olds—fight one another and none of the younger kids hop the fence or otherwise disappear. They are supposed to be quiet so that neighbors won't complain, because few suburban relationships are edgier than a homeless shelter in an affluent neighborhood no matter how progressive the neighborhood is purported to be.

Orlando is not skilled at keeping order. Gabriel is marginally better. The charity has volunteer teenage babysitters sometimes, some of whom are invested and others who are probably doing this work at the behest of parents, with an eye toward college admissions applications. The boys do their best.

He does enjoy kickball, though—has ever since preschool in Lancaster— and teaching the group to play helps to pass this totally isolated summer. The yard contains plenty of open grass for a real game. The kids boot the ball and chase and argue about what constitutes an out and what doesn't, what territory is foul and what isn't. They wear themselves out. Orlando and Gabriel captain the two sides and take their turns, awing the young ones with the distance of their kicks.

Orlando's world has demanded for a while that he act very old no matter how he feels inside, so he enjoys being able to act young here.

A home run over the fence into the neighbor's yard usually ends the game, though, because retrieving the ball creates a risky mission. Orlando chooses one of the more intrepid kids—often his sister Iris—and lifts her over the fence. This adjacent yard is covered in bushes. He advises which ones to look under, all the while making sure the neighbors don't emerge from the house. The mission is exciting, and excitement is needed for all of them during the school shutdown, which has shrunken their physical and social worlds to this island. But the same excitement speaks to the dichotomy of all their lives here, by which inside the Villas' fencing they are safe, nourished, permitted for the most part to behave like children. Outside the fence, even a few feet outside, they are interlopers and intruders.

During a normal summer, the kids in transitional housing would have school-like sessions and special extracurricular programs and on-site sports and childcare. But these days in mid-2020 are not normal. The kids enjoy a slightly lawless atmosphere, and a pervasive annoyance affects the families as they try to take care of little kids while also striving to find jobs and set savings aside. But at the same time the adults at the Villas share a sense of relief with knowing that they could so easily still be out there in the greater city, where all the new and old layers of mortal uncertainty lie. Instead, they've each taken an unlikely pathway to be here, where their children can be mostly unafraid even if they are stir-crazy.

They are right to be relieved, because the endemic homelessness that has been systemically swept into the city's unseen corners for decades, considered as a whole to be an unfortunate but tolerable background detail, has now burst forth to affect nearly all the square miles of Los

Angeles. The base numbers have not risen in 2020 much faster than they have in previous years. But the city's homeless have begun existing more publicly than ever, crossing some invisible membrane separating the unsheltered from the comfortably housed, and have made themselves no longer ignorable. Over the year 2020, the homeless citizens of Los Angeles in their street encampments and tent cities, in their panhandling and cart pushing and sidewalk sleeping, and in their unapologetic defiance of laws intended to keep them unseen, have gained some power never before wielded here by the nation's lowest socioeconomic class.

On Venice Beach, one of the county's most trafficked and weirdest tourist hubs, hundreds of camping tents and shanties cluster along the beachfront commercial district. Hundreds more line the adjacent grid of narrow residential streets. This specific point along the California coastline draws millions of visitors annually. Now it hosts the largest single concentration of homeless people outside of downtown. The situation casts a political paralysis over the city of Venice—a self-styled artsy, folksy community that also has a headquarters for Google and Apple and is home to thousands of multimillionaires.

A smaller but similar encampment community coalesces around the northern bank of Echo Park Lake, a man-made reservoir near Dodger Stadium that is its own modest tourist spot due to the serene environment in an otherwise urbanized area with its water lilies and a fountain that sprays fifty feet upward over swan-shaped paddleboat rentals and hipsters playing croquet. This encampment, shared with the geese who hatch goslings here annually on a tiny island nature reserve, has an organic garden and a commissary of donated food items. Two people are also murdered within its bounds in its first few months of existence, and assorted needles and vials are embedded throughout the grass. Similar to Venice, these dozens of tents and the hundreds of people residing in them create conflicting factions of homeowners in the surrounding gentrified neighborhood of apartment complexes and old Victorians.

In a nearby but entirely different milieu, a string of tents concentrates along the Los Angeles River, which is really a deep concrete culvert that provides the central channel for a water drainage network lacing the region. Though anything resembling nature was overlaid a century earlier to prevent seasonal flooding, a buildup of rocks and sediment along the system's floor now sustains its own ecosystem of foliage. The trees offer handy supports from which to string tarps, as well as shade from the sun and a measure of privacy. The silt bed becomes home for thousands and is absurdly dangerous since the entire system is designed to flood rapidly with even modest rainfall so as to convey water off the streets and into the ocean as fast as possible.

During the beginning of the pandemic, as much of the public obeys shelter-at-home policies and exits public spaces, those without shelter or home take up these environs, and in this progression a countywide confusion and unease sets in—escalating in some places such as Venice toward hysteria. Upset homeowners, business owners, and renters throughout the city voice valid concerns regarding health and hygiene, children and safety, and the city's enforcement policies, which continue to baffle anyone paying attention. Few of these voices mention that the city has permitted the largest settlement of homeless people in America, cordoned off in the center of its downtown area, to flourish for forty-four years—that what scares and infuriates them now is actually in accordance with long-standing, widely accepted policy.

♦   ♦   ♦

When Evelyn was told that mental-health treatment was mandatory, she groaned and made a face. When she learned from another resident mother that the therapist was a put-together white lady, she audibly scoffed and declared she couldn't meet with this person. "If I'm going to have to talk to someone," she said in the moment, "then I need to talk to someone who's, like, been in a gang and lived on the street."

Evelyn now sits alone with this therapist, who is older than her but not much older, maybe forty. She wears a floral-patterned mask and nice clothes. She has an iPad on the table beside her but she does not refer to the device or enter any information into it for the duration of their time.

With some awkwardness but also a certain softness, she asks Evelyn to tell her story. Evelyn stares downward at the carpet of the small, sunlit office.

"What part?"

"It's an open question. What I mean is, wherever you'd like to begin is where you should begin. Wherever you'd like to end is where you should end."

Evelyn giggles as a reflex. Then she races through a summation. She is not prepared and so she stammers often, skips around back and forth through time, constantly edits descriptions of people and decisions. The therapist doesn't say much beyond small prompts during pauses. Evelyn talks about each of her kids and the consistency with which she has prioritized their education. She tells a story of great intentions beset by bad luck and bad systems and bad people. As fast as she tries to speak and as much as she leaves out, her depiction still takes up her allotted fifty minutes. The therapist is both encouraging and believing throughout.

Once they run out of time, Evelyn says, "That's pretty much everything anyway."

The therapist replies, "Thank you for sharing. That was brave. Next week we will talk about what *really* happened to you and your family."

◆ ◆ ◆

Human consciousness handles moments of stress and fear with astonishing resilience. Regions of memory can absorb the most dreadful events in a person's life and soften those events around the edges or even block them out entirely—allowing someone like Evelyn to take her kids to school and arrive at her food service job on time the day after being choked and punched by her husband or after waking up from a nightmare of the abuse she suffered as a child or after sleeping in her car by an interstate with a baby in her arms. But when intense stress is sustained over a prolonged period, this neural armor wears down. Severe, continued hardship alters people.

Evelyn knows that—innately if not scientifically—and she knows she has been altered even if she is incapable of tracking the behavioral specifics of how. But she has strived over the past twenty-two months not to allow suffering to change her children, to shutter light from the windows through which each of them views life passing. That instinct in her is what transported the kids to the beach on weekends, and signed them up for dance classes and baseball at the rec center, and applauded the loudest at school concerts. That instinct helped convince Sofia and Marisol that nights in the car were family campouts and that the city was just like the woods. That instinct made dropping them off to the normalcy of a nice school each day her highest calling.

Overall she shielded her younger children from the precariousness and at times from the terror of their living circumstances. The success with which she did so is evident in the way they take to the other children and play spaces at the Villas. Gabriel and the girls join into the stable structures with apparent ease. Watching them, Evelyn feels that in spite of all the decisions she would make differently if that were possible, she might have done all right by them so far—and they might one day far in the future even remember her for having done all right.

But she will never know if all that she did for them was enough, and the not knowing makes her feel crazy.

She also can't change the way that she and Orlando experienced their family's homelessness for all its visceral ache and fear. So many weeks, days, hours, and minutes were anxiety-laced and damning. She and her oldest son carry all those moments with them with a clarity the others do not. Neither of them has an easy time finding the humor in day-to-day life like they once did. Neither possesses much patience. Both are easily angered. Both are high-strung around others. Now that they are safe and have some unencumbered time, all this repressed psychology presses down and spreads out.

During her first weeks in the Villas, Evelyn encourages her kids to play with the other kids there, but she herself maintains a distance from the other mothers. There are three Black families, two Latino families, two white families, and an Asian family, plus Evelyn's crew. They all in different ways carry the weariness that exudes from people who have spent time in the abyss and somehow emerged. Despite the safety and largesse here, a few of them seem overly possessive about their food or their kids or both—behavior reminiscent of 96th Street and some other places they've been.

Shared childcare is a part of the rhythm and the rules here, but Evelyn does not volunteer to watch anyone else's kids for even short stretches. When asked, she invents reasons to demur. Some people start logging official complaints about this. But she has no interest in ever again fighting with women about their kids and her own.

"Do all of yours have the same father?" A housemate named Rose asks this question as something like small talk. Much of the casual banter at the Villas revolves around fathers, how present or negligent they are, how much trouble and pain they have caused.

Evelyn is on the porch calling in her kids for their mealtime. The kids are all hiding behind trees and in bushes. She hears their snickers and sees a few errant feet poking out. Rose, who is a theater professor at a community college, has been sitting quietly on the porch with coffee, watching her own daughter do a crafts project on a picnic table.

"Different dads," Evelyn replies in a tone meant hopefully to avert the pursuit of specifics.

"Six kids in all?"

"Yes."

Rose whistles in a way that Evelyn opts to be put off by. "God bless you."

❖　❖　❖

The tests numb the mind at times: using a computer mouse to click and drag numbered files to folders with a corresponding number. She takes these tests over and over to measure both speed and accuracy. Other modules teach her the basics of Microsoft Excel, QuickBooks, and other software programs the world uses to organize itself. And these come only after she's completed a two-week course on how to operate a laptop computer.

She has chosen accounting as the focus of her job training. The tax code is not something she knows about or has ever considered much, let alone some passion to which she desires to devote her working life. But thinking practically, and after many conversations with the job-training specialists who visit the Villas, Evelyn concludes that everyone who earns above-board wages needs to file taxes, that accounting offices are everywhere, and that even small ones generate massive amounts of paperwork, so a person trained to manage these tasks will usually be hireable.

While toiling through the online practice modules, Evelyn imagines a future version of herself who files her own taxes with her own accountant.

For reasons she can't explain, the family's homelessness has activated in Evelyn a thrumming of obsessive thoughts about cleanliness. The hundreds of mornings and nights spent loading and unloading their worldly possessions into often disgusting motel rooms was an abnormal way to live, but those rhythms became normal over time, and so having an adequate space that they will not be kicked out of less than ten hours after arriving is to her a very jarring adjustment. And she somehow convinces herself that if she does not keep the space immaculate, then they will in fact be kicked out. The Villas does have a consistent cleaning staff and only asks of the families some basic care of their spaces and to relegate food to certain areas. But Evelyn sequesters a pile of rags, sponges, dusters, and soaps for different surfaces. In the evenings on weeknights and the mornings on weekends, while her kids idle, she cleans around them: the backs of cupboards, the corners of windowsills, the recesses of closets. This work is toilsome and she is not the kind of person who enjoys it. Rather, she is perhaps chasing some feeling of satisfaction or completion that—with six kids sharing the space—forever eludes her.

She still decorates their room with flowers. The wholesale market downtown is not accessible during this time. What she does instead is walk long loops around the neighborhood with Dev in the stroller and whatever kids she can convince to come along. Discreetly she picks flowers from the edges of yards. She tries to limit her collection to wildflowers and lush ever-growing foliage blossoms like morning glories and impatiens that will not be missed. But sometimes she cannot resist a rose or hibiscus or bird-of-paradise. During one of these sly harvests, as a thick stalk resists her, the homeowner opens the front door, a woman of young middle age. She surprises Evelyn in the middle of wrestling with the plant at the end of the walkway about twenty feet from her. The woman stands there with her hands at her sides looking dour and disapproving. Evelyn is scared but doesn't want to let the half-mangled blossom just fall to the ground. The two women stare at each other across the strange divide of the lawn. The woman looks as if she might say something but then seems nervous. Evelyn places the flower in the stroller's drink holder and walks on. The woman closes her front door.

The sills of their apartment all feature water glasses with this mishmash of her finds, and it is beautiful.

◆ ◆ ◆

School begins again online in August because the district remains physically closed. During the springtime school closure, none of the siblings could really engage with online schooling because of their technological lack. At the Villas shelter they are equipped to learn again with laptops and desks and supplies. Marisol is five now and beginning kindergarten. Sofia is seven and going into second grade. Iris is about to turn nine, starting fourth grade, and excited about the prospect of going to school without going to school—an excitement that will last all of one-half of one day of elementary classes via Zoom. Gabriel is starting seventh grade, and Orlando is entering his first year of high school. Evelyn has her own workstation for job training.

On the first day of school, hearing the girls virtually meet their new classmates and teachers, Evelyn closes her computer and takes a few moments to listen and be grateful that she and her children are here, that they are well, that they are connected.

Then the morning carries on and, as in tens of millions of other homes in America during that time, the structure of school dissolves into boredom and confusion on both ends of the online platform, and Evelyn's life is reduced to scampering from kid to kid in order to help them sign onto the right link and at least superficially engage with what education has become.

◆ ◆ ◆

For Iris, the Villas shelter is very much like its own kingdom. She has her online school schedule, and perfect attendance has become a matter of huge import to her after she missed so many online days last spring when the final few months of third grade were disrupted by the clumsy transition online. But at the same time her teacher this year does not seem to possess the rather arbitrary gift of engaging a large classroom of young students through a computer camera. After attendance is taken and she is logged onto the system as present, Iris struggles to pay attention to any aspect of school that is not art. Because her mom has her own online sessions, during which Iris is unmonitored, it is easy to blank the screen and mute the sound and slide away from the computer for stretches of time without consequence.

At first, these respites are akin to the short daydream periods that have always been a part of her actual school days; she takes breaks not far from her desk that usually involve her stuffed animals. As the interminable year of online school plays out, she grows more intrepid, her departures from the computer longer and farther. On the days when her mother is downstairs attending classes or meetings, Iris can sneak out of the apartment and this is when her life becomes really exciting: zigzagging along the shelter's central upstairs hallway to hide behind bookcases and within alcoves. Some of the other families keep their doors open during the day—Iris's mom is much too private here, bordering on antisocial, to do that—and Iris swoops past and imagines herself visible only as a blur of color.

She stays upstairs initially and sees how many times she can move back and forth along the width of the house before another child or parent sees her and sends her back to their apartment on the far end. Then that exercise feels less daring and she begins to make sorties downstairs, where her chances of encountering a Door of Hope staff member or—most dangerously—her own mother increase. Once she grows skilled enough to circumnavigate the entire house, she begins venturing outside, where being caught would mean more than a light, laughing rebuke, would potentially cause grounding or some other real punishment. Being in the yard by herself offers her a freedom that she has not experienced ever before in her childhood, the scary yet exhilarating state of being unbound. Iris's homeless life has been under a very tight oversight—not just in terms of her physical location but in what she divulges to teachers and to friends. Bad choices have been frightening for her until now, could bring harm to her body, could incur expenses they couldn't pay, could fracture the family and land her under the care of some stranger. Here in Pasadena on this property of soft grass and climbable trees, under the protection of a benevolent organization, Iris understands that she can press beyond some of the boundaries she has always considered absolute.

Predictably, what ultimately does her in is a tattling kid who spies her from an upstairs window and tells his mother, who tells her mother, who comes outside and lays into her with an intensity that might have been appropriate had Iris ever wandered off on Mission Road or in Skid Row but here at the Villas seems outlandishly frantic.

Her mother screams and tries to hug her at the same time. Iris cries and squirms. A few mothers and staff members appear around the front door and porch. Ultimately her mother clenches her wrist and yanks her back upstairs to their room. She tells the girl to sit at her desk and stay there throughout the remainder of the day, including breaks. Around their apartment, the older boys smirk and the younger girls appear scared on her behalf.

Iris nods in between quick breaths cut in half by residual sobs. She has never actually been in trouble like this before, never known her mother to scream like this. Her transgression does not seem so terrible: she did not place herself in danger, jeopardize her siblings, break anything, steal, upset anyone. She does not understand that what she really did was cause her mother to appear to the other mothers as someone who didn't take good care of her own kids—thus puncturing her mother's greatest source of identity.

◆　◆　◆

Door of Hope often shelters families who have experienced intense instances of domestic violence. The organization also takes in families that have been without stable shelter for a prolonged period of time. Evelyn and her kids carry with them both afflictions: they have together suffered the peak terror and confusion of violence as well as the daily uncertainty and shame of homelessness. Knowing this, the Door of Hope staff strives to address quickly the psychic marks that both experiences tend to leave behind. The strategy is to begin to provide some basic mental-health treatment without the kids feeling like they are in need of therapy. Some of the childcare and tutoring that the shelter provides while Evelyn undergoes her job training is given by certified specialists. These people play games and teach grade-level lessons while also asking noninvasive questions meant to identify the shape and thickness of the armor these children have each welded around themselves—not to poke or penetrate right away, but simply to delineate the edges.

Miss Abeba is not a certified specialist but might as well be after guiding the spiritual lives of Door of Hope families for almost three decades. She engineers this work mainly by observing new people from a distance after the first day: sitting in on the staff meetings at the main office, leading some light study with the children at the Villas, making sure that she bumps into Evelyn with some frequency but never in formal sit-down settings.

Miss Abeba believes that a rare dynamic is operating within this family unit, because a commonality among nearly all the families at Door of Hope is that a level of neglect has taken place. Very often, that neglect is the result of survival necessity more than ignorance or lack of caring; young parents in hard circumstances have to provide, and providing means not being there. When life is reduced to a relentless series of emergency situations, some functions of parenting invariably fade in significance behind the prerogative to stay alive—even basic hygiene routines and rote medical attention and physical contact like hugs and handholding. Once some education takes place, these parents are usually motivated to do better. Young children take to new rhythms with tremendous strength. In Miss Abeba's experience older children take longer to adjust—they can be wary of even the most fundamentally loving behavioral changes as if they are being tricked—but in the end are also glad to be treated like children.

When Evelyn's children enter her domain, Miss Abeba has a sense that although they have been homeless for a long time and have experienced a terrible event involving their father figure—the details of which are not yet clear because Evelyn minimizes them—these children have not known neglect of the sort that is most familiar. Their teeth are growing crooked in places because orthodontics aren't obtainable for poor people, but their teeth are clean with no visible plaque buildup. They do not complain of nightmares or other problems sleeping. None of these six children are overweight or underweight. They are all testing right around their appropriate grade levels and ahead in some areas. They show love toward their mother and toward one another. They fight but seem generally capable of refereeing themselves. Sofia and Gabriel are quieter sorts while Marisol and Iris are comically extroverted. Orlando is every bit a moody teenager.

The family's school records that Evelyn has kept on her email show that all these kids are above 90 percent in attendance and all their absences occurred during the previous spring when school was online. Orlando himself has missed zero days of school in Los Angeles, Gabriel four.

What concerns Miss Abeba is the strong attachment that governs this family: a group identity that she terms *us against the world.* This trait does not manifest as overattachment; the kids are capable of being apart from their mother and from one another, no doubt thanks to such consistent schooling. But Miss Abeba watches them pay keen attention to one another in relation to others. The kids are very quick to take offense, to frame themselves as victims in even harmless social scenarios and then bind together as a single defensive front. This happens during kickball games, arts-and-crafts hours, shared meals with other families. Something is always being stolen, someone is always being shortchanged, someone is always calling out a cheater. Playtime and mealtime can be anarchic with Evelyn's kids acting as sole arbiters of what is fair without searching for nuance within two-sided narratives. And their mother tends to be the loudest and fiercest and least apt to seek true causation.

Because the kids are young and adorable—also because they've been through such a harrowing ordeal together, which is not nearly over yet—the behavioral traits are easy to oversimplify and overlook as inevitable pains of adjustment to normative life. But Miss Abeba worries that as they grow older and begin to cast out more widely in the world, this quality will become a severe social hindrance and potentially dangerous to others. They might have trouble letting teachers and counselors into their circle. They might likely shy away from the sorts of friend groups that draw an identity from a specific affinity—sports, music, activism—and be attracted instead to peers who define themselves by the forces they see working against them. They might be reluctant to ask for help from anyone who is not their brother, sister, or mother.

Miss Abeba's priority becomes to gently open these children's various minds and spirits to all the support that exists for them, and to the fact that asking for that support and receiving it from people outside the tight ring of their family does not constitute weakness and will not lead to the foster system and is not some kind of refutation of their mother. The task will be hard, she knows.

◆　◆　◆

Evelyn remains anxious around Miss Abeba, who is almost cosmically kind in their many brief encounters but who seems always to be assessing them in an aloof way. Evelyn suspects there must be a personal failing that permits her to be suspicious of a person who is so earnestly spiritual and who gives to all the mothers and children recovering here a sort of limitless interest. But right now so many adults crisscross through their days and their lives that all these interactions have given rise to a general alertness. She has a sense when waking up that she doesn't know what questions will be asked of her in the hours ahead. As she did compulsively when her kids were going to school, she advises them to be careful about what exactly they share with whom and to always err on the side of withholding. The kids continue to carry secrets, to speak about their external lives in opaque generalities, and to try to talk about their internal lives as little as possible.

◆　◆　◆

"You talk about your kids a lot with a certain tone."

"My kids are my everything," Evelyn replies to her therapist in what must be their sixth or seventh hour together.

"But it is this tone, or this *way* you have, when you talk about them. How can I explain this? It's not a negative thing. But when you talk about them, it's almost like they're grown up—like you are talking about your adult children when they were little, things you went through with them a long time ago."

Maybe the therapist to this point has not illuminated every single shadowed nook within Evelyn's consciousness, but over weeks and weeks she has pried out far more thoughts and memories—the painful, the confusing, the hilarious, the tender—than Evelyn ever intended to give her.

"I think I get what you're saying," Evelyn says. "Like how my mom and aunts and uncles talk about me and my cousins back when we were all little."

"Right. So do you see why I bring this up?"

"Not really."

"Because your kids are not grown up. In fact they are all still very young. Most of the events you have shared with me did not happen a long time ago; these hardships are all very recent. They are fresh and raw."

"Okay," Evelyn says, still unsure.

"What I mean is that you are not through the passage yet. You are very much in the passage. That must be scary."

"It's scary to think about my babies grown up."

"But to have been through what you have already been through and also acknowledge and plan for the reality that you're not even close to done— you still have to raise your young children and take care of yourself. You have to do this for many, many years to come. Let's talk about what that means."

Evelyn evades for the remainder of their time that afternoon, because she does not desire to contemplate what that means at all.

◆　◆　◆

The Applebee's reopens in October 2020 at half-capacity, and Evelyn is invited to return to her management role. She takes the job part-time but, with the help of Door of Hope's childcare services, flips her schedule from what it once was: now she stays home all day in order to oversee her kids' Zooms, be with Dev, and progress through job training before driving to Applebee's for the evening shift. The restaurant is quiet and those who venture back to work do so out of financial need, like Evelyn. Most of the staff do not return. Charlotte is too scared to work because she's been smoking since age twelve. Others have moved on to different, perhaps safer jobs. The restaurant's large space being less than half-full on busy nights exacerbates the mournful quality. The pandemic has shaken the service industry but has not altered how ephemeral relationships are when they are formed on the margins of self-sufficiency.

Her schedule leaves her outside the shelter's tight social circles and she's lost contact with most of her work friends as well. Dinner is the natural time of the day for families to commune, and Evelyn is now often gone by then and unable to use that window to leaven her reputation for being posses-sive and quick to confront anyone who regards her children as anything but angelic. The outline of her story has been passed around among the mothers at the Villas and embellished through word of mouth. People know her as the one who has been raising kids on the street for years—who has actu-ally given birth while living on the street. They imagine her as some kind of savage human protecting her loved ones in the wilderness, someone to be at once pitied, admired, and feared. In the safe confines of the Villas, Evelyn has gained a kind of persona by which she, a woman barely north of five feet, casts long shadows. With six kids and a night job and an ingrained skepticism of other moms, she does not have the time to disabuse anyone of this mythology. And she doesn't actually mind the way conversations pause when she enters a common area, because after feeling like prey most every moment since Manny released his hands from her neck, she sees some advantage in being regarded as a fearsome person.

She is also known to be the one who has kept her kids in school—a good school—all this time and whose kids might not always be the best behaved but are well educated. While she is prideful of this effort and feels that she has useful information to share, the women who have had to move their kids around as a result of housing instability seem to view her greatest achievement as a character flaw, a moral affront.

"But you fooled the system," says one of the mothers during a mid-fall group meeting in the living room. They have all been talking generally about kids and school during a moderated discussion meant to be therapeutic and illuminating. Evelyn ventured to speak earlier about some of her kids' positive experiences with teachers at their Monterey Park school. This mother finds Evelyn to be smug and has been making some noise about that perceived trait to other families for a while. "You don't even live in that district but all these kids you have get to go there—seems wrong to me."

"I pay taxes," Evelyn argues.

"Not in that district, you don't."

"Our plan is to live there."

"What you *plan* and what *turns out* aren't the same thing."

"My aunt lives there."

"What does that have to do with it? I've got lots of aunts."

"Are you jealous my kids are smart?" Evelyn blurts.

The woman scoffs. She has been living at the Villas for only a few weeks longer than Evelyn has but behaves with an outlandish seniority. She has two young kids. She doesn't usually talk much, but when she does her voice tends to be negative and her intentions backhanded. "No," she replies. "I am *not* jealous of your kids."

Evelyn takes a few breaths. She has learned to do that here: concentrate on the physicality of breathing during taut moments, a few counts in and out. "Why not us?" she asks. "If the system is set up so good schools *are only in neighborhoods we can't afford to live in*—what's wrong with cheating? How

227

the fuck else do our kids grow up not to be dishwashers and lawn mowers? How the fuck else do they get to be engineers or lawyers or teachers if we don't cheat? Can you tell me that?"

The lady spends a moment trying to summon a worthy response, but as seconds pass she doesn't; she just makes a *hmmf* sound and looks around the room as if to gather affirmation from the others there. Evelyn believes that maybe she is the victor in the exchange. But she also feels guilty of some offense she can't articulate, some lack of merit. That dichotomy is becoming normal here.

◆ ◆ ◆

How strange it is to sit across from Manny. They share a table in a Pasadena café's outdoor area. The sun is bright and she will remember the intensity with which it shines off his shaved head. He's driven from Lancaster to meet her here, a little over a mile from the Villas—the address of which she hasn't shared with him. Dev squirms in her lap. She left the girls back in their apartment and walked here with Dev in a stroller. It is a midweek school day.

They immediately joke with each other over how awkward this moment is—a dynamic that itself is awkward but seems more worthwhile for her than staring at him silently and coldly. That is how she'd projected the encounter during the long days leading up to it: all her built-up pressure venting outward against his defensive front, likely followed by a back-and-forth of blame and excuses, the content of so many of his text message onslaughts translated into spoken words. Instead, Manny pushes his chair back from the table so that he can lean forward with his elbows on his knees in a sheepish posture. He keeps rubbing his hand from his forehead back over his bare scalp while gazing at Dev in a sad but unpossessive way.

"Thanks for meeting me here," he repeats a few times.

"It is really just to get my sister to stop calling me."

"Sorry, that is the only way I thought you might hear from me." Then, nodding toward Dev, "He's beautiful. God, he's really beautiful."

"He's my baby boy king," Evelyn says. "So is Gabriel, so is Orlando. They're all my baby boy kings."

Manny asks about their daughters. Evelyn tells him about the dancing and the Little League games and Taylor Swift and how good they are to one another.

In turn, she asks him about Lancaster and how he has been since moving back there. He shrugs and sips loudly on his coffee. "This place wasn't good for me, you know. It was just, like, too much of everything, and, like, life was not supposed to be as hard as it was to live around here. My life is too fucking short to be that hard, is how I felt. You know?"

"I get that even if it's not how I see it," Evelyn replies.

"How do you see it?" He appears genuinely curious as to her point of view.

"You do what you got to do for your kids. Their life's too short for me *not* to do what is hard."

"You are a good mama," he tells her, which is a sentiment she doesn't need to hear; his approval holds no value for her. "Can I have him for a sec? It's okay if you say no."

She does not want him to hold Dev, but the meeting is carrying on nicely enough such that she passes their son over. Manny was never that great with babies. He tensed up when holding them, as if legitimately afraid of dropping them, and of course they sensed his anxiety and cried and reached for Evelyn to take them back. This pattern was actually the source of some perennial conflict between them: she found him to be petty about her being

the preferred parent; he found her to be condescending over his shortcomings. But by this point in his young life, Dev is accustomed to being passed
around among his siblings and all the kids and mothers and staff of the
Villas—he is very popular there—and he lets his father gently, gingerly
sway him from side to side.

"He's solid," Manny says.

"He's a big boy like his papa."

Manny strikes her as being nervous but centered and physically healthy.
He does not snap at her or attempt any cheap arguments about how
messed-up it is that she kept his son a secret from him. A little over two
years have passed since the American Inn Motel. Most of his communication with her during those two years could adequately be labeled insane.
Here, now, he comes off as a grounded, older person. She knows from her
family—who indirectly incited this meeting when her older sister mentioned Dev's existence to Manny during a chance encounter in a 7-Eleven—
that in Lancaster he is in a relationship with a woman who has her own kids.
He is renting a place a few blocks from the street they used to live on before
moving here. Clearly, the desert is where Manny is comfortable and where
he can continue to try to be a good man.

"You been taking care of yourself and them and him this whole time?"
Manny marvels at one point, when their coffees are finished and she needs
to return to the Villas.

"We've been all right," she replies, and soon takes her son back.

"He's for sure mine?"

"Is that why you wanted to meet?" She laughs in order to conceal the
degree to which this question infuriates her. "To ask me that? You want to
take a test or something?"

"No, but ..."

"Yeah, he's yours. I wasn't with anyone else. But I don't want anything from you, all right? If that's what you're worried about."

He nods pensively and doesn't argue.

Before parting, he first offers to pay her back for the $400 he withdrew from their account when she was living on 96th Street. She tells him now that he had probably earned some of that money, too, and so he doesn't owe her anything. Then he asks her whether she would be willing to let him see his daughters the next time they are in Lancaster to visit Evelyn's family. Evelyn does not answer in one way or the other; she wants to neither cut him off nor lead him on toward believing she will let him be a steady part of their lives. She simply tells him that they do not visit home much anymore but that she is willing to keep in touch with him.

Evelyn does not desire to hate the father of her younger children the way she hates the father of her older children, the way so many of the women on 96th Street and at the Villas hate the fathers of their children. She has participated in so much vitriol devoted toward exes and is exhausted by it. Still, she can't help hating Manny a little bit.

She says before they part ways, "We still do need to get a divorce."

He nods distantly, laughs faintly. "Oh yeah, right."

❖   ❖   ❖

The phone that Orlando earns by keeping up with school during the shutdown and helping with all the kids at the Villas provides a conduit to the world outside the shelter again. But because he has changed school districts, he doesn't at first have many friends to call. So many of his peers in Monterey Park housed him and fed him for nights at a time throughout seventh and eighth grade. He hasn't saved all their phone numbers and will probably never see most of them again even though the townships are seven miles apart; such is the nature of geography in greater Los Angeles. In the meantime, new ninth-grade classmates in Pasadena live within a small area yet exist throughout the fall of 2020 as rows of faces within boxes often glitching and freezing on his loaner laptop. The Villas is by definition a transitional housing facility: a bridge for adults and children between destitution and self-sufficiency. For Orlando, the home on the tree-lined street is an in-between place, a scenic and comfortable limbo.

As time passes and the hysteria regarding the virus subsides—at least somewhat—he is given freedom to leave the property. There are two skate parks within easy range. With no other alternatives, as the fall segues into the holiday season Orlando finds himself at one or the other every day, sometimes twice a day. He meets some older kids from his new high school. Through them, he meets some girls. They are all young teenagers making their way during a year without physical school or sports teams or church.

In the regional consciousness, Pasadena is known for its old wealth, gated properties, private schools, Rose Parade floats. But the place is also a microcosm for the greater city in that it once drew a diverse population of working-class people who built modest homes on small plots of land and lived in multigenerational households. Over the decades, as the area's wealth increasingly concentrated among the upper crust, Pasadena became easy to characterize as a bastion for the entitled rich passing down assets through real estate. But as Orlando's world opens up, he quickly becomes acquainted with local working-class families who might earn money through small businesses or city jobs. The kids go to public schools. Many of these families are Latino and they are welcoming to him.

Orlando falls in with new classmates who have mostly grown up in Pasadena and yet do not view themselves as being *of* Pasadena. These kids roam the suburban environs in their baggy clothes on their skateboards, are loud, vape, play music, and generally derive some enjoyment from being low-grade nuisances to the rich Pasadenans because this is a form of entertainment in its own right and they don't break any laws. Police sometimes are summoned due to noise complaints or more overtly racist reasons, and Orlando's group has a decent rapport with most of the officers. No one tempts real trouble. A few of his friends' parents *are* police. Each individual kid with whom he hangs out has some sort of plan for the next few years of life that involves working, finishing high school, attending one of the local community colleges in some cases, joining family businesses in others. They do not present optically as hardworking and aspirational kids, but as a whole and in their hearts, they are.

As the New Year looms and Orlando becomes part of this roving crew of outliers, he spends much less time at the Villas.

◆   ◆   ◆

For much of her young adult life as she gave birth to a succession of babies and raised them through childhood, Evelyn maintained a vision of her growing clan as one that would have family movie nights together. This constitution never really came to be, mainly because her older kids grew out of certain genres of family fare as her young ones grew into them. Even while homeless and stuck in motel rooms with a TV most nights, they could never settle on one program. Nor could she take them to a movie theater because tickets and concessions were so exorbitant in this era. The closest they come to watching something together as a family now occurs when Gabriel or Iris happens upon a series of twenty-second YouTube clips that are zany enough to hold all their various attentions for a few minutes at a time.

At the Villas, with a true living room that has a large TV, Evelyn becomes determined to wrangle everyone into sitting through at least one film together. She begs Orlando to be home. She pries Gabriel away from his laptop math program. She spends too much money on fancy ice cream and fixings, sneaks all these supplies into the room brazenly against Door of Hope rules so that they can all make sundaes, and wills herself to not worry about the resulting mess until the little ones are asleep. She chooses a Pixar movie called *Coco* first, but the older three boo this one as being too saccharine, and she ends up letting Orlando put on a *Fast & Furious* movie. She remembers when the boys went with Manny to take pictures in front of a Los Angeles house that was used in the series during one of their first days in Los Angeles. Now they heap together on the couch and on some cushions she lays out on the floor. They have ice cream, then seconds and thirds. She thinks the movie is terrible but in a way that makes it more entertaining than it ought to be. The noise and colors of it hold Dev's attention for almost the entirety, though he does fall asleep in her lap on the floor eventually. She in turn lets her own head fall against Iris's shoulder and dozes for a time. Orlando sneaks out his phone and texts with people most of the night but she allows this because she is glad to have him there. And Evelyn feels during those couple of hours like a true American family watching a dumb movie and that is wonderful.

She hurts a bit when the night grows late and the kids move to their different rooms to do different things. Evelyn is still uneasy about the fact that having space and security also means that they aren't together all the time. Orlando in particular is testing his new geographical boundaries, moving ever outward day by day, away from her. And while her consolation is Dev and the years ahead raising another little boy, the quiet moments that having shelter provides let her see more clearly the still frames of this passing time and the inexorably waning days of motherhood. Until very recently, her children needed her all the time. The intensity of that need fueled her. But now its concentrated rhythms are diffusing—even Marisol is capable of logging herself in and out of school classes and organizing her work—and a portion of Evelyn's continued difficulty in adjusting to the people around her and what they ask of her at the Villas has to do with this drastic emotional shift.

◆　◆　◆

With hundreds of millions of dollars annually funding an array of public and private service providers, many dozens of different forms of aid flourish across the county. Mobile medical units rove the centers of homeless populations in order to treat illness, injury, addiction. Some organizations distribute tents, clothes, food, and hygiene supplies. Others provide education in the form of tutoring centers and special needs assistance. Trailer units containing showers and bathrooms are strategically placed. Certain parking lots are reserved at night with a security presence for people living in vehicles. Other lots are fenced and equipped with raised wooden pallets to create safe camping sites. Still other lots give rise to tiny-home villages: clusters of a few dozen shedlike dwellings, each about a hundred square feet with heat and electricity and a locked gate. Larger, more ambitious organizations procure land and build houses for families on the city's outskirts, or engage in the conversion of old hotels and offices. Firms experiment with quick-build modular construction and turning old shipping containers into apartments. Existing shelters receive more resources. The city government eases the permit process for homeowners to build accessory dwelling units. The construction of affordable-housing complexes is prioritized over the older idea of requiring a small number of affordable units in new upscale buildings.

Each initiative helps some people—a few dozen here, a few hundred there—but the challenge now in 2021 has reached a numerical scale that dwarfs even grand and expensive undertakings. By any calculation, the homeless crisis in this southwestern sector of America is out of hand, has been permitted to grow far beyond any solution that the political apparatus is equipped or motivated to provide now. There are currently as many people living in the region without stable shelter as there are living in many medium-sized American cities. The vast majority of these people cannot be housed in any current or near-future infrastructure. They can only be managed, warmed up or fed or treated here and there, moved around as necessary, folded in overall as a sad feature of the lived environment.

The overarching solution put forward by powerful people remains the same vague, slow, and unproven doctrine that has endured for all these many years, which pumps money into the construction industry far more efficiently than it provides shelter for the homeless: *build*.

◆　◆　◆

After spring break, the kids are able to be in school again on a rotating schedule. With most living and food expenses covered for the last eight months at the Villas, Evelyn has now saved almost $5,000. She has for the most part resisted the urge to spend money at the rate that she earns it. This impulse is common among mothers at the Villas, who before acceptance here suffered the heartbreak of watching their children lack so much for so long. Relieved of the typical financial sinks that once precluded them from affording anything beyond the basic staples of urban survival, the first itch upon saving some money is to buy stuff: toys, shoes, clothes, electronics.

The Door of Hope staff has deep experience with this cycle and the psychology that underlies it. The organization can advise but can't control its clients' money, and every new family arrives with a different financial situation and a different overall relationship with earning and spending. Women new to the shelter almost unanimously tend to spend all of their first few months' worth of savings on items that appear extraneous but are a vital step in the long process of feeling like a person of worth. They and their children very much need that physical experience of opening a box that contains within it a brand-new item—herby soaps and shampoos, makeup and jewelry and clothes, video games and sports equipment and remote-controlled cars—the pungent plastic smell of that packaging, the sensation of their hands being the first to have handled a thing since that thing's manufacture. But following such a moment, they also need to identify the illusion of newness, the distinctly American idolatry that equates new things with success and fulfillment. The families experience this revelation on their own, without oversight, through grim bank statement figures and monthly budget shortfalls. They make adjustments.

Evelyn has already known all these conflicting negotiations, known the elation of a job or promotion or temporary place to stay promising suddenly some freer and more abundant lifestyle. She's been through seven or eight instances of that. Always, whatever problems her fresh circumstances promised to solve trailed her closely.

Her kids, having been beside her throughout, do not ask for much anymore. Even so, to possess money and not spend it on everything she thinks they should have is a challenge for her.

The very same week in the spring of 2021 that schools reopen for in-person classes, Evelyn begins her new job as an assistant at an accounting firm in Pasadena. Her nervousness in the days before both transitions is nearly unmanageable. She has become so complacent in her time at the Villas—her kids' online class schedules, her uneventful shifts at Applebee's, her training modules, her therapy—that any disruption at all to these routines feels shattering. In addition, she will be separating from Dev in a more structured manner—leaving him in the care of Door of Hope volunteers for eight hours every weekday before he soon transitions into preschool—so she is undergoing that deeper, universal emotional conflict.

"Your kids are going to school and you are going to work," Miss Abeba states. "That is what normal kids and parents do. That is what normal is like."

"I don't know if they can do it. I don't know if I can."

"All of you can," Miss Abeba assures her. "All of you can live a normal life. Now, normal is not the same thing as easy. Actually, it's hard."

They are walking around the neighborhood in the direction of the larger, older Pasadena homes with porticos and columns in front of ornate doors. Evelyn still isn't totally comfortable around this woman. She has been monosyllabic in her responses for the first few blocks—*Yes, No, Good, Fine*—but as her heartbeat accelerates with the exercise, so does her anxiety and her need for support.

"What happens if I screw it all up?" Evelyn asks. "Like if I get fired or the school district finally kicks my kids out of school?"

"You've spent all this time learning about what the job is, training for the job?"

"Yes."

"I believe you will do fine. Just take it slow at first. Each task, think it through." Miss Abeba adds, "You know, I was a waitress, too, a long time ago. Office work is very, very much easier. Not easy, but easier. Listen to what you are told, ask questions about what you don't know, apologize for mistakes, be on time. You will see. You will finish well."

◆ ◆ ◆

Miss Abeba, sneaking sidewise glances during their walk, watches the visible opening of Evelyn's formidable retaining walls that for months have surrounded her anxieties and kept her silent and impassive through the majority of her training classes. The older lady prepares to absorb the subsequent outward-bursting flood. This absorbing is the absolute heart of her job. In her own mind on this peaceful, shady outdoor stroll, as Evelyn goes on about computer tests she scored poorly on and kinks of behavior that her kids adopted during online school that will not translate well to classrooms, Miss Abeba understands well that the young woman is not in fact anxious over her ability to manage office tasks or her kids' behavior in school. What troubles her actually is that the new job itself, and her kids growing older, signify progress in her life. For the families passing through Door of Hope housing, this progress can be as terrifying as any other manner of change in that the more of it they accrue, the closer they move toward graduating from the shelter. And graduation means finding her own place to live, paying rent, buying groceries and cooking meals again, sorting out her own childcare, and overall becoming responsible for her own outcomes. All the ways that this responsibility did not turn out well before color everyone's last months in the Villas.

What Miss Abeba knows, and what Evelyn will come to accept, is that she will have support in these changes, and that support is what makes comprehensive, well-resourced transitional housing programs far more effective in rehousing the city's destitute families than the kinds of emergency services Evelyn, out of these same fears, has relied on for too long—services designed to help families survive a terrible night, maybe a hard week or two, but not a month, certainly not years.

The accumulation of those years makes Evelyn's family, despite the kids' sound education and togetherness, a uniquely hard case for Miss Abeba. Her broad purpose and daily occupation is to bring women to a place where they can look forward with joy and hope rather than peering constantly backward with regret and fear. Evelyn carries many layers of trauma from her upbringing and youth—layers that have never been peeled back and likely never will be—and she still inhabits many horrid physical moments that have happened to her. This resistance to her movement through everyday life, this pullback toward the abyss, is tremendously strong.

◆　◆　◆

"Listen, I am the last person in the world who wanted to go to therapy," Evelyn expresses in one of her last individual mental-health-treatment meetings. "But in the end, I've kind of liked it."

"I've kind of liked it, too."

"I just have zero idea if it worked."

Her therapist folds her hands on her lap, fiddling a bit with the fabric of her expensive skirt. She looks upward and smiles. "How would you define *worked?*"

"Fixed my problems, I guess, obviously."

"I really don't see my work with this organization as fixing people's problems."

"Can I be the one to ask a question, then?"

"Of course."

"How do you see your work?"

"Partly I hope you can use me as an outlet for some feelings that, outside in the world where you need to be strong all the time, you can't express."

Evelyn thinks of all the dozens of times that she has cried in this room, in front of this person who for all their hours of talk remains a stranger. "I see you as that," she confirms.

"And I hope that as you move on into the next phase of your life, you will feel first that you are allowed to experience these feelings, and second you will be able to identify them and not judge yourself harshly over having them."

"Okay."

"And the absolutely most important number one goal of my work," the therapist concludes, "is that you will feel comfortable asking for help and deserving of the help you receive, whenever you need it, from me or whoever is best suited to provide for you and your kids." As a flourish, she beams a smile and spreads her arms wide. "Easy, right?"

Evelyn smiles back with as much confidence as she can manage, which probably doesn't amount to much. After their last meeting before her term at the shelter ends, the therapist asks permission to give her a hug, which Evelyn grants her.

◆ ◆ ◆

The graduation party in July 2021 is low-key, thoughtful, organized. All the young staffers and volunteers have spent a morning decorating the yard around the picnic tables. Streamers and cardboard sentiments of congratulations hang from tree branches like forest enchantments. One table is covered in food and cake, the other with crafts projects for the Villas children so that they can each write and draw messages of farewell. Coolers are filled with juice drinks buried beneath mounds of ice, and even that small effort points toward a time when keeping a drink cold was a difficult luxury, something she did not have the time or means to do. Evelyn has not made any truly close relationships among the mothers, but the kids have friendships that have seen them through the pandemic year, and those families emerge from the house first. Mothers with whom Evelyn has pronouncedly not gotten along come later. But the children of friends and adversaries alike all have a peaceful Saturday afternoon. The truth is that they have shared meaning and purpose and progress here, even if at times those almost mystic variables were accompanied by friction. The prospect of parting—of independence and uncertainty—is not happy.

Iris takes over the music playing on Evelyn's phone through Bluetooth speakers for much of the time. She goes heavy on Taylor Swift's canon—Evelyn has waited patiently for that phase to pass, and its grip has only strengthened—and she refuses other requests. A few of the mothers produce their own arts-and-crafts gifts for Evelyn, warm messages written around depictions of colorful flower arrangements.

"I was really scared when I first got here, and Evelyn made me less afraid," one mother testifies.

"Evelyn is not always, like, the easiest person to listen to because she's real and always tells it to me like it is. But it's important to know a person like that, someone who's been through the worst and come out with her same spirit."

"Evelyn and all these kids are strong people. I know they'll do great."

"Evelyn, I know you're ready for the next thing and to have a *home*."

The speeches are mostly short and kind. The other kids living in the Villas that summer pay attention for a while and then lose interest and organize a kickball game. Unfortunately, the day is quite hot and the food spread eventually draws flies and yellowjackets. They eat cake in the kitchen and begin cleaning up in the early evening.

Throughout, Evelyn feels a sorrow that has been constant these past few months as she's willed herself to grow accustomed to working in an office most of the day, most of the week. As she's expressed exhaustively to Miss Abeba, she is scared of many facets of life and scared of progress. But the sadness has more to do with the simplest elements of the past year: the grass, the trees, the toys in the yard, the porch swing, the rhythm of families coming and going, the sounds of kids playing, and other touches of a secure existence that homeowners in this neighborhood have all the time and through an almost impossible moment of good fortune she and her kids were allowed to enjoy for about a year. In an elemental way, she is angry at having to leave it, resentful of whoever will take her space next.

There is no word or phrase that she knows of in English or Spanish that encapsulates the complicated matrix of contrasting feelings overlaying her today, many of them positive and just as many not. And she has a sense at the party that trying to list each set individually would be tiresome to both her and whoever is listening, people who have their own anxieties. She leaves her emotions unvoiced.

Orlando remains close to her throughout the graduation party. Nearness to him is increasingly rare, so she savors this aspect of the party. He is growing older and he has friends and he is away much of the time. She accepts these dynamics and trusts his judgment while she busies herself with Dev and the little ones. But at their Door of Hope graduation party she sees that Orlando is very much feeling what she is feeling—the triumph of no longer needing the shelter and its staff, the weight of the responsibility

243

of not needing them, too—and that he is clinging to her now out of that shared tension of spirit.

At a certain point, once people begin drifting off but before any of the cleanup has started, she sits beside him at a picnic table. He is actually drawing, composing his own kid-like art project as if striving to travel back in time to when he himself was six or seven and drawing was the most anyone might ask of him. She thinks of how much affliction he has known between those ages and now. She puts her arm around him and he leans lightly against her.

PART VI

Crystal Lane

August 2022–January 2023

WENDI GAINES HAS JUST RETURNED home from work—one of the easy days in which no women or children experience any real emergencies, just a few imagined ones. She sits with Momo on the sofa watching a Netflix show about earth science that they enjoy. Rather, Momo enjoys it and she enjoys watching his delight. Momo is now nineteen years old, six foot one inch tall, and he weighs over two hundred pounds. He rocks around as the show plays. Wendi's feet are propped up on the coffee table while her phone charges on a shelf in the far corner of her small living room area in the Agape Court apartment.

When her phone begins ringing with calls and dinging with texts, she ignores the sounds at first. Her feet and hands ache badly today and her clients—over a dozen women who are living on their own following their Door of Hope graduations—have a habit of waiting until their own workdays end before calling Wendi to relay various crises. These might be schoolteachers telling them that their children are disruptive, or a notice from the gas company with additional fees that they don't understand, or an argument with the landlord over a clogged sink, or coming up short for the month after splurging on kids' birthday presents and needing one of the Amazon gift cards Wendi gives out sometimes to see them through to the next payday. Most commonly, her clients share a compulsion to call her just to complain about how difficult life is overall.

Wendi does strive to be an ever-present resource for these women, even if that means advising them to see how pointless the act of griping is, be grateful for the help they have received, be smart with the money they earn, and go spend time with their children instead of calling her. But she does not like to miss this time with Momo and so when the phone does not stop, she is already aggravated as she lumbers across the space. Blood drops back down into her feet and lights up the awry nerve endings there.

All the texts, missed calls, and new voicemails are from Evelyn, who graduated from Door of Hope a little over a year earlier, during the very same month that Wendi herself began working for the organization. In a way, Evelyn was Wendi's first client. She was not an easy client, and she still isn't. Even though Wendi maintains a special connection with Evelyn, the appearance of her name on the phone screen exhausts her.

She scans the garbled texts and then listens to the panicked voicemails. Momo grows quickly impatient, squirming and groaning and pointing at the TV. In the midst of his noise, though she can't make total sense out of all the communication on her phone, she discerns with rising dread that Evelyn's oldest son, Orlando, is in serious trouble.

◆ ◆ ◆

About an hour later, she sees Evelyn before Evelyn sees her. They are in the lobby of a police station in the township of Arcadia a little before 8 p.m. As usual, Evelyn has all her kids with her. Some of the advice that Wendi has given her over the past year—for the most part unsolicited advice to be sure—is that it is okay to be without her kids sometimes and especially in moments of stress that the kids don't need to see.

In Wendi's view, no matter what the situation is, those kids definitely do not need to see their mother contending with uniformed officers in a precinct at night while trying to find her son who has been arrested. Wendi watches for a moment from the entrance as Evelyn leans close to the protective glass that shields the front desk. She talks very fast and slaps her hand against the counter repeatedly. But she does not appear to be fully hysterical and that perhaps bodes well. Still, before Wendi actually enters the grim room, she steels herself for whatever is to come. Then she stands beside Evelyn and places a calming hand on her shoulder. The first words she says are "I love you."

Wendi begins to do her job, which often entails guiding fragile women and children through fraught environments and situations. She spends a few minutes calming Evelyn down and then seats her with her children away from the counter to talk to the desk attendant herself with some emotional remove that Evelyn doesn't have. Wendi learns that Orlando is not even here in the precinct. After processing, questioning, and the decision to charge, the department moved him to the Central Juvenile Hall in Lincoln Heights. This transfer occurred in accordance with protocol so that he wouldn't be held in the same facility with adults. Apparently, Evelyn has been told about this a few times but is having trouble understanding.

Wendi is not experiencing flashbacks exactly, but there is no way that she can support Evelyn through this night without recalling clearly her own experience with her oldest son's arrest almost twenty years earlier. She was in her early thirties then, right around Evelyn's age now, and her son was sixteen: Orlando's age. The similarities don't extend much further, as Wendi's son found trouble all the time and she was somewhat estranged from him, whereas Orlando has always struck her as a decent kid who loves his mother. What she remembers clearly tonight is how, through the whole protracted legal process and all the three-hour drives between Oakland and Fresno for dire court hearings and visitations, she had wanted above all things a friend willing to make those drives and sit in those rooms with her. She decides that she will be such a friend to Evelyn for however long this ordeal lasts.

◆ ◆ ◆

They take Evelyn's SUV to Central because Wendi's sedan can't fit all the kids. But Wendi drives while Evelyn rides in the front seat speaking continuously without really conveying information or making any points. The kids remain mostly silent in the back.

Wendi recalls learning during her introductory meetings with Evelyn that the family slept in this car regularly during their years without a home. Evelyn described how the driver's seat became the master bedroom, and the front seat was the living room, and the middle row was the dining room, and the way back was the kids' room. She imagines now these kids curled up together in this tight space that was also filled with all their bags of clothes and backpacks and homework; she considers how dark and airless and dangerous those nights must have been.

At the juvenile hall, she parks and participates in the process of getting everyone out of the car. Gabriel, who is a tall, frail, sweet boy in every encounter Wendi has with him, carries himself with a kind of blankness now. Evelyn holds Dev against her hip. He is growing too big to be held but Wendi doesn't say anything critical, even though this is exactly the kind of point she has a habit of making to her clients. She limps behind the family toward the jail's entrance. Usually her neuropathy affects one foot more than the other at a given time, but right now both feet are equally pulsing. Just inside the doors, they learn from the guard that the hour is too late to visit anyone and that the center will reopen to parents at 8 a.m. the following morning.

Wendi stills Evelyn before she can begin a futile argument in front of the kids and be categorized as *crazy* by these people from whom they will need guidance tomorrow.

"Let me drive you home."

"I'm not leaving," Evelyn says. She looks toward a wooden bench along one wall in the dim front lobby.

"You can't stay."

"They can't kick me out."

"The *kids* can't stay."

"We can sleep in the fucking car."

Evelyn's eyes dart all around. Wendi holds her by both shoulders so that she will steady herself. Evelyn breathes out. Dev is falling asleep against her shoulder, but at the same time he comes to alertness in brief fits and arches his body as if to wrench himself from her arms.

Wendi says, "I'll bring you back right at eight. Or even seven, so you're the first one in line. But the kids need to sleep."

❖ ❖ ❖

Orlando's arrest occurred earlier that day at a small market store east of Pasadena. A large group of high-school-aged kids was involved. Five of them entered the store: one girl and four boys. The store owner confronted some members of the group because he'd seen them pocketing items. He told them to return what they were trying to steal. They refused and this interaction escalated to the point where the owner decided to call the police.

When he turned around to do so, one of the kids struck him in the back of the head with a closed fist. He lost his balance and tipped forward such that the front of his head hit the counter and then the floor. He was unconscious and the kids all fled the store. Another customer immediately called 911 and—being as Pasadena is not a high-crime area—multiple cars responded fast. Within an hour they'd gathered three of the kids they believed to have been inside during the assault. Orlando was one of them.

Wendi takes in this broad information during the following day spent with Evelyn at the Central Los Angeles juvenile facility. Evelyn sees Orlando while Wendi helps set in motion the process of obtaining a public advocate to aid his case. Evelyn begins the morning in a messy, sleepless state, but once she spends time with her son she becomes calm enough to carry on a conversation.

"He told me he didn't do anything," Evelyn says. She is visibly relieved by her son's assurance of his own innocence. She adds, "Maybe he stole some ice cream by accident. But they'll figure it out and let him go soon."

Wendi knows differently; she knows that even if the son is being honest with his mother right now, Orlando nevertheless has been taken into a system that is time-consuming, expensive, and crushing in its rigidity.

"This is going to be an 'all hands on deck' kind of thing," Wendi tells her with a gentle, serious face. She uses the same sentiment later when reporting the situation to Miss Abeba and other pertinent staff at Door of Hope.

◆ ◆ ◆

Before meeting Evelyn, a little more than a year earlier in the summer of 2021, right after the family graduated from the shelter, Wendi was warned about how volatile and protective she could be, how her countenance could switch from amiable to aggressive in an instant and Wendi wouldn't even know what she might have said to detonate the charge. One of Wendi's first job assignments was to assist Evelyn's search for affordable housing. She expected Evelyn to carry a certain shine of gratitude since she had been placed directly onto Pasadena's Section 8 active roster without the torment of waiting lists—families earn preference by graduating from certified transitional housing programs—but as they drove around the picturesque streets between the freeway and the mountains that day, Evelyn primarily focused on her frustrations with her kids having to change schools now.

Wendi kept assuring her how wonderful the Pasadena public school system was. They looked at some very nice three-bedroom apartments and townhomes. All the spaces had drawbacks if inspected closely enough, and Evelyn never failed to find small warps in the floorboards or an oven dial on which the numbers had worn off. Compared to Wendi's own affordable apartment in the Agape Court complex, these places were well accommodated. Compared to the cheap motel rooms and car interiors that Evelyn and her kids had been living in before Door of Hope, they must have looked magnificent. But Evelyn was disappointed and short as if someone were trying to get one over on her and Wendi might have something to do with that.

Wendi was new to the process of apartment searching—she'd remained in the same place since graduating from Door of Hope herself—and brought with her a simplified, jaunty focus on only the positives: grass, in-unit washers and dryers, new plumbing fixtures. During those few days, Evelyn illuminated for her just how complex the very concept of *home* could be for people who had experienced time in which that word was reduced to what they didn't have.

Wendi strived to maintain cheerfulness with Evelyn, to conceal how annoyed she was by the general fastidiousness and lack of appreciation.

Once each day was done and she was home with Momo, Wendi actually reconsidered the decision she had made to leave her Huntington Hospital job for this—because at least the unpleasantness in the emergency room there had been mostly predictable, and she'd had a script.

But for nearly as long as Wendi had been leading Bible-study hours with families who had been homeless and women who had survived abuse, she'd held on to an abiding belief—one she could not express openly without inviting derision even from religious-minded people. The belief was that only those who live in the service of some higher power are truly capable of helping a helpless population of human beings. Cities, states, and nations could budget for services. Councils and supervisors could greenlight programs and earmark space for affordable housing. Charitable people in communities could come together to donate food, supplies, even some forms of shelter. Secular nonprofits could help with medical treatment and education and house construction and counseling. The voting public could enable legislation that increased funding. This entire vast sphere of government was vital but for the most part operated at a remove from the physical bodies of the needy—and in many cases existed in order to *maintain* that remove, with vast sums of money spent to ensure that housed people did not have to see or come into close contact with those seeking shelter.

To be in a room, side by side, face-to-face, breathing in the same air that they had breathed out, tending to those who needed so very much and had almost nothing to give in return—people who possessed virtually no means by which to have standard transactional dealings with the world—a human being really had to believe that some form of a God existed and desired this work to be done. That was how Wendi, who was attuned to many of the failings and imperfections in her own life, approached each day in her unexpected new vocation: as an instrument of service and not a rite of penance. Because in her experience the guilt that impelled most charity in this sphere was a finite and easily exhaustible form of fuel, and the people who needed her, like Evelyn, carried enough of it themselves without needing to assimilate hers.

In keeping with this framework, Wendi bore along with Evelyn's idiosyncrasies and helped her find a place to live. She believed then that the hardest part was over.

◆ ◆ ◆

In September 2022 the juvenile division prosecutors from the city's District Attorney's Office argue to keep Orlando in the city's custody due to a video they claim to possess of him taking part in the attack on the store owner, which left the man concussed and hospitalized. Evelyn at this point relies on a public advocate who is not yet familiar with all the details, and the judge approves the prosecutor's motion. Orlando is transferred from the short-term Central facility in the city to the county juvenile detention center in a neighborhood called Sylmar an hour's drive north.

There indefinitely while future hearings are scheduled, Orlando swears to his mother over and over that he had nothing to do with the physical encounter. Evelyn believes her son. She drives to Sylmar constantly. The facility is about halfway to Lancaster and sometimes her siblings come down to meet her there. Sometimes she has an appointment to see him and sometimes she simply shows up and is not allowed to see him. On those occasions she sits in the Highlander in the parking lot, staring at the facility's fencing and outer buildings. People tell her sternly that spending time this way is pointless, helpful to no one, least of all herself. But Evelyn considers that time worthwhile for being near him and having the space in which to cry.

Her employer at the tax firm is a religious man, a longtime supporter of Door of Hope graduates, and has been kind to her and patient with her on-the-job-learning mishaps for a year. He invites her into his office to talk, and she hopes the reason might be a gentle dressing-down for all the mistakes she's still making at work and not about all the days she's missed to spend in Sylmar. But a few weeks into Orlando's legal situation, her boss tells her that her employment is becoming untenable: at best, she probably needs to think about taking a leave of absence from the office so they can hire a temp worker in her place but reserve her job once she can work reliably again.

Any sense of security that has come to color her life over the last year since leaving the Villas tumbles away. Evelyn pleads with him to bear with her ordeal and promises that she won't miss any more days, which is a lie. She cannot hold a job right now. She doesn't know why she is pleading and promising.

Between the day of her Door of Hope graduation and the phone call from police a year later, she had been for the most part comfortable and self-sufficient. The town house on Crystal Lane that she and the kids moved into provided them with their own space for the first time in Los Angeles. Donors had contributed nice IKEA furniture and toys targeted toward each individual child: art pastels for Gabriel, a colorful abacus for Dev, a baseball mitt for Iris. Evelyn received a full set of nonstick pans because her inability to cook consistently over the past years had felt like the most vital element of motherhood lost to her. After a small move-in party with Wendi and other staffers, she watched their cars pull away down the pretty street at dusk. Evelyn was left suddenly with the full responsibility for herself and her children, which was a weight she hadn't known in its wholeness during their thirteen months at the Villas.

Throughout the ensuing fall her main anxiety revolved around the kids' various transitions to their new schools. But after a wearying year of instruction online, they were all so excited to be physically present in school that no one professed to miss their beloved campus in Monterey Park as much as Evelyn thought they should. The Pasadena schools felt less like a tight-knit community—in part because Orlando, Gabriel, and the girls were each on different campuses, in part because her work schedule did not permit nearly as much volunteering, and in part because the white moms who seemed to run all the volunteer committees formed exclusive cliques. But the academics were stellar, the schools had large grass fields instead of asphalt recess yards, and they offered more free extracurricular after-school programming to make the days full and active.

The reliability of Evelyn's new administrative job made the hours boring, especially since she was so accustomed to the constant and often zany human interactions of the service industry. But in the rigid nature of tax organization she also experienced a certain freeing of her mind from the present tense. While working at Applebee's and other restaurants, interior distractions like children and relationships and money meant screwing up orders, bumping into people, annoying her coworkers, and angering her managers. Even as a homeless mother of six she learned to shut down certain sectors of her consciousness while working the restaurant floor. Now that her job required no real physicality and a much more repetitive kind of cognitive operation, she had the bandwidth to daydream; she could fret about the kids and come up with lists of questions she would ask them about their days when she saw them; she could think about ways —some realistic, some fantastical—she wanted to furnish and decorate the town house on Crystal Lane.

Because Door of Hope had placed her directly into a voucher program that in Los Angeles had been frozen for years, a third of Evelyn's income went toward her rent and utilities. The remainder was subsidized by the city of Pasadena and the state of California. What the subsidy meant was that she could live, work, engage with school, sign kids up for dance and baseball at the local rec center, and generally participate in this community without arranging her financial life entirely around shelter and food. Nor did she need to factor in hour-plus-long commutes and lousy home school districts in order to hold on to what was an entry-level, $40,000-per-year job. The voucher and the salary did not automatically meet all their needs without sacrifices; Evelyn said the word *no* so often to her children and to herself that the word seemed to live as an echo in their new home. She miscalculated and overspent sometimes. But the figures worked. She had not known functional math in a long time, had not known the feeling of being able to absorb small unforeseen costs and even her own errors without potential collapse.

She took her Highlander to a garage to have all its many ailments diagnosed and repaired. There, a flummoxed mechanic told her that there was no way the vehicle should still have been running with all the breakages and friction inside it. She asked him if he could coax another year out of the engine, and he did his best.

In the evenings that fall, she spent as much time as she could on the front step. Their town house was the one in the complex closest to the street and so she had a nice view down the bend. She liked to plant herself there and stare into the distance that was lined with old-growth oaks. That was just where she was sitting when she learned that Orlando was in jail.

◆　◆　◆

In juvenile hall, Orlando moves through his days uneasily: not understanding all the orders he is given or the language and behavior of those around him, desperate to obey despite being constantly remanded and threatened. Juvenile hall is something classmates and friends have referenced mainly in jokes: *I've gotta pass this math test or I'll end up in juvie.* He is here now in the Barry J. Nidorf facility with over a hundred other kids. The campus is an expanse of bumpy green-brown grass surrounded by multiple triangular structures that house the kids and their cells and various spaces for activities. Orlando does not know that for years this facility has been under constant threat of shutdown because of staff shortages, allegations of abuse, the general optics of such an archaic operation in a purportedly progressive city and state. But children in the juvenile justice system have a powerlessness similar to the land's homeless population: moneyless, voiceless, typically sequestered in far-flung, unseen, ignorable spaces.

He was brought here in shackles two days after his arrest and was then led to believe by his unraveling mother that he would be here for a few days while the investigation into the crime progressed and the store security video confirmed Orlando's story. But weeks keep passing and now he has been a month inside a metal fence.

Because Orlando's alleged crime involves serious violence, he lives in Unit 6. Here he carries on alongside the saddest and most rageful children he has ever encountered. Due to understaffing, they spend a lot of their time in their cells or in a common area. The level of pent-up energy coursing through these spaces—his own and that of others—is frightening. Over the first few days he learned which kids had set property on fire, which had attacked people and beaten people and raped people, which had killed people. For his own safety, Orlando goes long stretches of time without speaking except to respond succinctly to the guards' orders and questions. Few conversations that begin between two kids here end without some sort of conflict.

During a lunch in his second week here, a boy sets his tray down beside Orlando's and then punches Orlando directly in the side of his face with enough force to knock him from the bench onto the floor. The quick blast of knuckle against cheekbone had not been instigated: a stranger taking an opportunity to vent anger on another who probably wouldn't fight back. Orlando doesn't retaliate but a mark is logged on his disciplinary record for being involved and he loses common-room privileges for three days, made to remain in his cell alone instead.

When he is alone, Orlando's mind wanders often toward a heartbreak he experienced the previous school year. He'd had a few doomed romances in Monterey Park even while homeless—when he didn't have a phone and the onus to be in Barnes Park by 5 p.m. each evening in order to drive to some undetermined motel or sleep in the Highlander on Mission Road or convince a friend to let him stay over had all combined to make impressing girls nearly impossible. He was also twelve and then thirteen and then fourteen years old and trying to figure out what sort of person he was while surrounded by angst and uncertainty.

The girl who changed him began as more of a fringe member of his group in Pasadena: a friend of one of his friends who did not go to their school. She hung out only sometimes at first, and Orlando, over the course of that previous summer and fall—a passage of time that included graduating from Door of Hope and moving on to Crystal Lane—found his mood revolving around the prospect of seeing her on any given day. He and a few of these friends began earning some money loading trucks for a junk-hauling business operated by one of their families. With that income, he paid his mom so that she let him have a phone again, and over these months he texted with this girl dozens of times a day. Sometimes the two of them walked together away from the larger group and just moved around neighborhoods in a very old-fashioned way, talking, bumping shoulders, holding hands, making out. They had spots that felt like their very own. He confided in this girl about his years of homelessness. She came off as an unusually sensitive person and so in a calculated fashion he predicted that the vulnerability would attract her to him more. But she was also a teenager and he feared that the knowledge of his continuing poverty might also turn her away.

Now, in retrospect, it is possible that both results came to pass. His honesty did seem to bring them closer, add more meaning to the gazes shared between them among the larger group, deepen their conversations, bring her to trust him with the troubles in her own fractured family and insecurities regarding her future. But then after a time she pulled away: she joined the group less often and rumors reached him of her spending time with other groups and other guys. When she did hang out, he was not able to draw her away on their own excursions. The tone of her text messages became less intimate and then the messages became less frequent. Then without definitive explanation she stopped really interacting with him at all.

Overall these wonders and joys, these confusions and dashed expectations, these jealousies and fears were ten months of his life. In keeping with the extreme emotional swings of being a teenager, they occurred over the same period in which he gained placement in the school's advanced math track that was focused on geometry. His English and history classes both presented American studies in a way that was meant to embrace multiculturalism, and he was receiving praise for his writing. He enjoyed chemistry and had good teachers and for the most part continued in the solid academic patterns that began when they moved to Los Angeles. He struggled to marry these aspects of life that were clean and fulfilling with those that confounded him and caused pain.

A small and oddly lasting memory occurred over that previous spring break, when Aunt Talia came over to Crystal Lane and two friends of Marisol's from first grade were there. His mother was overstressed trying to cook for everyone. Even though their home was huge relative to their standards since moving to the city, the rooms were actually narrow and they crowded easily. The acoustics amplified noise. Orlando noticed that Aunt Talia appeared cornered by the noise that the little kids were making. So he took the kids outside for chalk drawings in the driveway. He outlined some cartoonish monsters for them to color in. While he oversaw the activity, his mom found him. She put an arm around his shoulder and thanked him for helping her out. He told her that it was no problem, he was happy to be there with everyone.

Now he is incarcerated and striving to entwine all these hanging strands of his recent past in a way that ought to explain why he is where he is, but doesn't.

◆ ◆ ◆

A Door of Hope alum calls very first thing in the morning, just as Wendi settles at her desk in the quiet office and enjoys a quick glance at the many photos of her children that make a semicircle around the back of her workspace. The woman is in a deep panic. Her landlord just notified her that she's being evicted and has to move out. She howls over the phone, "I can't be on the street again! I can't be on the street!"

This client, who has four young children, is of Palestinian descent and Wendi cannot understand her very well when she is in a high emotional state and speaking rapidly. She lives in an affordable-housing complex and works at a hospice care center.

"You're not going to be evicted," Wendi tells her calmly. Now over a year into her job at Door of Hope, she is gaining a superb command of how word choice, voice tones, and simple declarative sentences work together to help her daily interactions make sense and produce results.

Her clients live in a constant terror of eviction and their landlords often manipulate this terror either to dodge their own property management responsibilities or in some instances—Wendi feels—simply to exercise power for its own sake. The behavior is simultaneously repugnant and typical; the women's sensitivity to it is tragic, evidence of the wells of pain they have carried back from the places they have been.

Wendi does not believe that she will make much progress with this client over the phone, so she drives to the apartment. There, the mother hands her a small stack of unpaid rent notices from the previous six months. She spreads her arms and widens her eyes in some sort of reference to the meanness of the universe they all inhabit. Wendi, still maintaining outward calm, asks why she hasn't paid the rent in so long. More important, she wants to know why she didn't contact Door of Hope much earlier for guidance in the shortfall before it escalated. The woman says that she has been sending money home to relatives in the Middle East. "You are a good person," Wendi assures her. "But nobody's good enough to not pay rent."

The woman claims that she has money but can't access it. Wendi suspects that this might be a lie. Some clicking around on phones does not clarify anything and the language barrier really is an issue today, so Wendi drives her to the bank. After some waiting, they speak to a teller and Wendi learns that in fact the woman has over $6,000 in a basic savings account while her checking account is nearly empty. The figure is enough to cover the back rent with more than $2,000 to spare. All that needs to happen is for the confused bank teller to press a button transferring funds from savings to checking. Outside, the woman makes gestures of prayer and hugs Wendi with the full weight of her body, as if Wendi has given her the money out of her own pocket.

Wendi tells her, "That is your money. You earned it working and you saved it by being smart. We just need to get you some more education about bank accounts so you know how to use it. And you need to call me *when a problem comes up.* Not call me *after the problem is six months old.*" She isn't sure what percentage of this message lands.

That is the first half of her day and it resembles in its tenor the first half of many of her days as a problem solver to the formerly homeless and abused mothers of this region.

The second half of her day she spends packing pencils, notepads, organizers, and stickers into bags as gifts for kids at the annual back-to-school party they throw at each of the shelters. While bag stuffing, Wendi talks to her much younger coworkers and volunteers about the progress all the families are making, the various tiffs that at the moment are unfolding between certain individuals, the challenges they can address, the challenges they can't—those that are ingrained by homelessness and that never leave people. This second half of her day is pleasant and reflective.

And then there are Evelyn and her children.

During the summer of 2022, after Evelyn had been working at the tax firm and living in the Crystal Lane town house long enough to be settled—but before her son's arrest—Wendi arranged a series of semiformal sit-down meetings with Evelyn in the Door of Hope office. The purpose was to create a space in which Evelyn could think out loud through her financial future without feeling like she was in a class being quizzed and assessed. Wendi's goal was to help draw a picture in Evelyn's imagination of living a life in which she spent less than she earned. Without using any pie charts or Excel spreadsheets—without writing anything down or even having a laptop open—they simply talked about this notion.

People who have spent time beyond the boundaries of financial stability—particularly people with children—can often lose their relationship with solvency. In that wild place where they are required to spend more than what they have on materials of survival—and to supplement remaining gaps with emergency services and city services and charity and more primal strategies—rational means of accounting cease to factor over time. There are only the pressures that bear down now; there are only the needs that are lacking now.

Evelyn had not resorted to the extremes that many of Wendi's clients had, but she was still struggling to step back into an organizable world.

"A third, a third, a third," Wendi kept hammering over and over during those conversations. "That's all it is; that's all you have to think about." She meant: a third of Evelyn's income on housing, a third on living expenses for her family, and a third aggressively saved.

During these discussions, Evelyn nodded in appreciation for the equilateral geometry without committing to it. When Evelyn grew frustrated and felt condescended to, or Wendi became tired of listening to herself repeat the same basic tenets over and over, the two women would break and instead laugh about their primary bond, which was that they were both mothers to many children, had experienced the ostracism and the pain and the joys of that journey:

The time Momo sat in the driver's seat of a real fire truck.

The time Orlando decided to be a professional basketball player when he grew up, before Evelyn informed him that most of those players on TV were nearly seven feet tall while Orlando's parents were both short, and he cried for two hours.

The time Wendi's youngest daughter, Tiara, tried to turn their entire tiny Agape Court apartment into a princess castle and how Wendi was still picking glitter out of the cheap carpeting a dozen years later.

The time Sofia tried to hide Marisol inside her backpack so that she could bring her to school for a day.

The time Gabriel drew a portrait of Evelyn for a school project.

The time Momo, seven or eight years old and big for his age, spent a full night sleeping curled up on top of Wendi's head.

The time Evelyn explained who the Jackson Five were after hearing them on the car radio and how Iris then tried to turn all her siblings into a group of her backup singers and dancers for stage performances in Barnes Park.

They marveled over how many wonderful memories each had managed to create out of their respective hard lives. And as their financial planning meetings progressed and they became closer, they also touched on the harder memories such as Wendi's four older children at times cutting off contact with her, how Momo's autism cost her so much time as to make some of these estrangements irreparable. Evelyn in turn shared her guilt in possibly showing more love to some of her children than others—Sofia, Gabriel, now Dev, the ones who absorbed it more easily. And she shared her fears of Orlando's increasing willfulness as his soul took shape independently of her desire and ability to mold it.

"The problems get bigger as the people do," Wendi concluded. Over that recent summer the small meeting room became their private space for wistful, giggly reprieves from stressful days and resolutions. They prayed, too, because sometimes all the talk of money could only lead them there.

◆　◆　◆

Evelyn has about $4,700 saved at the time Orlando is arrested—nearly the same figure that she and Manny first brought with them to the city to start a new life in 2018. And just as their initial, reactive set of decisions immediately began to deplete their money and the hope it once seemed to promise them, so now does the American juvenile justice system face her with similar costs and demands: her employment, her savings, her capacity as a mother, her stability, her sanity, everything.

The visiting area in the Sylmar juvenile hall is designed to feel slightly less jail-like than the rest of the facility in that some art hangs on the wall, some unfiltered natural light makes it through the windows, the chairs have cushions. Surrounded by the low, tight murmurs of others and the occasional rebuke from a guard, this is where Evelyn and Orlando spend what time they have together in the fall of 2022. During some of these hours they are in retreat from each other. During others they strain to keep each other uplifted.

Evelyn learns early in the court process—from Wendi and corroborated by basically every mother she encounters—that if she does not actually hire a lawyer, then the chances of her son being sentenced to jail increase exponentially and independently of his innocence. In this sense, the juvenile justice system operates similarly to the American public education system: promising a standard to all while making its finer resources available only to those who can afford them.

Evelyn can't afford representation, but she pays for it anyway. She keeps paying while the case bumps forward short distances during cursory court hearings and then pauses for long stretches between. She is told that evidence has already made it clear that Orlando did not attack or hurt anyone; video shows him in the back area of the store near the ice cream freezer when the brutal confrontation plays out. The complication is that his fleeing the store along with all his friends has given the state room to argue that he was an accomplice. This area of law is much murkier and involves the testimonies of other people who have their own interests and loyalties that could potentially cloud the truth. The gathering and piecing together of these testimonies are why Orlando remains incarcerated indeterminately. Visit by visit, in a kind of time lapse, Evelyn watches her son's hair grow out and his skin pale and his muscles erode and his eyes dim. The latter change is the hardest to see anew each day as she devotedly makes the trip from Pasadena to Sylmar at the cost of the time and attention that her other kids badly need.

◆　◆　◆

"You need to let him go now—let him go and focus on the children you have. You can't lose them all in order to save him. Believe that he will come back home when it's the right time."

Wendi's advice breaks her heart and activates her rage.

"The right time is that they never should have taken him away," Evelyn replies into the phone. She initially placed this call to ask what will happen to her when her savings runs out while she is still on leave from work and she can no longer pay rent—she honestly doesn't know the Section 8 rules and whether COVID-19 eviction relief measures are still in effect.

"Listen, you know I love you and I love your son," Wendi replies. "But he isn't worth everything you have."

Evelyn hangs up on her.

She does not take Wendi's calls or reply to her messages for three weeks. What makes her anger heavier is knowing that the advice is not given lightly, that it derives from Wendi's own experience with her own children, that it is painful to say and is meant only to help Evelyn and the younger children survive without relinquishing all the triumphs they have made together.

Evelyn spends most of her free time during those weeks in the Highlander, either in the juvenile hall parking lot waiting for meetings, outside her kids' schools, or driving in between these locations. The Highlander has been acting up again despite the recent repair, obscure warning lights flashing on for a few days and then inexplicably turning off. She cannot face any more components in her life breaking down.

As Evelyn outlays thousands of dollars' worth of fees and legal charges, she depletes the savings she has built over the past two years and enters into debt again. She picks up afternoon shifts at the Applebee's and out of desperation asks Manny to drive down from Lancaster a few times a week to help take care of the younger kids. The new managers at Applebee's are kind about letting her set her own schedule. Manny, too, for the moment is generous about taking off work. Aunt Talia fills in the gaps. Always Evelyn is in motion, either physically working and child rearing or else on the phone begging and pleading with legal actors or making a ruckus in the juvenile hall itself—about her son's safety, mental health, hygiene—or sitting across from Orlando and struggling not to let him see her cry for him and the way he looks.

While she contends with her son's incarceration, she also does her best to bury thoughts of the too-real prospect of being on the street again with her children. Even with her voucher assistance, Door of Hope support, a civil relationship with the property owner, and the continual progressive movements within her city, the state's pandemic eviction relief measures

269

expired during the past summer and the underlying truth is that Evelyn's family can be replaced in their townhome in less than a day. Hundreds of thousands of people in the city have struggles akin to hers. Millions more can pay their rent on time and in full every month. This imbalance does not favor her effort to remain housed, and her predicament does not matter much outside her own orbit.

Wendi's advice to cease devoting all of herself to Orlando might be well-intentioned and rational, might be Evelyn's only pathway beyond this awful moment. But she disregards the words and forsakes her friend.

◆　◆　◆

At the end of October 2022, Wendi organizes a pumpkin patch event in the Los Robles shelter yard. She is a year and three months into her job at Door of Hope and planning a low-stakes event for children is a beautiful break from managing the constant crises of parents who don't always appreciate her. She has a few dozen pumpkins and bales of hay donated and placed around the yard. On one of the picnic tables she orchestrates a jack-o'-lantern carving station, on the other some less goopy arts and crafts for the kids. She designs a tiny maze for the preschoolers and makes scarecrows out of old clothes that families have left behind. She hides small prizes like stickers and bubbles around the hedges for a scavenger hunt. During the party she mostly sits by the crafts table with Miss Abeba and reflects on the time she herself spent here at Los Robles.

"Momo must have been what—four, five?" Wendi tries to recall the exact timing of her journey.

"About that," Miss Abeba says. "Actually, maybe he was three?"

"And we were sure younger, too."

"We were."

Wendi says, "If you'd told me then that all these years later I'd be here in the same yard doing this now"—she whistles sharply, up and down—"I'd have told you that you are a crazy person."

"Oh," Miss Abeba replies in her typically sly and knowing manner, "I always had a feeling you weren't going to leave us."

Wendi is nervous when she sees Evelyn and her kids there, because she knows that their last conversation hurt Evelyn—that she overstepped the parameters of both their working relationship and their friendship with the bluntness of her message to let the system process her son. She doesn't want to be yelled at in front of everyone else here. But Evelyn, despite appearing tired and wan, is in a happy mood. She sends her kids off running through the yard and comes to sit with the two older women. She bends over to hug Wendi and greets her as if no tension exists.

"It's so pretty here!" Evelyn peers around the yard in awe. "Did you two do all this?"

Miss Abeba nods toward Wendi, and Wendi says, "I just ordered other people around."

The three of them sit through the afternoon, not talking about money or trouble, just idly being together amid the pumpkins and children.

Evelyn does not speak of current circumstances until everyone is leaving, when she states almost casually, "I think we're going to lose our home."

Wendi wishes that she could assure her otherwise, but she can't.

◆ ◆ ◆

At the Halloween party Iris joins the different activities with her sisters and with kids who currently live in the shelter. She is in fifth grade now and the art projects and games skew young. She grows bored quickly and begins bugging her mom for the phone to play games. But her mom refuses and Iris wanders the yard adrift. The space at Los Robles is similarly situated as that which she'd known at the Villas. That yard seemed gigantic when they lived there, its own frontier. She had been electrified by the depth and greenness. Standing here now feels like standing in a regular yard.

She observes the kids and can easily differentiate those who have lived here for a few months from those who are new, just recently escaped from whatever their versions of disaster were. The longer-term residents are less clingy with their parents, more at ease with adults and one another, a little haughty about their groups and ownership of the space. The new kids, even the few that are older than Iris is now, move about the festivities with quiet caution as if any overstep or altercation might result in their being placed back outside. Iris doesn't remember behaving like that; in her recollection she and her siblings arrived and practically took over the Villas. But maybe her memory is flawed and they did in fact resemble these scared children. Maybe they resemble scared children again now with Orlando taken away.

She has had a feeling of late that the happiest and safest year the family will ever have occurred in the Villas and has passed them by.

A hand sticky with pumpkin innards takes hers and yanks: Marisol. Iris follows her to the jack-o'-lantern table to help with the carving tools while Sofia draws crooked outlines of facial features. Their mother helps for a few minutes but loses patience and seems generally distant. The girls are accustomed to this bearing. Iris thinks that she understands, thinks that her mom misses Orlando the way that she misses Orlando. Losing her brother has altered her life—she doesn't enjoy school as much, she is meaner to her sisters, she tries to act older and more knowing than she is—but Iris is certain that he will come home soon because that's what her mom keeps telling her. And she believes with a church-like surety that when he does, the energy in their home will revert to how it was.

A clod of seed and pulp hits her in the back of the head. The little kid who threw it claims it was an accident but Iris knows that it wasn't and she returns fire. The adults are quick to stop the volley and they are genuinely mad. Iris is not scared or bothered. She knows that even if they do take things away from her—privileges, possessions—the world won't change or care very much. Her brother is in jail and she can carry on through anything.

◆ ◆ ◆

Just before winter break, Evelyn reaches out to teachers from their old school in Monterey Park. She explains the situation: the juvenile court judge currently is awaiting an argument from the District Attorney's Office that Orlando somehow was involved in planning a premeditated robbery and assault even though the same judge has stated that testimonies from others involved in the case, including from the victim, have established the attack as spontaneous. She asks for letters of support that describe Orlando's character. Her son has been in custody in Sylmar for over four months.

Many of the teachers don't respond to her, perhaps uncomfortable with any association with the justice system. Orlando's favorite teacher, Mr. Garcia, replies immediately and the letter references a class presentation Orlando once gave about how his family believed in the same Catholic religion brought to this continent by the conquistadores who had murdered an entire civilization of his ancestors for its land and its gold and who had

273

used their God to justify the genocide. The presentation involved Orlando's struggle with the presence of this God in his and his mother's life. Mr. Garcia makes a point in his letter to say that he knew Orlando had a challenging life outside of school, and he was in awe of the positive spirit he brought to class with him each day. *Orlando in my experience with him is a great influence on those around him. I definitely never saw him intentionally hurt anyone's feelings, let alone engage in any physical altercations with anyone during the two years he was a student in my school and classroom.*

Evelyn also secures Orlando's school records, which show his unfailingly excellent attendance rate even during the pandemic shutdown. She pays for extra copies of his transcripts, mostly As with a B+ here and there over the past four years since beginning school in Los Angeles County. She did not herself save much of his work—there'd been nowhere to store the paper—but she has report cards that were online and she finds a note that a science teacher scribbled on a homework sheet that he is a pleasure to have in her class. Any existent record she can excavate of her son having been a normal kid who showed up at school every day with his siblings she transfers to her lawyer so that he can bombard the judge with them. The time and effort is expensive in every sense, but if she were not paying a lawyer then she would not know how to submit any of this documentation officially into the court—this evidence that her son is not the delinquent boy that he has been drawn as, that she isn't the neglectful mother.

In January 2023, a week after winter break ends and almost five months after he was first arrested, Orlando is released by the juvenile court. He is cleared of all serious charges but is given three months' probation for robbery: store security footage revealed clearly that when he fled the store, he took with him ice cream that he never paid for.

◆ ◆ ◆

The last time he was in the town house, back in August, Orlando slept in late, wrestled with Gabriel over some inconsequential disagreement, played for a while with Dev, then grabbed his skateboard and headed out along Crystal Lane and Walnut Street. In that moment on that day, he was a decent high school student nearing the start of eleventh grade. He had just experienced a full school year with his mom in a salaried job and their home secure and his siblings mostly taken care of, a year in which he could invest the sustained effort that straight As demanded and earn a little money of his own and nurture strong friendships. College was a real prospect in his life. He had qualified academically to be a math and science tutor for a school club that provided extra help to struggling students and those with special needs. At the end of that summer of 2022, an ethereal optimism hovered about him.

That aura winked out abruptly a few hours later in the day.

Orlando still doesn't really know what happened. The kid who attacked the store owner was not a core member of his friend group. They both were incarcerated in Sylmar at the same time but in different units, and Orlando mostly stayed away from him throughout those months, following the explicit advice of the lawyer his mother hired. What he knew was that an argument escalated for no real reason, a teenager lost control of himself, and a person was badly hurt. Orlando was nearby and associated with the perpetrator of the violence. He spent the first half of his junior year of high school in a juvenile detention facility—a rough one. His mother nearly lost her mind during that stretch as well as her job, her savings, and probably her home. He lost his friends and his clean record and his stature at school as a "good kid." His siblings lost some still-undetermined piece of what their family had been before.

Gabriel and Iris are awkward with him at home—cagey, as if they are scared of him—and so Orlando spends most of the days following his release hanging out with Sofia, Marisol, and Dev. The little kids pile across him as if no disruption of time has occurred and the brother they are with now in winter is the exact same brother who left at the end of summer.

His mother spends most of these few days in bed. The sustained physical energy and emotion of the autumn leaves her curled up in the dark.

◆ ◆ ◆

The eviction notice, when it comes, has been anticipated for long enough now that it doesn't ruin her day. What Evelyn does do as the ninety-day grace period commences, after which they need to move on from the town-home on Crystal Lane, is make a conscious decision to stop modeling exhaustion for her children and do what she can to rise. During the week that means working as many Applebee's shifts as she can procure. On Saturdays it means venturing again into the city's rental market. On Sundays it means taking all of them to church, a habit that she has fallen out of.

None of the kids appreciate this latter return to their old ways, when part of the impetus of going to church when they were homeless had to do with having an indoor activity and free, home-cooked food. But Evelyn herds them into the Highlander and drives the distance to Boyle Heights. They sit with Aunt Talia and take up half a pew. The kids zone out during the prayers. Evelyn makes sure that Orlando sits close to her, with Dev and Marisol in between them. During services, she is attuned to each of her children: the barely whispered jokes and elbowing and tremendously tall yawns, the eyes wandering upward during the sermons to the beams above that look old enough to split under slight pressure, tracking the long cracks in the paint on the walls, then returning downward to the pews and whatever entertainment they might find there with each other. Evelyn spends much of these hours clutching Dev in one hand and Aunt Talia in the other hand and praying for reprieve with as much sincerity as she can gather to a deity that doesn't seem all that concerned about them.

Surrounded in church with other believers in the midst of their own trying lives, she can sometimes feel a certain truthfulness behind all the worship. But during the weeks in between, as she takes her kids to school and habitually cleans the home they are being forced to leave soon, faced with charting a course beyond the immovable date of departure, she does question the utility of believing in anything at all that doesn't directly help her find shelter.

PART VII

Magnolia Gardens

January–December 2023

IN 2020, AGGRESSIVE TENANT PROTECTION measures enacted in California made evicting even nonpaying renters difficult. The enforcement of this temporary law no doubt helped keep housed hundreds of thousands whose incomes had been disrupted by the pandemic. But the protection had a largely unreported countereffect by which landlords—not keen to take on tenants of whom they could not easily rid themselves—became far more selective with lease approvals. Even in cases when this "selectiveness" meant lowering the rent by increments, avoiding potential squatters who might use the relief laws in order to live as long as they could for free was deemed to be worth the hit to monthly collections. Suddenly large numbers of schoolteachers, caretakers, service industry workers, administrative support employees, and other types of working people could not find new leases in the city—even in units with rents they could afford. The number of homeless on a given night in Los Angeles County rose 10 percent between 2022 and 2023 to over seventy-five thousand. A study concluded that about half of all people who had sought services over the course of the year worked or had recently worked. Some city leaders touted these numbers as progress.

In the fall of 2023, the Door of Hope organization has made strides toward opening another transitional housing site on a pretty street in

Pasadena. Reverend Andy Bales, a central figure of homeless services in greater Los Angeles who for twenty years has led the faith-based Union Rescue Mission in central Skid Row, has sold his own Craftsman home to the organization at a 20 percent discount from the market rate. Once zoned and converted to transitional housing, this property on Marengo Avenue will become Door of Hope's fifth shelter and increase the organization's capacity by another twenty families.

However, the surrounding community revolts against the prospect of another concentration of needy families among its owned homes. Each of Door of Hope's new shelter openings over the years caused a stir, typically in the form of op-eds in local papers and some hollering at city council meetings. Across all the five hundred square miles of Los Angeles County and the hundreds of small organizations and churches spending hundreds of millions of dollars to help tens of thousands of destitute humans, it is all but a given that any progress made on behalf of the unhoused invariably angers the proximate housed. But never has this organization's staff encountered vitriol so fierce, sustained, and organized. Potential future neighbors whose homes are all valued in the range of $2 million or more gather their resources to hire lawyers who in turn raise all sorts of obscure construction regulations and hypothetical dangers to prevent the conversion. During office meetings, Wendi and Miss Abeba and the rest of the leaders and staff take to reading some of the quotes aloud to one another to laugh at the level of pure selfish inanity on display. But even in amusement and with the foreknowledge that they will open this shelter in the end, they cannot contend with the hassle without feeling saddened that in 2023, forty years after the first Door of Hope shelter opened—and with the greater city in peak crisis without visible end—these objectors are not anomalies but are in fact utterly normal.

❖   ❖   ❖

With Evelyn facing imminent eviction from the Crystal Lane town house, Wendi and multiple other Door of Hope employees are all keenly focused on placing them somewhere livable—a challenge when the average rent for a two-bedroom on the market exceeds $2,900 per month and is rising. Evelyn complicates the search because her foremost priority is that her children not have to change schools again; she seeks a home within a couple square miles of some of the region's most valuable real estate. The specificity is maddening in a way they've grown accustomed to during two years of working with Evelyn.

Wendi and others plead for Evelyn to consider that the county holds more than five hundred public elementary schools and over two hundred charter schools, and many of them are well-resourced and well-run. Kids change schools all the time and remain healthy and bright, they tell her; kids are resilient beyond measure. Evelyn takes to hanging up the phone whenever this rationale arises.

Her family has a little over forty-five days remaining at this point to search. With a Section 8 eviction for failure to pay rent now on Evelyn's record, her expectations sound impossible, deranged. But Wendi knows as fact that when Evelyn states that she is willing to become homeless again if it means keeping her kids in their current schools, she is speaking with absolute honesty and precedent.

❖   ❖   ❖

In February, Evelyn is reinstated at her tax firm job in a part-time capacity. With about a hundred extra dollars a week between clerking and waitressing, she begins gathering again the first increments of the safety net she expended on the legal system.

The rest of her time she devotes to apartment searches and to reconnecting with her oldest son, gauging the degree to which incarceration has altered or damaged his spirit. They don't talk about anything all that substantial, but an urgency emerges that has to do with Orlando's new aversion to school. His friend group has dispersed in the aftermath of the store assault. A few of them transferred to other schools and others were ordered by their parents not to associate with anyone near to the crime that day. He feels as though some of his teachers, including those he likes, treat him edgily now. The official findings of his innocence of all but ice cream theft hold no bearing in his actual movements through the world; in the sector of society they live in, incarceration itself is a signifier of guilt. Orlando, whose months in juvenile hall have not desensitized him to the opinions others hold of him—who if anything seems to his mother even more reactive to his environment and the people in it—comes home from school in a fragile state at the end of many of those midwinter days, unequipped to balance the anger and sadness and sense of remove. Evelyn, who is usually in between returning from her four hours at the tax office and embarking on the forty-minute drive to her seven-hour Applebee's shift, can hug him and loudly scorn others who she believes wronged him, but she can't console him or ease his life. Her fear is that this downturn will manifest in bad grades during this determinative stretch of his education, just when he can no longer afford to have them.

◆ ◆ ◆

On Saturday afternoons, Wendi hosts small workshops for alumni. She invites guest speakers such as local professional people to talk about different employment sectors—realty or HVAC installation or nursing—and the barriers of entry; community college instructors who specialize in various vocational degrees; a mortgage broker who talks about the steps of homeownership, even though the women who attend that class have a sour reaction since the average home price in the area is now $1.3 million and the presumption that any of them might ever enter that market seems mocking. Usually seven or eight women show up. Wendi always offers some snacks and coffee. They end with a few rounds of bingo in which the board prompts have to do with that day's life-goal theme.

Evelyn agrees to attend one of these weekend workshops in the spring along with two other alumni in order to give career advice to more recent shelter graduates. Over the years when Evelyn has come to Door of Hope for any kind of gathering, she has been asked to talk about the school system and how she navigated it with all her children. Evelyn was skilled at these presentations: she could talk about everything from how she behaved during parent-teacher conferences so that the schools never marked her as an indigent parent to the least time-consuming volunteer jobs to interacting with the affluent cliques of moms to how she coaxed her kids to finish homework on the nights they were sleeping in an SUV. Mothers, staff members, and especially the donor set all loved hearing her speak, captured by her forcefulness and the sharp dramatic arcs of her anecdotes.

Once word of Orlando's arrest made its way through the Door of Hope community earlier in the fall, Evelyn ceased in her willingness to speak to the topic of child rearing and school. She became afraid that people would be more interested in judging her parenting than listening to what she had learned.

But Wendi does not want to lose her as a guest, because she feels that doing so might be the first step toward losing track of Evelyn altogether, which happens sometimes in her work: mothers can fall out of her protective sphere. Sometimes this happens gradually, as they receive less daily support and contact. Other times Wendi loses people suddenly after an argument, a phone number change, involvement with a new man, a move. The ultimate fragility of her connections is possibly the saddest aspect of the work. Losing people now makes her think of Yasmine, the young woman who helped with Momo when Wendi lived in the shelter, who disappeared.

These days, in the early spring of 2023, nearly two years after they'd first met and with Evelyn in another of her long succession of desperate and time-sensitive situations, Wendi feels that she still has some role to play in Evelyn's life as it continues to progress chaotically—and as Evelyn continues to weaponize that long-ago interaction in which Wendi gently advised her to spend less of her time visiting Orlando in Sylmar, and to consider letting go of her dream of what the future once held for him. Wendi now and always will regret giving that advice before she came to understand the level of devotion of which Evelyn was capable. She fears that if this family were to fade away, they could all end up back on Mission Road.

"What am I supposed to talk about?" Evelyn asks her regarding the workshop Wendi is planning for her to attend. Evelyn sounds breathy over the phone, as if she is cleaning and cooking at the same time, which is typical. "Because whenever I talk about my kids now, ladies get pissed and they talk shit back, so I don't want to talk about school or anything like that."

"No, no," Wendi assuages. "That's not what I'm asking. I'd like for them all to hear about the housing situation you are in and how you are not giving up, how you never give up on your family."

"Well, you're doing all the work," Evelyn says, softening. "Why don't *you* talk to them?"

Wendi smiles privately to herself. She is more than half a century old now and has built her whole identity and vocation around her Christian faith, but she is not above feeling prideful when she does receive some credit for her efforts—maybe because it doesn't happen too often.

She says, "The help we're giving you is part of the conversation. It's important for these women to know that they can ask for help from us—that they will *need to* ask for help from us. Because a lot of them are going out into the world and it's going to get cold on them fast and they don't like to reach out saying they can't handle things. A lot of them would rather suffer than admit to that, you know?"

"Yeah," Evelyn says, veering between indignation and reflectiveness. "That is important."

◆　◆　◆

Their next home is a two-bedroom apartment in an affordable-housing complex on Magnolia Street. Beneath all the official policies and channels by which a person might secure housing support, the truth in desirable residential areas is that a place to stay really requires incredibly fortunate timing combined with someone with knowledge and connections within the market willing to perform some dogged, targeted work. To secure this unit for them, Wendi leveraged all of Door of Hope's local influence as a decades-old community organization just days before Evelyn and the kids were going to be evicted from Crystal Lane. She probably spent seventy or eighty hours in total—with at least a quarter of them on the phone with property managers in order to assure them of Evelyn's solvency and character—trying to keep this family from becoming homeless again.

Wendi believes those hours ought to earn her some blanket forgiveness for the advice she'd given Evelyn during a delicate, impossible moment. What Evelyn does instead is make Wendi's work life even more difficult by taking in a small, loud rescue dog not a month into her new lease. As Evelyn's primary reference, Wendi receives many of the manager's complaints directly.

Their new home has low ceilings, narrow windows, too-small rooms, and no playable outdoor space. The front door opens into a living room and a short hallway with a bedroom on each side and a bathroom at the end. The building is called Magnolia Gardens. They split up the rooms by gender, the four girls on one side and the three boys on the other, though Dev wanders back and forth throughout each night at his own whimsy. The dog—whom the kids begged for but Evelyn now takes full care of—is a five-pound poof of dirty-white fur, but her more or less continuous barking has the effect of further shrinking their space. Living here does not feel easy the way the town house on Crystal Lane did.

But she is balancing her two jobs and building a cushion, they have Orlando home with them, they are all healthy, they have a place she can afford and schools with tremendous programs and resources. Day-to-day life feels predictable. For all these reasons, Evelyn knows that she and her kids have cause to be grateful now perhaps more than ever.

Yet Evelyn has a new premonition that the feeling of imperishable togetherness that she and her kids have sustained across the city is beginning to thin. No one seems as happy as Evelyn feels they should be; no one seems as proud to be a member of this family. Generally, the kids seem resigned in advance to whatever misfortune will occur next.

She asks Gabriel outright, since he is the most observant and attuned, "What can I do better?"

They are in the apartment's kitchenette, which is a tight space. He shrugs. "Nothing."

"You have to tell me if anyone's upset with me."

"No one's upset with you that I know of right now."

Those two innocuous words—*right now*—strike her as important, because even while speaking evasively to spare her feelings, he encapsulates what she already knows: her kids have been through enough repeat cycles of their whole world falling apart around them that they live now in a steady state of waiting for the next time that security dissolves and the money is spent and they will be driving aimlessly in the Highlander at night. They don't trust her to provide stability; they have forfeited some understanding of the notion of security. In her heart, Evelyn herself can't really hold faith that she is competent. These years have taken that simplicity from all of them.

Evelyn next reaches out to her therapist from Door of Hope, who schedules one appointment over the phone. Evelyn begins this conversation by speaking very, very quickly about Orlando's experience, in a stressed state of trying to include the greatest number of details in the shortest amount of time. She stops repeatedly to apologize for being all over the place.

"Maybe that's the issue," the therapist tells her.

"What is?"

"Needing to communicate too much, holding too many different threads, striving to be too many characters to too many different people."

"Okay, but what's the answer to that?"

"Do you ever meditate?"

Evelyn laughs at her.

"Unfortunately, the answer is probably time."

That word is what Evelyn does not want to hear, because time is a commodity she never has—neither in the course of a regular day nor in the context of children growing older without pause. In August, Orlando begins his senior year in high school, Gabriel his sophomore year, Iris seventh grade, Sofia fifth, Marisol third, and Dev begins preschool. These are crucial years in each child's life.

"How much time does it take for kids to be good again?"

"There's no single answer. But a general rule is that once lives are stable for longer than they have been unstable, kids can begin to feel comfortable in their surroundings and find purpose in relationships and hard work."

That amounts to five years, Evelyn realizes. She also realizes she doesn't have that long to make repairs; in five years, most of her kids won't really be kids anymore.

Every few weeks she makes the drive to downtown Los Angeles, a place that once physically loomed over their lives but now exists somewhat on the fringes, the buildings visible in the far distance now and again at certain points of view near their new home. She rings around the edges of Skid Row—unchanged by the pandemic or any of the billions of dollars earmarked for the homeless crisis, as far as she can tell with her eyes—to the flower market. Usually at least Dev and Marisol are with her and they hold hands while strolling past the many stores. She tries to let the kids direct her as long as they don't beg for anything too exotic or expensive. Together they spend ten dollars or less and usually bring an armful of flowers back to Magnolia Gardens, and the kids line up plastic cups half-filled with water to make their small arrangements and decorate the apartment. Sometimes their enthusiasm draws the older, more jaded siblings like Iris over to consult on some petal color combination. Evelyn still loves those afternoons more than most.

◆　◆　◆

The family begins visiting Lancaster more often again, as they did during the early months of the pandemic, the first months of Dev's life. The rhythms there do not change in Evelyn's estimation even as both the adults and the children in her extended family age in noticeable ways. A desert city—even a large one like Lancaster—carries the feeling of being on an island, the settled land's finite boundaries dropping off into earth that is uninhabitable and punishing. For most in her family, that demarcation holds some mode of security. Community there is circular and without many unfamiliar places. Even in youth, Evelyn was always closely attuned to that feeling. She never enjoyed it; she remembers feeling marooned there more than protected, hence the ever-strengthening pull toward the city, where she and the kids might live in a continuum of humanity, cross their own pathways with a million other pathways, become expansive people together.

Evelyn isn't sure if that imagining has actually come to be yet or if it will—Orlando's imprisonment threw into disarray all her precious thoughts of what they could become—but she is confident that it still might.

The drives to Lancaster make her more and more nervous because the Highlander is failing, finally, leaving Evelyn in a common vehicle owner's plight of gauging whether the big work required to coax ten or fifteen thousand more miles from the engine will cost more than the SUV itself is actually worth. In her case, the numbers are clear but the calculation is not as simple because even with whatever she might receive in a sale—a couple thousand dollars, tops—she cannot necessarily afford a replacement with enough seats for her family in the current used-car economy. High demand and shortages of parts have inflated prices absurdly. In the meantime, she has a local shop that performs short-term fixes for reasonable rates and she drives the Highlander as little as she can. Magnolia Gardens is within a few blocks of multiple useful bus routes and she takes those to work and for errands. But to go home around mountains and over desert will always be a drive.

On one of these trips to Lancaster in mid-October 2023, well before Christmas, her entire family presents her with an early gift. Curious, she opens the envelope and unfolds a picture one of her nieces drew with crayons. She needs a moment to recognize the busy images as a plane ticket alongside a bright red arrow pointing from a stick figure drawing of her to a yellow circle with a vaguely palm-tree-like form sticking out of it. The gist is that her family wants to send Evelyn on vacation.

"That's crazy," she protests. "I'm not letting you all pay for *seven plane tickets*. That would be, like, thousands of dollars, no."

Her mother holds up a finger to shush her, then explains that they want Evelyn to go on a vacation on her own. While her family is not aware of very many details of her journey over these past years—and certainly not the most harrowing or embarrassing ones—they know enough to feel that this excessive kindness is important right now.

The conversation becomes an argument, the kind of argument her family has engaged in with one another hundreds of times over her life, complete with self-righteousness and martyrdom, guilt, half-truths, many bottles of beer, people raising their voices to be heard without having much to say. Evelyn is a full participant in the discord, and at points she is its driver. Her angle has to do with an aversion to both the suggestion of charity and the wasting of money on something so utterly nonessential and short-lived as a vacation. She also resents the awareness that everyone here probably talks about her with some regularity, likely as some sad example of rash, poor decision-making. Her instinct is that they are giving her this gift to feel high-and-mighty about themselves. The tenor resembles times when she and her siblings and cousins were teenagers bickering over slights they can barely remember now. Just like those long-past moments, this night ends with most of them laughing about their own collective foolishness. But the matter at hand remains unresolved for a few weeks.

The family argument causes reflection on a certain contradiction of her life. Evelyn at turns speaks with contempt about gifts given out of guilt—and yet she will never be able to calculate the monetary value of all the benefactions she has received over these past five years from Aunt Talia, from random clerks and social workers, city services, Door of Hope, Section 8, employers and coworkers and hospitals and teachers and school administrators. She considers herself to be worthy of most of what she has been given; she works hard, doesn't hurt anyone, brings her children to school looking nice and with their homework completed. She believes those children to be deserving of a decent life. That she hasn't lost her mind seems to merit some recognition. At the same time, she has no idea how to quantify these matters when thousands upon thousands of mothers and children are trying to survive here. In church, she tries to envision a God sorting it all out. The rest of the week, outcomes seem closely entwined with luck and some intangible qualities of spirit.

In their apartment, she mulls over these facets of her life aloud for days after the visit, striving to square them all and having a hard time. Usually she is cleaning in the slightly frantic manner she deploys when her life outside Magnolia Gardens feels disordered. Eventually her arguments with herself become so incessant that they even distract Orlando—who learned in juvenile hall how to shut out any noise and motion that happen beyond the two feet in front of his face. In their compact space Iris can be singing and dancing to Taylor Swift at high volume, and Dev and Marisol can be brutally fighting each other over what show to watch, and the garbage truck can be roaring its way along the block outside, the dog barking—and Orlando can read for long stretches at a time, because in the midst of his ongoing social dislocation, he continues striving to catch up on the half year of school he missed. So Evelyn understands that she must be making a mighty fuss about the underlying significance of the vacation idea when he scoffs and glares up at her from his textbooks.

"Mom," he says. "You don't think you deserve nice things or good times. But you do. It isn't charity, it's a present from your family that still loves you. So take it and stop going on and on. It's all right for you to be happy."

Evelyn has a Swiffer mop in one hand and a lint roller in the other so that she can clean the floor beneath the sofa and the cushions on top of it simultaneously. "Who's going to watch all you kids?" she asks meekly.

"There's a lot of people that can watch us; we'll be all right."

◆ ◆ ◆

In early October, on a weekday evening, Wendi attends a meeting of the Pasadena City Council. Momo is with her and sworn to his best, quietest behavior. They sit with Miss Abeba near the front of the half-filled room. The few dozen board members, church congregants, donors, employers, and former residents who have come here in support of clearance for the new Marengo Avenue shelter dwarf the eight or nine objectors from the neighborhood willing to publicize their discomfort with being near poor people and the struggles they bear. Wendi recognizes two of them, a man and his wife, from her church but doesn't think they recognize her.

The meeting moves along slowly as the council ratifies the previous meeting's minutes and tends to some of the more mundane tasks of managing a city government. The part of the agenda involving Door of Hope and the property additions required for the new shelter—which have already been approved and bonded by the city—is included in the meeting as something of a formality. The council makes time so that the people in opposition can feel like their voices are being heard even though the legal efforts to undermine the shelter, costly as they are for all sides, are nonstarters.

The objectors' voices are loud and predictably focused on imaginings of crime and violence and drug traffic that they proclaim are sure to overtake the peaceful neighborhood the moment the charity's clients take up shelter there. One elderly lady openly weeps at the microphone, lamenting the ruin that Pasadena is becoming. A middle-aged man brings his two elementary-aged kids to the front with him and keeps jabbing his finger down the line of council members while accusing them of behaving "like sheep in a time that requires leaders to act like wolves," and the point of this language mystifies everyone else in the room, including his children. The complaint that a few of them land on that seems vaguely defensible has to do with the fact that the house in question was sold and fast-tracked for conversion without anyone bothering to inform residents, and so they feel disregarded when perhaps they could have participated in the planning and made the new shelter a true community collaboration. Wendi nods thoughtfully if somewhat skeptically at those comments even as they are all but drowned out by the self-righteous indignation of the smaller, louder sect who don't understand why this kind of charity can't just stay in downtown Los Angeles, where it's been contained for longer than a generation—as if Skid Row represents some kind of urban-planning success story.

When the microphone is turned over to the Door of Hope side, a long line forms. First the organization's leadership promises to be more respectful and inclusive of neighbors moving forward. Then mothers and children begin giving testimony of the ways in which the housing provided for them in the three active shelters has saved their lives. Some neighbors of these shelters testify as to how, far from attracting crime, the Door of Hope residents contribute to the richness of the neighborhood and how in certain ways they care more about its well-being than the homeowners, how the owners in turn have become wiser members of the city they live in: statements that are saccharine yet earnest and important to hear in a serious forum. After a time, the head of the city council stops the testimonies and asks everyone in the line to raise a hand if they plan to say something praiseworthy about Door of Hope. All the hands go up.

Wendi notices then that Evelyn has arrived late and is sitting in the back with her three youngest children. All their hands are stretched high.

The city council then recognizes the support while sparing everyone remaining actually having to talk, and the meeting moves on to the next agenda item. With much satisfaction but without visibly gloating, Wendi watches the opposition neighbors file from the room cantankerously. Momo laughs at them, and Wendi lets him go on for a few moments before gently shushing him.

◆ ◆ ◆

During the summer before his senior year of high school, Orlando works part-time at a Petco not far from their apartment. He spends most of his hours stocking shelves and handling animals dropped off for grooming. He doesn't hold any special affection for animals and would much rather work the cash registers, where he could interact more with humans and absorb fewer odors into his clothes. But possibly because of his record—the stolen ice cream means that he has one—he is assigned to the floor. The money is meaningful.

His dilemma is that his high school has a program by which seniors tutor underclassmen from underprivileged backgrounds in core subjects. This program does not pay anything, nor does it earn school credits. But the work is supposed to be fulfilling and also look pleasing on college applications. Orlando qualified for the program the previous year before being pulled from school. One of his teachers offers to fast-track him back into it to help build a counterweight to his arrest and all its academic repercussions, which include a steep dip in his GPA, summer school classes, and a host of other potential red flags embedded in his imminent college applications. He has to choose between earning a few hundred dollars a week carrying huge bags of pet food and taking on a challenging, uncompensated task under the premise that it might raise his chances of enrolling in a two- or even a four-year school. The choice between money-earning and résumé-building seems much weightier the longer he contemplates its ramifications, as if he is deciding now what kind of person he wants to be.

His mother says, "How is this something you even have to think about for two seconds? Or even for one second?"

"Maybe because I'm broke," he replies.

She sits beside him and grips his shoulders in her hands. Orlando has muscles and facial hair now, and he came out of juvenile hall with a new, intimidating glower as part of his resting facial expression. He is looking down at her but still experiences the powerful authority that she holds over him as she talks. "It's not just about you," she says. "It's about who your brothers and your sisters see when they look at you."

"I didn't ask to be the oldest one," he says a bit lamely.

"So what if you didn't ask? It's who you are."

He opts to join the tutoring program.

The kids he works with are freshmen and sophomores who are unhappy and typically struggling badly in their classwork. In their hours together during study-hall periods and between 3 p.m. and 5 p.m. after school, Orlando learns that in order to accomplish more with them—in order to accomplish anything, really—he needs to lead each kid to feel that he, Orlando, *wants* to be there with them. And that alone can be really hard. Two of his assigned students take over a month, well into November, to exhibit even faint traces of trust in his guidance. With another, the process takes longer. Orlando becomes fairly certain that this boy—who is Black, slight in stature, and reserved—is homeless. The student never confides this; he barely speaks at all beyond the sounds of *yes, no,* and *hmmm.* Orlando just gradually picks up on the fact that when they finish their work on Tuesday afternoons, he leaves the classroom with the bearing of someone on his way to nowhere.

During this same early stretch of his senior year, he decides to sign up for the ACT standardized test. These tests have become optional in the admissions process to many of the country's universities since the COVID-19 pandemic began, because the various entities that govern this process can't seem to decide whether the tests themselves stoke or reduce inequality. Orlando passed on taking it the previous spring when most of his classmates did, because he was just out of jail. His counselor urges him to take it not just for the score but in order to demonstrate initiative and engagement, to thicken his file, and to build out his story. The ACT is thought to measure rational thinking and real-world applications of school knowledge versus the more traditional SAT. The counselor helps him through the grind required to waive the eighty-five-dollar exam fee, gives him a few books to study and practice tests to take home. College application forms also ask him to begin contemplating responses to questions about what people and forces have shaped him, who he is now, who he wants to become, why his existence matters at all.

At the end of October he shows up early at an area high school along with hundreds of other high school juniors and seniors. These kids are all amped and nervous knowing that their performance over the course of the morning will determine some unknown aspects of their lives over the next few years. Orlando himself is a bit numb or perhaps inoculated by his imprisonment to the anxiety coursing through the space as he sits in his assigned room with his scratch paper and sharp pencils and the computer screen. He actually feels calm here, as if some new sort of motion is underway and if he can stay balanced then he can ride it.

❖　❖　❖

Every so often, the liberal governor of California casts a public threat to pull homeless services funding from cities that have not reduced their transient populations or cleared encampments. While the state has not closely audited its spending on this budget sector, outside agencies report that roughly $5 billion per year has been invested in different facets of the housing crisis since 2019—around $25,000 per unsheltered person per year—and during that span the population of such people in the Golden State has risen by thirty thousand. Government is an innately reactive entity, and the numbers over the past two decades have shown homelessness to be uniquely resistant to its sporadic, backward-facing interventions: a generational plight that stymies broad solutions and undercuts political ideologies and is a confounding sinkhole for immense sums of money. That is how the cycle has played out in the past and how it continues to play out now.

Maybe the many folds of bureaucracy that lie between proposals and results hold too much space for grift and evasion to deliver what is promised; maybe the current economic tides sloshing across America are too great a force to counteract with mere billions of dollars; maybe the tight handshake between the finance and real estate industries that propels city growth invariably presses down upon those who lack holdings on either side of the deal; maybe those nearest to the bands of power will rarely prioritize people who can't donate and don't vote at the expense of those who can and do. The fundamentals of why such aching poverty persists beneath expansive, celebrated wealth are perhaps irreducible. The opportunities to escape it are narrow and limited. The collective attitude of the greater populace remains tepidly concerned and resistant to accountability. Service providers on street level continue to perform triage while officials in different tiers of government rhetorically push blame away. These constants persist alongside the enduring truth that for people without shelter to find it and keep it, they need above all to feel that they are not alone.

◆ ◆ ◆

Wendi is fighting with Evelyn again in the middle of that fall. This cycle of argument and amends has repeated so often that she ceases to keep track of who instigates a given loop. The cause is almost always the same anyway: Evelyn calls her to ask for something specific such as a volunteer babysitter, an extra Amazon gift card, a bundle of bus fare credits, or some handout for car repair work for her Highlander; Wendi says no, she can't budget for this need right now, it is not part of the program; Evelyn begins accusing Wendi of not caring about her and her kids; Wendi assures her that she does care but she is also very busy with dozens of clients who are in their very first weeks of life beyond the shelter and she doesn't have gift cards overflowing from her purse; Evelyn hangs up on her.

The resolution is also the same: they don't speak for a week or more; Wendi calls a few times to check in and is ignored or rebuffed; then Wendi either comes up with whatever Evelyn asked for or else Evelyn asks for something new that Wendi can provide; all is forgiven and reset.

The current spat involves birthday party planning for her daughter Sofia. Evelyn asked Wendi if she could throw a party for Sofia and her school friends in the Villas' yard. She was thoughtful about the proposition in that all she wanted to use was the outdoor space itself, and she promised to leave alone the shelter's stores of food and drinks, plastic cups and paper plates and coolers, toys and decorations and party favors, even bathrooms. Wendi was skeptical of that, and she also vaguely remembered having the same argument with Evelyn the previous year regarding Iris's birthday party. But even so she passed the request up her chain of command and was told, predictably, that the organization could not indulge this mainly because allowing them to have a party at the Villas would set a precedent and incite dozens of graduate families to begin asking for the same privileges.

Wendi informed Evelyn that the yard could be used this way only by current residents.

"I've thrown a lot of birthdays on the cheap, though," Wendi added, and she recommended a few local public parks that gave free reservations of picnic spaces.

"Every park is full of street people laying around under the trees," Evelyn scoffed.

"Do you ever listen to yourself talk? Because you *should*."

"I don't mean it like that, like I'm judging them."

"How do you mean it?" Wendi asked.

"Listen, I don't want to throw a kids' party around a bunch of street people, all right?"

"So you'd rather have it at a shelter?"

Wendi laughed and hoped the absurdity would lighten Evelyn's bearing as well, but Evelyn was already pissed off and the conversation ended there.

Immaturely, Wendi now shares the nascent squabble around the office, where Evelyn is well-known for her frequent demands, her prolific retractions of friendship, and the reversals of those retractions. The Door of Hope staff always appreciates something trivial to laugh about as a salve to the secondary trauma of contending with others' suffering every day, multiple times a day, mostly that of women and children.

Miss Abeba gently chides Wendi over her own pettiness that afternoon. "You're better than that," she says.

"But you have to grant that Evelyn is sometimes a pain in my butt," Wendi replies.

"You were a pain in mine once," Miss Abeba says. "Though, my goodness, do I dislike that expression."

"I wasn't perfect but I must have been pretty easy compared to some," Wendi says.

Miss Abeba laughs. "You and your kids had a lot that you asked for. And none of you liked hearing the word *no*, either. *And* you were very messy. So don't give Evelyn such a hard time. At least she was clean; I never had to rush to her room before inspections and shove clothes in the closet!"

Wendi grumbles childishly to herself and tries to remember those months nearly twenty years ago. Times were very different then. Not everyone had cell phones or laptop computers. Looking for jobs and dealing with kids and school involved more legwork and hustle and face-to-face interaction. She must have been a very harried person. She must have asked for help with her kids often. The sheer terror she had known at times while sheltered at Los Robles isn't a sensation she can summon viscerally anymore, now that she knows her children survived that phase of their lives and are leading self-sufficient existences if not glamorous ones, and she knows that she herself has the means to take care of Momo until she can't.

She seeks Miss Abeba out the next day with a nagging need for reassurance. "I must have been more gracious than a lot of these women we see now," she posits. "Tell me at least that I said *please* and *thank you* and that I showed you all some gratitude."

Miss Abeba smiles to herself in a way that will drive Wendi mad for weeks afterward. "Most of the time, you were," she says.

When Evelyn forgives Wendi for the birthday party conversation sometime later—having since thrown the party at one of the parks Wendi recommended—she does so to make another request. Evelyn now wonders if Door of Hope offers any kind of free, formal college-application guidance that Orlando might use. She sounds humble and a little desperate.

She says that she asked some parents at Orlando's school and did some research online, and normal college-application tutoring costs thousands of dollars.

Wendi has to be honest: "No, we don't have anything like that." She waits for Evelyn to start yelling at her and hang up.

But Evelyn simply replies, "Oh. That's okay; that would be a lot. I'll try to help him myself."

"But we should have that resource. I will look into it and see what can be done on our end. You and Orlando hold tight."

Evelyn blurts with pride, "He scored a twenty-eight out of thirty-six on his ACT. That's above average at a lot of schools, you know."

Wendi smiles because she is proud of Orlando—and also because she realizes that the main reason Evelyn has forgiven her and made this outreach is so she can brag about her son.

In the moments after this call, and during the following days while many other employees and interns brainstorm ways to provide some help, Sister Wendi reflects on the fact that Evelyn's habitual, reactive anger followed by these bursts of sincerity might be annoying traits but they are also part of the skill set that she has developed in order to be alive now—because parents on the street who don't attach high emotions to pleas for help do not often receive it. They definitely do not keep six children performing well in school while avoiding entirely the child welfare system.

Wendi believes she can understand the pattern, even as it remains aggravating and endless.

In the meantime, Momo has joined a local basketball league for young adults with special needs. Twice a week Wendi disconnects entirely from her work to watch his games. Her son towers over most of his teammates and his opponents. His dribbling is poor but he can make baskets at close range, and whenever he does, he performs a little shimmy and the gym erupts with parents from both teams mirroring his glee.

◆　◆　◆

The sight of the nearly white, fine-grained sand moves Evelyn immediately into a mental space of strange detachment. The first hour, she sits on the beach in front of her hotel and scoops up handful after handful of the powdery stuff and lets it seep through her fingers into small piles. She has brought a novel with her, the first book in a crime series that someone at work recommended. She liked to read as a child in school but has barely read any books for her own pleasure as an adult—though she has read many of the works that her kids have been assigned for school. She can talk fluently about Sandra Cisneros, Kate DiCamillo, Chinua Achebe, and a dozen other authors whose work weighted her kids' backpacks and stuffed the car footwells through all the different grades. She thought she might experience again that old sensation of plummeting into a story, losing time to it, maybe being changed by it. But she doesn't end up reading at all during her trip. She plays with the sand and stares at the sea instead.

Flying was scary. One of her best friends from Lancaster, who has accompanied her on this trip, held her hand during the takeoffs and landings of their three connecting flights. Her friend, who has her own children and is divorced, is interested in meeting men here—or at least looking at and talking about men—but Evelyn isn't. She thinks about relationships sometimes in an aloof way, such as when she happens by happy-looking couples or when women at work share details about dating and marriage to pass the days of organizing strangers' taxes. But her active memories of the serious relationships she's had are among her most terrible overall, and so she does not focus any minute of this trip on meeting people except for the ones required to humor her friend.

They stay in a very modest hotel a few blocks from the beach in St. Croix. Evelyn's mother is staying in the Magnolia Gardens apartment with her kids. Evelyn has not spent a full night more than a few feet away from her children since 2018, five years ago. The one child she permitted some freedom to ended up in jail and that devastated her, jammed her with guilt, probably shortened her life by some years. In the days approaching this trip, locked in anxiety, she listened to multiple lectures given by Wendi and Miss Abeba and Aunt Talia about how parents are mere shepherds for their children and need to loosen their grip at a certain point so that the kids can build independence. But Evelyn refuses to believe that her kids will be all right without her remaining very close by in the years to come. The world has proven itself to be full of danger and ledges and people who don't care.

She uses FaceTime to check in a few times each day and becomes panicked in the instances when no one answers. Overall, she has a hard time enjoying herself. She walks along the shore with her friend, swims in warm, shallow water, has a few drinks, and overall tries very hard to act like a thirty-five-year-old woman on vacation—to act like the many people around her for whom excursions like this are maybe an annual fixture or at least a normal outing. For Evelyn, these days are decidedly not normal, and even while her friend admonishes her to quit wasting their getaway by feeling as if she doesn't belong, Evelyn can't keep herself from feeling this way—not necessarily that she doesn't belong, but that there's a wrongness in her being here. And as annoying as a certain four words must be for everyone around her in the tropics, she can't refrain from repeating them a few times per day: "I miss my kids."

◆ ◆ ◆

After spending over five years investing daily effort and enduring a severe emotional toll in order to keep his housing situation—often his lack thereof—a secret from friends and teachers at school, Orlando now hears from his high school counselor that touting his family's homelessness as a banner of survival, parading that experience through each segment of his college applications, will greatly increase his odds of acceptance and financial aid to desirable schools both in state and out of state. Not only will this narrative help explain the aberrations in his overall solid GPA, but it also provides moving fodder for the various essays and scholarship attachments. Orlando learns that in the world of college admissions, there is actually a genre of writing called the trauma essay that is known to be one of the most effective tools an ambitious kid can wield.

The school counselor works with the entire senior class, because due to their district location, Orlando goes to the kind of school in which basically every senior is looking toward college. So he doesn't see her often. But in their meetings throughout the fall—and after his decent ACT score comes back—she encourages him to be open about growing up as a homeless domestic-violence survivor. This counselor does not quite understand the depth in his soul at which his mother has rooted the idea that anyone at his school finding out about his family means that he will lose both school and family. Even these private conversations in the counselor's office throughout his middle stretch of senior year bring on numerous physical symptoms of anxiety: his heartbeat accelerates, his fingers and toes twitch, his eyes dart around the room and the many university flags that decorate its walls. One of his first thoughts is that his mom will freak out if he writes anything about homelessness. She will interpret anything he composes— even the most fawning tribute to her strength—to mean that he is blaming her and that readers will judge her poorly. Orlando does not want to hurt his mother, even at the risk of diminishing his college chances.

He asks the counselor, "What am I even supposed to write about when I write about being homeless?"

"Write about what it was like and what you learned," she advises. "Include details: things you saw and heard, things you smelled, what you were feeling."

"What if I didn't really, like, learn anything, except maybe how to do homework in the back of a car, how to get my friends' parents to cook me good food?"

Her eyes flash brightly, and she nods. "Both of those are great details."

"I probably learned a lot more in jail—just about life and surviving."

She replies, "You probably do not want to write about being in jail. You don't have to mention it and they're not allowed to ask. It would probably be very hard for you to write about anyway."

He likes this woman and knows that she's been doing this job for a long time. But she does not understand what he is trying to communicate.

He thinks that Sister Wendi might understand, even though he doesn't know her very well. She always seems to carry some wisdom or at least some zany stories regarding these sorts of junctures in life, the confusing transitions.

The holidays are approaching and so Wendi is on regular rounds among alumni distributing gift cards and inviting people to workshops about how to navigate this time of year—the very hardest time of year for poor parents. While his mother tends to some drama with Dev, he explains his predicament to Sister Wendi out of her earshot. The lady lets out a sharp burst of laughter.

"So the counselor says that fancy colleges now *want* to pick kids from off the street?" She chortles some more and then explains: "Listen, Orlando, I am someone who didn't go to any fancy four-year school like you're getting set to go to. I went to community. When I was your exact age I already had two kids and a third coming. But I always did spend a lot of my time thinking about education. And so with this essay, if you're asking my advice, I would say just don't fret over it. Maybe just do what the lady says and write what she says to write even if it doesn't feel quite right. Because you've already done all the hard work. So now it's time you go get what's on the other side of that. Don't let your feelings and others' ignorance get in the way of that anymore. You've dealt with all that enough and now if you can use it to get them on your side, I say go ahead. Do you hear me and what I'm saying?"

He thinks he does, and he nods even though he is a little disappointed because he expected her to be far more precious and guarded, like him, about what he has seen and done. She leans closer and grins at him. "Also, if I were you I would not talk about this to your mother, because that would be a whole *thing*. I'm trying to make it easy on you and she is going to make it hard. Nothing against her, but do you see?"

"I do," he replies. "But she'll probably find out about it eventually."

"If or when she does, she'll probably be mad," Wendi says. "But your mom always does come around."

◆ ◆ ◆

Sofia's homework has to do with standard algorithm math strategies, which to Evelyn, even after helping three older kids through the same unit, seems like a way of taking very simple arithmetic problems and jamming them through rubric diagrams that confuse everything. She knows the answers to the equations but she doesn't know how to solve them in the way the teachers want them solved. But she loves being beside her kids while they do their homework—both to ensure that they do it and to show them how much she cares about it. She's developed a routine in the evening such that between each step of cooking dinner she sits with a different kid. While waiting for the rice water to boil, she sits with Gabriel. While the rice cooks, she sits with Iris. Once the rice is transferred to the Pyrex with vegetables and chicken and baking in the oven, it is Sofia's turn to have her mother peer over her shoulder.

Later on, she will look back and find it appropriate that Orlando chooses this regular point of a regular evening to tell her that he's been accepted to Arizona State University with full financial aid. But in the actual moment, she is taken aback and angry with him that she is in the midst of making a normal quick dinner, with no special dessert or anything celebratory on hand to mark the announcement. She's had a crummy, harried day at work and is probably going to Applebee's soon because someone asked her to cover for a childcare emergency, which may or may not be a lie, but Evelyn is sensitive to those situations and always needs the money. Their dog is barking. A neighbor already pounded on the door once to complain. Her car has been grinding inside again. The way this sacrosanct moment happens—with all these normal-life logistics occupying her mind just before her oldest child tells her that he has fulfilled the peak dream that has carried her through these brutal years—is truly confounding as well as emblematic of their survival.

She stands on her tippy-tippy-toes to hug him. All the children join in the hug. And Evelyn thinks that even if this minute isn't exactly how she would have arranged it, it is not necessarily her minute to engineer. She is glad that they are in their home on Magnolia Street and the home is clean and the atmosphere is warm with food smells while all the kids are doing their work. In that sense, the scene and the embrace they all hold within it are close enough to perfect.

◆ ◆ ◆

A few weeks later, she sells the Highlander for parts to the mechanic who has been keeping it in operation for the last thirty thousand miles, which is about sixty thousand miles more than its lifespan was designed to be. He likes her and gives her a fair price—money she will use for Christmas presents in a few weeks and then sock the remainder away on top of the money that she is always gradually socking away. That figure is beginning for the first time to feel like more than the minimum amount she should have— to feel like an actual buffer that might protect her and her kids from harm someday, even though she knows that in the great scheme it probably isn't much at all. But the extra money does make her feel a little more confident than she's ever been before that the bad times, when they come—because they always do come—can be withstood.

Symbolically, she shakes his greasy hand and zippers the check into her jacket pocket. She keeps double-checking that the slip of paper is still there as she walks from the garage to the bus stop. She's been researching used cars and what the best makes and models are and how to find deals on them; she is in the market for a smaller vehicle, one that can still fit the whole family on the infrequent instances they need to be in it such as visits to

Lancaster, but a car that is easier to park and will use less gas. This trade-in is a part of the greater recognition that her family doesn't need to be in a vehicle together very often anymore. They are all growing older, more independent. Orlando is leaving soon. He has built the model of going to college and Gabriel is definitely on track to follow him, then probably Iris. Her family will become smaller. This truth makes her gloomy even while she understands its power.

At the bus stop, a shirtless, shoeless man sleeps on the metal bench in the bright sun. Evelyn happens to have an orange in her purse, and she places it near him for when he awakes. She then stands a few steps away and waits with a group of other riders who are, like her, on their way home.

A Note on Reporting and Sources

AS MENTIONED IN THE BEGINNING, I met Evelyn and Wendi and their families after these stories had in large part transpired. This approach to reporting felt appropriate over a more direct observational method because in writing about the subject of homelessness, I struggled ethically with the prospect of spending weeks or months or any amount of time embedded alongside a family's saddest, hardest, darkest moments on the street and then leaving them there at each day's end to return to my own home and work on a book about my observations. What seemed more humane and ultimately more faithful to their truth was to reflect on a family's past circumstances once they had found a path toward stability and had time to process what they had endured. I also believed that meeting people in a grounded state of mind meant that I could earn their consent in a more genuine manner and—importantly—I would not have affected their stories with my own physical presence and inquiry. On a more personal level, I sought to avoid the position of standing alongside people I cared about, trying to ascertain the degree to which current journalistic practices permitted me to help—materially and otherwise—as desperate and traumatic circumstances pierced their lives.

The above considerations are suppositional and yet representative of past experiences I have had writing true stories. They are extremely relevant to this work and the human relationships that undergird it. And the truth is that no depth of reportorial immersion could enable me to understand what homelessness actually looks and feels like—but through abundant and expansive conversations, I could ask questions in a safe space that was conducive to listening at length. And I could do this work steadily over a period of years in a way that accommodated the colossally demanding schedules of those who lack housing stability and those who help others find it. At the end of it all, this method of research allowed me to weigh fully how each decision that people such as Evelyn, Wendi, Orlando, and others made along the courses of their journeys—even those decisions with disastrous outcomes that might appear ill-considered from the outside— felt rational to them in that time and place, in the context of the pressures set upon each. In my view, that understanding is a fundamental aspect of nonfiction writing and of human connection.

Wendi and I met in August 2022, and she introduced me to Evelyn shortly after. If you have read this far, then you might recall that during this period, Orlando was in juvenile hall and Evelyn was devoting nearly all of her time, spirit, and savings to his case. Having recently finished writing a book about the juvenile justice system at the time, I was in a position to help her with connections to advocacy organizations, but she really didn't need help; his innocence was already clear in the evidence and she was an unstoppable force in pushing his case toward its conclusion. Once Orlando was home and Wendi helped resolve the family's subsequent housing crisis, Evelyn and some of her kids decided to begin telling their stories. Her belief was that if she could spare another parent the level of negative judgment she experienced for having children without shelter, then the temporal and emotional demands of putting her narrative forward would be worthwhile.

The few hundred hours of conversations that followed, plus a great deal of contextual work and fact checking, resulted in this book.

Beyond these many generous, courageous human testimonies and the documentation provided—such as schoolwork, school reports, whatever housing and financial records had been saved—I relied heavily on publicly available LAHSA reports; transcripts from government council meetings in Los Angeles, Monterey Park, Pasadena, and other townships; and trends in coverage of the landscape of homelessness by local and national print outlets over the last twenty years. My own interpretations of some policies and events are also a part of this composition and delineated in the text.

The sections of this book that involve the Door of Hope organization emphasize the success of its model of support as well as the limitations inherent to providing service in a city with as much sheer disparity as Los Angeles. The intention is not to serve as a promotion for the specific charity or its religious underpinnings. At the same time, in giving a true telling of individual experiences within this network, I am compelled to advocate for the core mission of providing transitional housing and robust work support for families in communities where they can live and work, where they can use public transit easily, where kids can have decent experiences and friendships in nearby schools. Thousands of organizations across the country undertake a similar mission and they often do so against intense and historically successful opposition from local homeowners who fear potential financial devaluation of their real estate as well as the nearness to—the daily probability of interaction with—poverty, lack, and need. I am positive that the first fear is a motivator because it is documented in many years' worth of public forums. The second fear is harder to confirm because most people do not explicitly admit to it. Here, I am making an inference, but I am nearly certain of its truth.

As of this writing, the most recent official count of the number of homeless families in Los Angeles County lists 3,303 households comprising 10,477 individuals. Many, many more are unaccounted for. With four shelters in operation, Door of Hope currently houses and supports thirty-six unique families at a time while providing homeless prevention services to hundreds of others. Los Angeles holds more than one hundred distinct neighborhoods and if each provided space and funding for even one similar organization, then family homelessness could be reduced significantly and without exceeding the region's current funding level. The resources of the Department of Children and Family Services could then be much more targeted, the pressure to provide homeless services within communities that already support high numbers of low-income residents could be spread more equitably to affluent areas. Homeowners in those areas would have a closer relationship to those surviving without shelter.

This relationship is crucial. Just like the issue of homelessness, that of disparity is easy to oversimplify along the binary axis of rich and poor. Such clean lines are easier to visualize and digest. But even the most privileged people in America, the ones who live on the top floors of the tallest buildings and in the grandest houses in the most exclusive neighborhoods, the ones living almost entirely free of financial struggle, still are part of a continuum; interactions between people of all backgrounds are constant and necessary for the economy—for society—to function, not just in the context of services like restaurants and cleaners but for complex, vital needs like health services, early child development, and quality public education. Daily life hinges on a codependent relationship between classes. American power brokers and power structures are not realistically going to produce policy measures that will reduce the wealth that is the basis of their power; any expectation that they will is unrealistic. What can happen on the ground, in the world that we share, is that people with firm voices and adequate means might stop wedging people without either of those commodities into the farthest neighborhoods with the barest infrastructures, the least reliable transit systems, the thinnest health-care options, and under-resourced schools. In cities in particular, those who own the land and its dwellings might embrace the idea of a shared landscape and a culture of access over entitlement, which can be achieved by supporting measures for residential shelters, an expanded voucher system, and funding for childcare. So much current thought—much of it subconscious thought—bends toward removing people in crisis from communities when the beginnings of a solution to the current widespread suffering lies in better incorporating them.

Many of the hardships Evelyn and her children endured would have been avoidable—or at least much easier to navigate—if she had not been so afraid of the consequences of asking for help. She was afraid of her aunt losing her own home, afraid of her kids being taken out of school, afraid of bearing additional financial fees, afraid of being forced to cede parental rights to her husband or to the city or to a stranger, afraid of losing one or more of her kids entirely. All of these fears were valid not just because of institutional policy but because of a national ethos of suspicion and blame and a tendency toward making the easiest presumptions in the most complex milieus.

True poverty, especially the relentless vulnerability and mortal danger of being homeless, is a state of invisible burdens, warped logic, and hopeless decisions. A widespread understanding of that state as a measurement of human strength and even a testament to our capacity to love—for children above all—will go a long way toward helping families like Evelyn's be less stigmatized and feel far, far less afraid.

Acknowledgments

Colin Harrison of Scribner continues to be such a sharp, wise, caring editor. As a person, he exhibits a kindness that inspires. For every book drafted, every sentence deconstructed, every conversation enjoyed, every enlightening truth learned about pear orchards and stone walls and parenthood, I am grateful.

Also at Scribner, thank you to Emily Polson for working closely as an editor and during all stages of multiple books now. She is so careful, so patient, and so very smart—a person who helps make book publishing a special sort of universe. Thanks to Nan Graham, an intellect and spirit whom I am beyond grateful to know. Thanks to Paul Samuelson, Brian Belfiglio, Jaya Miceli, Kathleen Rizzo, Victor Hendrickson, Alan Bowie, Stephanie Evans, and everyone in the Scribner orbit for all manner of support. There is a collective kindness and warmth within this publishing house that I still can't quite wrap my head around. Especially meaningful is the sensitivity shown by all toward the real people in these difficult stories. Scribner is a wonderful home.

Every day I am thankful for David Black's representation and friendship. He continues to teach me greater lessons about telling stories and being a person.

Acknowledgments

Michelle Weiner at CAA has changed many lives with her intelligence and talent and love of books, mine among them. Kim Stenton remains a true wonder to our family and a person who really does make the community better for being in it.

Thank you to the Guggenheim Foundation for supporting this book from an incipient stage when that support meant a great deal. The connections I have made through this fellowship are inspiring, and to be a part of the community formed by it is humbling beyond measure.

Close friends are always a source of meaningful connection, book recommendations, and of heart: Aubrey and Adam Siegel, Thomas Hocker, Dan Riley, Helen Thorpe, Charles Barber, Alex Kotlowitz, Anne Fadiman, Lily Brooks-Dalton, Brad and Antonia Pennington, Rawson and Sarah Thurber, Dan and Katherine Villalong, Jeremy Weiner, Kate Lloyd, Marty and Bellinda Scott, Doug Grimes, Alfredo and AJ Manrique, Kate Brown, Poppy and Posy Brown Honikman, Richard and Cissy Ross, Katherine Bradley, and Matt and Staci Eddy.

Jackie Peace, Dante Peace, Syreeta Lum You, Diandra Peace, and the entire Peace family have been incredible friends and inspirations of the heart over many years now. All time spent with this family is special.

Thank you to Lucy and Whit for being curious about, patient with, and supportive of this work—and for being such adventurous, giving, loving people. Thank you to Rebecca for being the beautiful center of us.

Mom, Dad: for everything, then, now, always.

At the Door of Hope organization, Barbara Pettit was so generous, phenomenal, and necessary in enabling and nurturing this process, as were Megan Katerjian, Miss Abeba, Carmella France, Lesley Assistio, and many others in the community. Denis Danziger, Amy Friedman, Ms. Mendoza, Ms. Leung, Ms. Li, Mr. Hernandez, Tina Gruen, Reverend Andy Bales,

Acknowledgments

Kitty Davis-Walker, Gilbert Zavala, Ahmad Chapman, and many others contributed a great deal of time toward teaching me about education, social work, emergency services, and the annual homeless count in Los Angeles.

Wendi, Evelyn, and both of their nuclear families gave a tremendous amount of their time and shared some of their hardest, most private and precious experiences in the hope of easing the lives of those who struggle and tempering the judgments of those fortunate enough not to struggle.

About the Author

JEFF HOBBS is the recipient of a 2023 Guggenheim Fellowship and the author of *The Short and Tragic Life of Robert Peace,* which won the Los Angeles Times Book Prize; *Children of the State; Show Them You're Good;* and *The Tourists.* He lives in Los Angeles with his wife and two children.